D0677593

CELL TOWERS
Wireless Convenience?
or Environmental Hazard?

Proceedings of the "Cell Towers Forum"
State of the Science/State of the Law
December 2, 2000

Edited by B. Blake Levitt

Sponsored by:
The Berkshire-Litchfield Environmental Council

The Nature Conservancy (Northeast)
Housatonic Valley Association
Berkshire Natural Resources Council
Orion Afield
Sharon Audubon
Scenic Hudson, Inc.
Lake Watch Educational Institute
E.F. Schumacher Society

CELL TOWERS
Wireless Convenience?
or Environmental Hazard?

Proceedings of the "Cell Towers Forum"
State of the Science/State of the Law
December 2, 2000

Edited by B. Blake Levitt

ISBN 1-884820-62-X
Library of Congress Catalog Card Number 2001090854

Printed in Canada

Cover photo: Jeffrey Anzevino, Scenic Hudson, Inc.

Safe Goods/ New Century Publishing 2000

New Century Publishing 2000

Head Office   US Office
60 Bullock Dr. Unit 6   561 Shunpike Rd.
Markham, ON L3P 3P2   Sheffield, MA 01257
905-471-5711   413-229-7935

Table of Contents:

Foreword

The Berkshire-Litchfield Environmental Council (BLEC) was established more than twenty-five years ago by a group of concerned citizens in response to an ill-advised public works project that would have had far-reaching, negative impacts on this area's environment. The organization has evolved into a regional effort, comprised of active volunteers addressing the broad-based environmental concerns in Berkshire County, Massachusetts, and Litchfield County, Connecticut. We also support numerous worthwhile environmental efforts far beyond our own region.

BLEC does not mindlessly oppose change but rather seeks solutions that minimize negative effects in order to preserve the unique beauty and character of this region. We have some of the largest unbroken tracts of land on the East Coast of America. We are on a major Eastern migratory bird flyway. We have numerous rare and endangered species of plant and animal life, as well as abundant historic sites dating back to the founding of the country. Our night skies are still dark enough to see the stars, absent as we mostly are of urban light pollution. Our ridgelines are unfettered with communications towers. Our air is mostly pure. Our lakes and streams are still neutral in pH.

The area is currently being considered for National Heritage status. There are only 13 such designations in the country. We are stewards of a beautiful and unusual region and we have an obligation to protect it for future generations.

BLEC's work is characterized by a coordinated regional effort to inform and inspire citizens and community leaders toward appropriate environmental solutions. That was the motivation for sponsoring the Cell Towers Forum on December 2, 2000 in Litchfield, CT.

We thank the co-sponsoring organizations that participated to make this event possible: The Nature Conservancy (Northeast Chapter), the Housatonic Valley Association, the Berkshire Natural Resources Council, Orion Afield, Sharon Audubon, Scenic Hudson, Inc., Lake Watch Educational Institute, and the E.F. Schumacher Society. We also thank the regional and statewide planning agencies for providing mailing labels, as well as the Connecticut Bar Association. We sincerely thank the New England Grassroots Environment Fund for much-needed grant money, as well as the AKC Fund.

We are particularly grateful to our speakers who traveled great distances to share their expertise, and for granting permission to use their presentations in this proceedings book. Their work and dedication forms the backbone of a solution to the problems we are trying to address with telecommunications technologies.

We also extend warm thanks to those speakers who do not have presentations included in this volume — Ed Barron, Deputy Chief Counsel for U.S. Senator Patrick Leahy; Whitney North Seymour, Jr. of Landy & Seymour in New York City; and Connecticut legislators Andrew Roraback and Philip Prelli. Their contributions to the conference greatly helped the audience understand the complexities of the subject from a legal and legislative point of view. Thanks are also in order to Nina Anderson and Stephen Hawkins of Safe Goods/New Century Publishing 2000 for bringing this book into being.

And lastly, we thank BLEC members and friends who helped establish a benchmark for the way wireless communications and their environmental/health impacts will be understood. Ambient non-ionizing radiation is a new environmental issue unlike any we have faced to date. The challenges are serious and legion.

It is our hope that the information contained in this book will be a significant help to other communities trying to navigate this complex issue.

Starling W. Childs,
President, Berkshire-Litchfield Environmental Council

Graham Davidson,
Chairman of Trustees, Berkshire-Litchfield Environmental Council

Chapter 1

Telecommunications Technologies – An Overview: Wireless Convenience? Or Looming Environmental Problem?[1]

By: B. Blake Levitt

Towering Questions

Cell Towers. They seem to be popping up everywhere, like intergalactic mushrooms. We see them inappropriately placed in residential neighborhoods, on school grounds, on pristine ridgelines, along beautiful country roads and scenic highways — usually over the vehement objections of neighbors, parents, and environmentalists. Towers are often reluctantly sited in these hallowed places by the very people we have elected to protect our communities.

Many of our municipal agents have been intimidated by an onerous provision in a federal law — called Section 704 of the Telecommunications Act of 1996, and by an aggressive telecommunications industry that threatens to sue at the hint of a rejected application. Towns, fearing staggering legal bills, have come to think their hands are tied and that somebody's neighborhood must be sacrificed for the sake of the larger community.

But with so many new antenna arrays needed to support more and more wireless buildout, everybody's neighborhood now faces "sacrifice." No neighborhood, scenic vista or historic structure is off-limits.

Municipal agents feel maddeningly frustrated and powerless in the face of a multi-billion dollar industry that appears to have Congress on its side. It is as if we have become candles in the wind of the wireless juggernaut, even though serious scientific uncertainty about the safety of this technology continues to exist.

No community is unaffected by cell towers today. Siting them is one of the most contentious areas of land-use law in America, as well as in many European countries where far more stringent exposure standards

---

[1] The opinions expressed are those of the author, not of the sponsors or other presenters.

have been set[2] for ambient environmental radiofrequency radiation — the area of the electromagnetic spectrum used for this wireless technology.[3]

Just a few short years ago this was not the case. Indeed, the rapacious buildout of this technology caught most communities completely by surprise.

How did we get to this place where we feel we have lost fundamental control over our most cherished right to protect the health, safety and welfare of our communities, and to preserve our property values? How real are health concerns regarding this technology? How can we restore our rights? What is reasonable to ask in light of the fact that many Americans want cellular service?

A one-day conference was held in Litchfield County, Connecticut, on December 2, 2000, featuring speakers with extraordinary expertise, to help answers such questions. This proceedings book from that conference hopes to share that expertise with a broader audience. No community should be without this information because one thing is certain — millions of people love cell phones, but no one loves the infrastructure needed to support a wireless, civilian phone system. New wireless technologies are already out of the gate — wireless TV, wireless computers, wireless faxes, wireless modems, to name a few. All will require additional spectrum and antennas with accompanying radiation — with no clear understanding of the biological consequences to humans or to other species.

It is imperative that we acquire far more wisdom in balancing the competing needs of those who want such services with those who do not want to live near the infrastructure, including the recognition that it may be time to fine-tune the technology away from ground-based networks altogether.

About The Forum and
The Berkshire-Litchfield Environmental Council (BLEC)

The 2000 Cell Towers Forum was organized and sponsored by the Berkshire-Litchfield Environmental Council (BLEC). It was the second such conference by that organization. Founded in 1970, BLEC is a two-state, nonprofit environmental group located in the rural northwest corner

---

[2] See Carl Blackman's presentation, Chapter 2

[3] For more information on the radiofrequencies, see Henry Lai's presentation, Chapter 3.

of Connecticut in the foothills of the beautiful Berkshire Mountains of Massachusetts. (This area of Connecticut and Massachusetts shares long borders with the environmentally-sensitive New York Hudson River Valley corridor.) With over 300 active members, BLEC serves as a science-based advocacy and educational resource for numerous environmental issues, working for conservation and preservation of the region's precious natural and historic resources.

While our topography in this tri-state area is certainly beautiful — dotted with old New England towns with many municipal offices staffed by volunteers whose families go back generations — we are not dissimilar to many other areas of America. We all want to protect our communities. When it comes to cell towers or other unwanted antenna arrays, we are all affected in the same way.

BLEC often works with other environmental organizations toward common goals. This conference was co-sponsored by eight like-minded environmental organizations — all concerned about cell tower siting. (BLEC received additional funding from The New England Environment Fund, as well as the AKC Fund.) It is the first conference of its kind to be initiated through environmental circles.

A 1997 Conference

BLEC sponsored a similar conference in 1997. That effort was aimed at planning and zoning commissions who were faced with the subject of tower siting for the first time. At the '97 forum, the audience was presented with hands-on zoning tools to help those on the frontlines of decision-making understand that the time to enact effective regulations was before tower applications came in — not afterward.

We had discovered that the large national and state planning agencies had early on been subtly co-opted by the industry's offerings of regulations and tower-siting schemes that only minimally protected communities. Any issues regarding health and safety had been summarily dismissed with statements like "you're not allowed to consider that," or "the facilities are within federal guidelines, so don't worry." As a consequence, people making decisions were only partly informed, and most did not make the further effort to study the scientific issues.

BLEC decided it was time to offer the towns a much fuller picture of the problems, uncertainties and possible solutions for this fast evolving area of land-use regulation. At that first conference, we offered sample moratorium language and stringent planning & zoning regulations. These regulations included detailed engineering requirements, strict liability language, large setbacks, and radiofrequency radiation monitoring protocols, among other things. We also made engineering expertise available. It was a radically different way of regulating, and it was legal. (Our panel in 1997 included two attorneys.) This way of regulating really did afford the towns some control and protection.

The conference was a resounding success. It resulted in some of the most stringent telecommunications regulations in the country being adopted by numerous towns on the East Coast. Towns across the country have also adopted variations on this approach.

New Conference For New Problems: Health v. Aesthetics

By 2000, many communities were struggling with different issues, largely due to the advent of the digital wireless systems that required antenna installations every 2-5 miles apart, unlike the older analog systems at 8-10 mile increments. Even good regulations weren't addressing fundamental questions regarding safety and citizen concern. Towns were now being hit with multi-tower grids, often as part of one application.

Plus, independent tower companies began to troll for sites — companies that are not themselves wireless service providers, but rather businesses trying to develop "vertical" real estate — often at the expense of abutting neighbors' property values. Such companies try to hide behind the same legal provisions afforded to the service providers but nothing in the federal law was intended to preempt local zoning for tower companies. The Telecom Act provisions were intended to facilitate the deployment of the service. There is a distinction between the two.

For historic rural environments with a gracious sense of yesterday, the continuing rollout of this technology has become a nightmare. Residents with a deeply held "sense of place" are feeling under siege. And there is no relief in sight without another act of Congress.[4]

---

[4] For the last three congressional sessions, U. S. Senators Patrick Leahy (D-VT) and James Jeffords (R-VT) have introduced legislation that would reverse Section 704. The bills have not made it out of the business-friendly Commerce Committee, headed until 2001 by Senator John McCain. [With the shift in the majority leadership in the Senate back to the Democrats in 2001, the Commerce Committee is currently headed by Ernest F. Hollings (D-South Carolina).] Senator McCain had not allowed testimony during these hearings from anyone other than the telecommunications industry. See Appendix C for

Despite the fact that by the year 2000 many towns had enacted good regulations, planners & zoners had fallen under the spell of "stealth" siting as the answer, meaning if the antennas are hidden or camouflaged, there's not much to worry about. That's because they have been forced to leave out the science piece by the Telecom Act. It has become common to hide antennas in church steeples, on barn silos, atop billboards and tall buildings, indeed almost anywhere — again over the vehement objections of nearby neighbors. Often towns themselves become brokers in such deals, leasing space on municipal water towers and other town-owned land. But, this "aesthetic" approach has an inherent flaw. At its core, this is a medical issue. Aesthetics are easy. Public health questions are difficult.

The problems that communities face now are more fundamental and worrisome: health & safety issues; adequacy of the response at the federal level; liability passed on to communities from tower and service providers; property devaluation, and many other problems with overt legal and societal implications. It was time for a different kind of conference. We needed a broader range of expertise and a more thorough examination of this technology.

The 2000 Conference: About the Speakers

In putting together the speakers panel for the 2000 conference, BLEC set the bar high. BLEC decided that if the forum was to be called "State of the Science/State of the Law," it in fact had to be that. BLEC wanted the audience to hear from the scientists actually doing the research, not someone with credentials merely doing a roundup of information. We wanted the people in government agencies with a stake in this subject to help us understand what was happening at the federal level. And we wanted to hear from the lawyers taking the telecom cases to the higher federal courts — not local municipal attorneys who we envisioned as part of the audience. We thought it was time to go to the next level; to give the towns a real glimpse into how public policy is made, as well as where the safety gaps are located in the system. We thought this was the only way to responsibly deal with the subject.

---

the Leahy/Jeffords bill from the last congress. Edward Barron, Deputy Chief Council for Senator Leahy, gave out copies of this at the 2000 Conference. Mr. Barron was a conference participant. New bills are being introduced in 2001. Anyone interested in keeping abreast of these bills should check the EMR Network's website at www.emrnetwork.org.

We did invite industry researchers, notably from Motorola, which has a renowned research lab, but their scientists had scheduling conflicts. We also invited the chairmen of the boards of two satellite-based companies, Globalstar and Teledesic, but they too had scheduling conflicts.

We were not interested in industry spokesmen. No one at the local level is unaware of what this industry has to say, or what it is willing to offer in exchange for the privilege of locating in our communities. We were also not interested in high-profile industry consultants with science credentials. We considered them part of industry public relations. We wanted people actually doing the research, working in the government agencies, and trying the cases. That was our criteria.

Those who agreed to be on our panel recognized the professional standard we had set. We were blessed to have some of the top people in this area agree to speak at the local level. Such expertise is rarely available to citizens and municipal agents. We thank them wholeheartedly. What follows in this book are their presentations. (Videotapes of the conference are also available through the BLEC Office. For ordering information, see Appendix H.)

The Telecom Act of '96: The FCC and Section 704

This is section 704 of the Telecommunications Act:

Section 704 of The Telecommunications Act of 1996 amended Section 332(c) (47 U.S.C 332(c)) of the Communications Act by inserting this section:
Preservation of Local Authority –

(A) General Authority – Except as provided in this paragraph, nothing in this Act shall limit or affect the authority of a State or local government or instrumentality thereof over decisions regarding the placement, construction, and modification of personal wireless service facilities.

(B) Limitations –

(i) regulation of the placement, construction, and modification of personal wireless service facilities by a State or local government or instrumentality thereof –

(I) shall not unreasonably discriminate among providers of functionally equivalent services; and

(II) shall not prohibit or have the effect of prohibiting the provision of personal wireless services.

(ii) A state or local government or instrumentality thereof shall act on any request for authorization to place, construct, or modify personal wireless service facilities within a reasonable period of time after the request is duly filed with such government or instrumentality, taking into account the nature and scope of such request.

(iii) Any decision by a State or local government or instrumentality thereof to deny a request ... shall be in writing and supported by substantial evidence contained in a written record.

(iv) No State or local government of instrumentality thereof may regulate the placement, construction, and modification of personal wireless service facilities on the basis of the environmental effects of radio frequency emissions to the extent that such facilities comply with the Commission's regulations concerning such emissions.

(v) Any person adversely affected by any final action or failure to act by a State or local government or any instrumentality thereof that is inconsistent with this subparagraph may, within 30 days after such action or failure to act, commence an action in any court of competent jurisdiction. The court shall hear and decide such action on an expedited basis. Any person adversely affected by an act or failure to act by a State or local government or any instrumentality thereof that is inconsistent with clause may petition the Commission for relief.

The Telecom Act looked innocuous at first glance to the uninformed eye, especially the prohibition regarding radiofrequency (RF) environmental effects. Few at the local level understood that a debate had been raging about the safety of this particular area of the electromagnetic spectrum (the ultra high frequency/microwave bands) in science circles for decades, and that the jury was still out.[5]

Nor did many people at the local level know that the nascent tele-communications industry had already petitioned the FCC in late 1993 to override all local zoning. The FCC wisely refused because to do otherwise would have been outside their authority and possibly against the U.S. Constitution. When industry could not get what they wanted through the FCC, they realized they would have to get Congress to do its bidding. They found a champion in Senator Klug from Wisconsin who introduced the preemption clauses into the huge and complex telecommunications bill.

There was a reason the industry needed this preemption. They knew RF technologies rarely won approval at the local level when the health card is played. If they could not get the FCC to override local zoning, they had to get the health piece taken off the table.

Prior to the Telecom Act, communities were free to turn installations down flat based on legitimate health concerns that could be backed up by science. And turn them down, communities did. Without a provision in federal law, the telecom industry would never have gotten off the ground.

Activists and legislators alike who understood that there were potential problems tried to remove Section 704 from the Telecom Act, but to no avail. Congress had never before preempted local zoning where it intersected with public health, especially with a long-standing, contentious, unresolved area of the science such as this. Public health/zoning decisions had been strictly under state and local control up until the Telecom Act. A bipartisan amendment introduced by U.S. Senator Diane Feinstein, a California Democrat, and Senator Kempthorn, an Idaho Republican, tried to remove the preemption clauses. Their effort was defeated by a slim 56 to 44 margin.

The Telecom Act was a by-product of the Republican sweep of the 104th Congress. By most accounts, many new members were ideological pro-business neophytes. This was reportedly the first time that businesses

---

[5] Concerns first surfaced about the health effects of microwaves and radar during World War II when the U.S. Bureau of Ships documented infertility and other adverse outcomes in midshipmen who were exposed to the then-new technology. Nicholas H. Steneck, in *The Microwave Debate* (MIT Press 1985), documents the "politics" of this area of the science. Little has been resolved about the safety of this part of the spectrum.

were actually invited into congressional chambers and asked what their "wish lists" were. (The Bush Administration has repeated this invitational behavior with numerous industries.) In the case of the Telecom Act, the industry actually wrote the language.

Democrats were equally involved with the advent of this technology. Telecommunications quickly became a centerpiece of the Clinton Administration. Important distinctions between wireless technologies, including any lingering concerns about RF risks, and other Internet capabilities for safer wired technologies seemed to blur early on. Technology was seen as good. Anything that stood in its way was bad.

Cozy relationships also existed between Clinton Administration officials and top regulators. Then-Chairman of the Federal Communications Commissions (FCC), Reed Hundt and Vice President Albert Gore were personal friends. They had gone to the same high school.

Under the Clinton Administration and Reed Hundt's directorship, the FCC took on a new activist role that was out of character for the previously lackluster, technology-centered agency. It was under Hundt's FCC that the spectrum auctions began. Huge swaths of the public airwaves were auctioned to private businesses with almost no outcry from the public — which owns the spectrum.[6] Billions of dollars went into federal coffers. It was a fast way to decrease the federal deficit.

This new activist role was odd and didn't seem to fit the temperament of the FCC. Martin Nolan, the Boston Globe columnist, called Hundt's FCC "a cheering squad for the industry it supposedly regulates." Hundt and the Clinton Administration came to see the role of the FCC as an extension of the economy with a mandate to foster competition among providers. But as a regulatory agency, that is not the FCC's role. It is rather like the FDA deciding to stimulate the economy through competition among pharmaceutical companies. It would be wholly inappropriate.

---

[6] When other public assets, such as oil drilling rights in national forests, are being considered, there is always an outcry from the public interest sector, often through environmental organizations. But environmental organizations have not yet embraced ambient energy as an "environmental" issue even though non-ionizing radiation is a form of air pollution. Most public interest groups covering the FCC are concerned about pricing structures for various entertainment services, like cable TV franchises. Most of the press coverage of the FCC is by technology writers for technology publications. Medical/science journalists do not cover the FCC. Consequently, there is a major reporting hole regarding health issues for ambient energy issues.

But unfortunately this mindset has become endemic at the FCC and has been embraced through the Bush administration.

Following Hundt's tenure (after which he became a private consultant for the former industries he regulated), William Kennard became chairman under the second Clinton term. Broadcasters and the telecom industries made it clear that they expected to have a voice in who was appointed to that agency. Kennard was the former assistant chief counsel for the National Association of Broadcasters and was "approved" by the business sector before he was appointed.

In just a few short years, the FCC has gone from a backwater licensing and engineering agency to one of the most significant government agencies today. It is ground zero for the technology revolution and the billion-dollar fortunes riding on it, and many of its functions uncomfortably intersect with public health issues that are far beyond its purview and expertise.

More than a subtle shift has occurred at the FCC. The spectrum auctions continued under Chairman Kennard. Under the Bush administration, not much is likely to change. Whole new swaths of spectrum in the infrared bands are up for auction. Spectrum in the microwave bands very near to the frequencies used in microwave ovens are already being used by the wireless technology sector. Very little research exists to document safety for this. It's a giant technological experiment with the presumption of safety going to industry.

In the meanwhile, there are huge gaps in our regulatory agencies regarding this subject. There is virtually no funding for unbiased government research, even as this buildout continues to escalate.[7] Budgets at the lead agencies such as the Environmental Protection Agency (EPA) under whose jurisdiction environmental RF exposures fall, have been

---

[7] According to "Wireless tower boom creating local static," *Denver Post*, April 8, 2001, page 33A, the Cellular Telecommunications & Internet Association (CTIA) states that the number of antenna sites in the U.S. now tops 95,700. A private company, Tower Map.com, puts tower sites higher at 120,000. There are no records of how many antennas have been sited on or in other buildings, or mounted on other structures. The FCC does not keep a complete database for the number of towers or antenna arrays in the country. They issue licenses for regions. Actual siting is under local jurisdiction. Another industry estimate holds that an additional 100,000 antenna sites will be necessary for the digital buildout because the FCC sold more of those licenses. But with PCS antennas needing to be placed every 2-8 miles apart, that would require 100,000 new sites in a state like California alone.

slashed.[8] And the FCC has been greatly co-opted by the businesses it is supposed to regulate.[9]

The FCC's own budget was also slashed in 1996 — right when the Telecom Act was passed. As a consequence, the FCC was forced to close nine field offices. Today, it has no funds to monitor any industry for compliance with emissions regulations. This is something that always surprises officials at the local level. How could there be this kind of preemption of health concerns at the federal level, yet no research, and no monitoring by the lead agencies?

The FCC will make a field visit with RF testing equipment only after problems have been detected, usually at significant expense to a community which has hired an RF engineering & testing company. The cards are all stacked in favor of RF industries.

Democracy Undermined: Property Devaluation;[10]
Neighbor Pitted Against Neighbor; Citizens Against Their Towns

We are paying a steep price at the local level for the Telecom Act and an activist FCC. Not since the buildout of the railroads at the turn of the last century has there been such a land grab in favor of one industry. Some of our most cherished democratic rights are at stake.

The price to democracy is very real to those whose property has been devalued — in some estimates by up to 40 percent — when a cell

---

[8] From 1990 through 1995, EPA research expenditures for RF totaled $821,000. Since 1995, only one-half of a staff member is presently funded at $25,000 and assigned to perform EPA's role in RF radiation health effects research. See Appendix A, p. 27, *Citizens for the Appropriate Placement of Telecommunications Facilities et al., vs. Federal Communications Commission and The United State of America*, Petition for Writ of Certiorari, Whitney North Seymour Jr., Counsel of Record, Landy & Seymour.

[9] See Chapter 2, "The Difficulty With Setting Standards," *Electromagnetic Fields, A Consumer's Guide to the Issues and How to Protect Ourselves,* by B. Blake Levitt (Harcourt Brace 1995) for a more extensive discussion of government agency responsibility and radiofrequency radiation.

[10] According to "Couple Wins $1 Million in Suit Over Cell Tower Near Home," *Microwave News*, March/April 1999, a jury in Harris County, Texas ordered GTE Wireless to pay a Houston couple with a cellular tower installation 20 feet from their property line: $720,000 compensation for nuisance and invasion of privacy; $225,000 for mental anguish; $28,000 for property devaluation; $230,000 for legal fees plus interest — for a total of 1.5 million dollars.

tower is located nearby.[11] Often citizens are pitted against their own local governments when their towns form alliances with industry.

The price to democracy is reflected in our taxes when towns must cover lawsuits brought by the telecom industry — many of which are slap suits meant to intimidate. Telecom giants have also named individual citizens in lawsuits who try to stop such installations, even though such citizens were acting within their lawful democratic rights. Something very unjust is occurring and most people who collide with the politics of cell towers are appalled by it. People rightly sense that something is very wrong with the Telecom Act.

The price is very real to our psyches when our enjoyment of the environment is taken away by towers plopped down in our pristine viewsheds. The psychological price is high when neighbor is pitted against neighbor, after one person is tempted by the licensing revenues over the objections and fears of others. And unlike other unpopular proposals — nuclear power plants, trash incinerators, toxic waste dumps, etc. that would serve to unite a town in opposition, cell tower applications tend to isolate individual neighborhoods. People living on another side of town might sympathize, but they often will not lend organizing support for fear that the tower will leapfrog to their side of town instead.

The civic price is high when we cannot depend on our local elected officials to do their jobs to protect our neighborhoods because their hands have been tied at the federal level, and because the telecom representatives have convinced them that citizens objecting to the technology are hysterical NIMBY's (Not In My Back Yard).

---

[11] Estimates range from 2% to 40% devaluation, depending on location and other factors. In "Property reassessments can be controversial call," by Phil Brozynski, *Pioneer Press Barrington Courier Review*, Jan. 28, 1999, a 26-year Chicago real estate appraisal firm, Howard Richter & Associates, found as much as 15% devaluation in a home within 270 feet of a cell tower. Twenty-one residents of North Barrington, IL sued the Village of North Barrington and Ameritech Mobile Communications for property devaluation. Ameritech paid half of the town's legal expenses thereby pitting the industry and the municipality against the citizens. In other studies, it has been found that the more expensive the home, the greater the impact. In one survey, a $200,000 home lost 2% of its value, while a $400,000 home lost 10%. In some cases, homes remain unsellable at any price. (See "Cell Phone Towers Are Sprouting in Unlikely Places" by Christine Woodside, *New York Times*, Connecticut, Section 14, January 9, 2000.) When sales offers simply do not come in for a property, there is no way to measure percentage losses in value. People are stuck with properties they cannot sell. Furthermore, properties are often taxed at before-tower evaluations, forcing citizens to sue their towns for reevaluations. Lower real estate values generate less tax revenue for host towns.

Municipal agents do not feel they can legally fulfill their obligation to protect the health, safety and welfare of citizens by taking RF exposures into consideration without ending up in court — and they are correct. But according to typical state statutes, that's the very reason zoning exists. The Telecom Act did not alter a zoner's legal obligations, only their ability to do their respective jobs.

Citizens have lost the right to petition for their own safety, or to choose what level of risk they are willing to assume for themselves and their families. This is the most fundamental right that exists in a free society.

People who have unwanted cell towers forced on them can move and take a loss on their property. Or they can stay and live in fear and bitterness. That's about it. The unfairness of this federal provision strikes at the very heart of our democracy, and it hits us right where we literally live.

First Amendment Rights Undermined

What happens at local zoning commission meetings regarding tower and/or antenna proposals is often contentious and sad — for everyone concerned. Citizens who raise the health issue at public hearings are often summarily shut down by zoning officials who say, "We aren't ALLOWED to talk about that…"

Since when aren't we "allowed" to talk about something in America? When did non-ionizing radiation become contraband information in public discourse? We can talk until we are blue in the face at public hearings about ionizing radiation when a nuclear power plant is planned, but because of Section 704 we cannot talk about ambient microwaves? How did this happen? This is in clear violation of the First Amendment.[12]

---

[12] According to *Bulletin – the voice of the personal telecommunications industry,* March 28, 1997, the Personal Communications Industry Association (PCIA) asked the FCC Wireless Telecommunications Bureau to implement procedures to prohibit zoning hearings from entertaining comments and statements about the health effects of RF exposure unless it could be established that the carrier in question had failed to comply with FCC's emission standards. The PCIA stated that such a rule is required because zoning hearings have become forums for the discussion of the adverse health effects of RF emissions, even in cases in which the licensee in question fully complies with all federal standards. "The discussion of these adverse health effects is generally prejudicial to the zoning applicant and is not always mentioned in the decision denying the application, thereby making it difficult to challenge such decisions…" wrote PCIA President Jay Kitchen. At

Despite what industry says, the driving concern that motivates citizen opposition is the health issue. People understand this subject on a powerfully intuitive level. They understand that abnormal, artificial energy is a potential threat — be it from power lines or from cell towers, or from high-powered broadcast installations. They do not need to understand the minutia of the science, or the different engineering definitions between one technology and another, although it is amazing how fast lay-people come to grasp these things when they need to. People know that there is a safety concern about this technology and that it is legitimate. That's enough.

Concerns about health are almost immediately followed by concerns for property devaluation and aesthetics. Often, when citizens at public hearings are allowed to talk about the health issue, zoning officials adopt a long-suffering attitude as if they are in the presence of cranks holding forth on junk science. The discourse can be condescending and insulting. In many cases, those citizens have done more homework than the zoning officials have. But the zoning officials have extended a presumption of trust toward the telecom industries and the federal government instead. The presumption is, "The government couldn't really be jeopardizing the public health, could they? It can't be *that* bad — and these companies must be liable!"

But, as soon as someone gets their teeth into the background driving the concerns, that extended trust quickly fades. The facts become clear: there are huge holes in our regulatory agencies, the concerns are legitimate, and this is not junk science.

Stealth Siting: Historic Structures and Churches

Like the Telecom Act, the notion of stealth siting is innocuous at first glance. Why build ugly towers if there is a less intrusive option? Who could argue with that?

The fundamental problem with stealth siting is that this is a medical issue. Aesthetics are secondary. Because the health piece has been

---

that time, the PCIA also requested the FCC make it illegal for towns to force service providers to prove they are in compliance with federal regulations, and for the FCC to create a streamlined process that would allow the FCC to overturn local decisions when applications were denied. Prior to that, the industry asked the FCC to declare all moratoriums over 90 days illegal.

declared "illegal," aesthetics then get bumped up as the primary concern. But stealth siting is a smokescreen for the larger elephant in the room.

From a RF safety standpoint, tall towers that are isolated away from the population, with large setbacks from adjacent property lines, are easier to maintain and monitor. They also offer the best co-location options to group many service providers together. But towers are the least popular — for good reason. They are intrusive and ugly. People have an almost visceral reaction to them. (Early on in the towers debate, the telecommunications industry stated that in time the population would become inured to the presence of towers the way we have to the utility poles running along every street. That is wishful thinking on their part. There's no way to turn a blind eye to a mammoth tower, no matter how often one passes by.)

Land-use consulting services, as well as state and local agencies have developed extraordinary expertise in stealth siting.[13] Whole industries have been developed to make cellular installations look like something they are not. They can now look like surreal metal pine trees, or abnormally tall and thin barn silos, or disproportionate flagpoles. Rectangular antenna panels can be mounted to the sides of buildings and clipped to billboards. Antennas can be made to look like Victorian grillwork. The list goes on... At least the above mentioned are still visible.

The worst thing, from a RF safety standpoint, is to hide antenna arrays in places where they cannot be seen, or to encourage micro-systems with very small antennas that can be mounted virtually anywhere. But camouflaging is exactly what we are encouraging, especially in churches with tall steeples. Churches are usually in the centers of towns, very close to residences and businesses. Their steeples can be on a lateral plane with the top floors of nearby buildings. In old New England towns, buildings can be less than twenty feet apart. These can turn out to be significant RF exposures for the neighbors of churches today. Whoever thought living near a church would be a danger?

The issue of siting antennas in church steeples is contentiously dividing religious congregations across the country. People are leaving

---

[13] See Executive Director of the Connecticut Siting Council Joel Rinebold's presentation, Chapter 8, and Jeffrey Anzevino, Regional Planner, Scenic Hudson, Inc., Chapter 10. Both of these presentations emphasize creative options in antenna siting. Stealth siting is also what Albert Manville, of U.S. Fish & Wildlife Service, recommends to offset bird kills due to the presence of towers, Chapter 4.

their congregations over the subject.[14] Often, the board of a church will be approached by a telecommunications provider and asked to lease space for a monthly fee — typically $1,500 to $3,000 a month. To cash-strapped congregations, this is like money from heaven. The deal is often framed as a win-win situation. The church gets the money, the community is spared ugly towers, and — it is often suggested — the church will be performing a civic duty because people need wireless service for safety reasons — especially the homebound elderly. These are specious arguments as will be examined in the section on satellite systems.

Churches rarely have access to the whole picture. The literature the telecom providers hand out is often misleading. One national PCS provider has a brochure likening the radiation from the antennas to the heat of a campfire or to that of the human body. The human anatomy does not generate pulsed, digital, ultra-high-frequency radiation. Neither does a campfire. And nothing is ever going to change the physics of those facts, despite misleading brochures. The misinformation is also based on the presumption that power output from antennas and tissue heating are the only things of concern regarding such exposures, but this is simplistically untrue. This will be extensively explored in the science section by this author, and is examined throughout the other presentations.

Churches that strike deals with telecom providers soon come to realize that rather than a win-win situation, it's more like a devil's handshake. Once a lease is signed, the companies will not let them out of it, no matter how divisive the issue becomes to the congregation, or to the surrounding neighbors. Churches are supposed to bring people together. But that's not what is happening. Some liken these deals to the biblical moneychangers, who Christ drove out of the temple, being invited back in.

Churches are not the only vulnerable organizations. Historic structures — often cash-strapped, too — are prime targets. The National Trust for Historic Preservation released a very expensive, very detailed, lengthy guide on how to site antennas in historic structures. Almost no mention of health issues — or potential liability — were included.

There is a real inappropriateness in using our historic structures as cash cows for a private industry, especially an industry that plays political

---

[14] The author gets calls weekly from congregants who are opposed to the siting of antennas in their church's steeple. When their objections are overridden and antennas are installed, they leave the church in search of another that will, in their estimation, be more responsive to spiritual and environmental issues. Many fear for their children's safety in churches with RF radiation.

hardball at the federal level with our most cherished rights. This course of action will likely come back to haunt the organizations that follow this path. The price will be exacted in the lost goodwill of neighbors, fewer supporters, declining memberships, legal fees if nearby neighbors become ill or when equipment fails in a detrimental way — which it frequently does[15] — and in the loss of integrity of the original historic structure itself.

No matter how carefully the antennas are installed, the building will not be original. It will have been tampered with. Filling our magnificent old buildings and their accompanying historic significance — national treasures that belong to us all — with antenna arrays is a travesty.

Some have raised the question of whether churches and historic buildings should continue to be afforded nonprofit status once antennas are installed since they are clearly hosting for-profit businesses after that. The issue has not gone into the legal arena yet.

Are Telecommunications Services Public Utilities? Centralized Siting at a State Level, v. Local Authority[16]

The way telecommunications services are classified and regulated differs from state to state. In some states, like New York, wireless services are considered public utilities while in other states, like Connecticut, they are not. From a zoning perspective, the distinction is critical because public utilities are allowed by right in all areas, including residential zones and environmentally sensitive areas after certain review hurdles are overcome.[17] Public utility status removes additional local control and is particularly frustrating for those attempting to site telecommunications installations in a responsible manner. It can be like a Sword of Damocles over the heads of citizens. It is a much-craved designation for this industry that has been attempting to gain public utility status at the federal level through a number of channels — most notably the U.S. Commerce Committee. Last year, they had some success in that direction which will be discussed in the following section on the E-911 Act of 1999.

---

[15] See Appendix E for websites on various hazards from telecom installations.

[16] For a discussion on how the Connecticut Siting Council functions, see Executive Director Joel Rinebold's presentation, Chapter 8.

[17] See Jeffrey Anzevino's presentation, Chapter 10, for more information on state environmental review requirements and siting issues in a state where wireless services are public utilities.

Another venue that limits local control is centralized siting at the state level. Connecticut is the only state in the country that has a State Siting Council, although other states have departments within select agencies that serve a similar review function with varying degrees of authority.

Connecticut is the poster state for how the industry would like other states to regulate. In fact, telecom providers have tried to force centralized siting on some states through back door methods.[18] Anything that would allow them to avoid dealing with individual towns — and the accompanying differences in zoning regulations — is what they are after. This industry sees a victory at the federal level as a victory in all fifty states; and a victory at the state level as a victory over however many municipalities exist within that state. The last thing they want is to have to deal with Everytown USA.

In Connecticut, centralized siting has an up- and a down side. The down side is that individual towns do not have complete control. The up side is that a state agency — with all of the legal authority that entails, has the big picture of what is happening with public works projects at any given time. They have the authority to make telecommunications providers, for instance, exhaustively prove that they need additional installations since the council already knows what their existing network is. Nothing is done on speculation. The burden of proof is on the provider, not the council or the host municipality. Telecommunications providers are less likely to try to intimidate the council with threats of lawsuits, too, since they expect to do future business with the council and an adversarial relationship would be counterproductive. A certain level of fairness comes into the process for all concerned.

---

[18]In the mid-1990s, telecom providers attempted to get Vermont to adopt centralized siting. After local resistance, the Vermont state legislature declined. In 2000 in Massachusetts, six telecom providers worked behind closed doors with the Massachusetts Municipal Association (MMA) – the statewide group that lobbies at the State House on behalf of municipalities – in an effort to restructure local and state authority. A bill was proposed that looked good at first glance but which served to ultimately undermine local authority. A number of significant tradeoffs were made by MMA that eroded local control, particularly by allowing antennas attached to an existing structure as a by-right use that would bypass zoning review. Through massive protests from citizens, lawyers, municipal agents and zoning officials, the bill was dropped. Before this effort, telecom providers had unsuccessfully attempted to get all siting review under the control of the Department of Telecommunications and Energy (DTE), in effect mimicking how Connecticut handles telecom siting. Similar efforts were launched in New York State. See Jeffrey Anzevino's presentation, Chapter 10.

The difference between Connecticut and nearby states regarding towers is obvious to anyone who crosses into Massachusetts or New York where towers are more numerous. Connecticut happens to have a particularly good, thorough Siting Council that will not hesitate to turn a project down if it is inappropriate in some way for the host community. Nevertheless, people either love or hate them — depending on decisions they have made in any particular town.

For a few short years, Connecticut towns did get to site the newer PCS systems that function with frequencies the Siting Council did not control. Some towns did better than others. After dealing with the complexities of such siting decisions, many municipalities gained a new respect for the Siting Council. But at the end of 2000, a state court awarded control of the PCS frequencies to the council, which had been sued by U.S. Sprint. Sprint maintained that the council did in fact control the PCS frequencies because they are functionally equivalent services with the older analog systems that were already under the council's jurisdiction. Sprint won, and all siting control has reverted back to the state. Some towns were relieved. Others were not, after having put in extraordinary hours to develop good land-use regulations. It remains to be seen just how this will integrate over time. There are proposals in the state legislature that would require the Siting Council to legally consider a town's regulations in conjunction with all applications, as well as other bills.

The Connecticut Siting Council originated in the 1970's with a small group of environmentally-minded citizens who did not want to see the state carved up with utility projects — high-tension lines, gas pipelines, power generators, TV/radio towers — according to whether a community was rich or poor. They wanted massive utility projects to be sited intelligently for the benefit of all. But such centralized siting likely wouldn't work in large states. The council is a judicial body that holds public hearings in towns with pending applications. Council members crisscross the state daily. Plus, a centralized siting agency that did not understand its mission and primary obligation to the public, or a council that was activist in forcing utilities on communities that did not want them, would be a nightmare. That is not the case in Connecticut thus far.

There are major regions in Connecticut that do not have cell service, and with any luck it will stay that way. Litchfield County, for instance, is rural. A major portion of the population is comprised of weekenders with second homes seeking to get away from urban sprawl and all of the things that go with it — including cell phones. The Interlaken Inn, in Lakeville, where the conference speakers were lodged, advertises itself as "a distraction-free environment." That's become code in the hospitality industry for "your cell phone doesn't work here." Most rural hoteliers will say that this is a drawing feature. People like to get away from the technology, despite what the industry claims.

Safety Issues: Cell Phones, 911 and Radiofrequency Interference

Safety issues are often raised in wireless-free areas, especially for those traveling secondary highways with few houses or services to call upon in times of need. In fact, safety issues are the trump card that the telecom industry plays to pit neighbors against each other, portraying those who do not want to live near antenna arrays as NIMBYS endangering the lives of others who need the service in emergencies. But that is hogwash.

In fact, cell phones are likely causing more accidents than they are being used to report, and are often jamming the 911 lines with so many calls about a given accident that other important calls cannot get through. The jammed lines are then used to argue for more wireless capability. It's a round robin of our own creation.

Let's look at this subject with more scrutiny... When people use cell phones to report their own emergencies, there are no tracking abilities if someone has gone unconscious, or cannot otherwise identify where they are located. So a cell phone doesn't give people the kind of blanket protection they think it will in unfamiliar territory. With wired landline phones, emergency personnel automatically can tell where the call is coming from. People are actually better off walking to the nearest house or pay phone to seek help.

There is a current proposal to put tracking devices in all cellular phones but this brings up important issues about privacy, and engenders other safety questions. For instance, in cases of stalking, tracking devices may actually increase danger to some people. And phones with such devices will constantly transmit an additional signal, thereby creating more radiation near the user even when the phone is turned off. So the subject is far from simple.

In addition, the serious problem of radiofrequency interference (RFI) from cellular installations often affects local police abilities to use their own radio systems.[19] This is particularly ironic because local police are often used by the industry as allies when tower siting problems arise. It is not unusual for the local police to be asked to speak at public forums, especially in rural areas, about the need for wireless capacity. But as more wireless installations are erected, police and other emergency service personnel find they cannot rely on their own radio systems to work within miles of some installations. The situation is complicated by stealth siting, and by the fact that the telecom industry constantly changes its coverage footprint, as well as its frequency bands. Every time a new site is added, the whole configuration of an existing system changes accordingly. Emergency radio dispatch cannot keep up with such changes. Police in some communities often do not know from one minute to the next if their radios will work.

The sudden unreliability of a public safety system can have dire consequences. In Tigard, Oregon, a dead zone caused by a cell installation silenced radio transmissions a few blocks from the police station. On several occasions it prevented officers from calling for backup when faced with armed suspects. And in communities near Phoenix, Arizona, area police and fire radios did not work correctly within three quarters of a mile around Nextel towers. Because of such experiences, Tigard police officials cautioned that community's school district not to allow telecommunications companies to place towers on — or near — schools. In light of shootings at schools, police could not guarantee that they would be able to communicate with emergency response teams going in or out of the affected RFI area.

This problem is a by-product of the FCC licensing bands of the spectrum traditionally used for public safety to private industries. Under the aegis of public safety, the industry purchased empty or available bandwidth laced throughout the spectrum segment reserved for law enforcement. As a result, if there is a cellular/PCS installation — whether tower mounted, hidden on or in existing buildings, or otherwise camouflaged — RFI with emergency service radios may occur. If an emergency radio service call is being made, and if the cellular service is being activated by another user at a frequency close to the emergency signal, the power from the cellular installation may override the local system, making

---

[19] "Sounds of Silence: Cell Phone Towers Are a Police Radio Nightmare," *Law Enforcement News,* March 15, 2001.

it impossible for emergency personnel to transmit or receive messages. Police can no longer be sure where they will encounter a dead zone.

Some think that the only solution will be when the FCC moves the telecom providers out of the public service band area altogether. But there is only so much bandwidth. It's a natural, finite resource. This situation argues for far fewer telecom providers.

Vermont uses a satellite-based system for all of its 911 emergency location needs. It is one of the few states to do so. Using a satellite system is less prone to weather problems and is more reliable, especially in large-scale calamities like floods, hurricanes or earthquakes when ground-based networks often become dysfunctional. The satellite capability already exists. So much for the one-size-fits-all "safety issue" the way it is framed by the industry. On closer examination, it doesn't hold water. Vermont also considers non-ionizing radiation an air pollutant — which is exactly what it is.

E-911 Act of 1999

The Telecom Act is not the only federal law that preempts local regulations regarding telecommunications facility siting. Another bill was unanimously passed in the U.S. Congress that could prove as detrimental to local rights, but very few people know about it. It's called the Emergency-911 Act of 1999 and it affords certain protections for the industry that came about through more backdoor routes. Again, the language seemed innocuous at first glance and the legislation was as "mom and apple pie" as it gets. And again, legislators may not have had a clear understanding of what they were putting in motion.

The bill proposed to declare 911 the universal emergency response number throughout the country. Most people thought 911 already was a universal number but in fact many local jurisdictions had other numbers for emergencies. People trying to make emergency calls from cell phones did not always get through to emergency personnel if they didn't know the local number. That part of the legislation was certainly a good idea but like the Telecom Act, stealth clauses were tucked into the language and it was obvious that the industry was lobbying hard for this bill because of a hidden agenda.

The telecom industry didn't really care about creating a universal emergency response number. What they wanted was to get their industry declared an emergency response "public utility" by having wireless services afforded interstate commerce status — which would override all local zoning. Entitled S.800, the bill also conferred the same level of liability protection for wireless carriers as the wireline providers. The problem is, wireless services function in a much more worrisome area of the spectrum than the traditional wireline services which use direct current in the extremely low frequency (ELF) band, or the new fiberoptic systems which use glass light fibers encased in thick conduit. Wireless services will never be as environmentally safe as the wired networks so why should they have the same liability protection?

But under the E-911 bill, the telecom industry was granted liability protection for the operations of their wireless systems, which presumably could include health and environmental effects from RF. So what they hadn't been able to secure directly from the FCC, or completely through the Telecom Act — meaning preemption of all local zoning and liability protection — they finally secured through the Commerce Committee, then-chaired by Senator John McCain. The industry had been petitioning this committee for three years, seeking interstate commerce status. McCain would accept no testimony from anyone opposed to the various bills.[20] Eventually what the industry really sought came through the Trojan Horse of designating 911 as the national emergency number.

The 911 bill also gave the industry access to sites on all federal land and buildings — including prisons, federal courthouses, and branches of federal agencies outside of Washington, D.C., as well as to our national

---

[20] In 1997, the telecommunications industry petitioned the Commerce Committee, chaired by Senator John McCain (R-AZ), for interstate commerce recognition. Senator McCain was one of two Republicans who voted against the Telecom Act in 1996 so he was thought to be a potential ally in the cell towers issue. When it was discovered that the industry was trying for interstate commerce status, Cathy Bergman, founder and president of the EMR Alliance, an international activist organization headquartered in New York City, petitioned the committee to publicly address the safety issues of RF exposures from cellular technology. Others also petitioned. Industry was scheduled to testify. But rather than allow public testimony, Senator McCain tabled the bill. An aide to McCain told Ms. Bergman to stop calling; that the reason Senator McCain voted against the Telecom Act was that it was too restrictive to business, not the other way around as she had assumed. (From a private conversation between Cathy Bergman and the author.) Subsequent attempts by the industry at the Commerce Committee met with similar refusals to activists who wanted to testify. It wasn't until the 911 bill was formed, and support looked overwhelming, that the bill made it out of committee. By then the EMR Alliance was no longer in business and another activist organization called the EMR Network had taken its place. The EMR Network sent information packages to senior aides at the Commerce Committee but their educational efforts were not successful.

parks — with an expedited review process and only a 60-day notice to the host community.

So far, only a handful of communities have seen the 911 card played with multi-tower grids being proposed all at once. But this provision is like a tiger waiting to strike deeper at the heart of our cherished rights. And it was completely unnecessary. Congress could have designated 911 the universal number without giving away so much to a private industry. That the congressional vote was unanimous is telling... the language was so slick no one in his or her right mind wanted to vote against it. Many emergency response groups and safety personnel supported the bill. Without knowing the legitimate health and science issues that still exist for RF technologies, why not? Who could be against public safety?

Satellite Systems

Safety issues have proven to be a successful rationale for the telecom industry wanting to force ground-based installations on communities that do not want them, but are the issues real? And if so, is it *only* a ground-based wireless network that can fill the gap?

Often when citizens fight specific tower proposals, the subject of satellite-based wireless systems comes up as the answer to ground-based towers and antennas that bring RF exposures close to the population. But, how viable are satellite systems? How reliable?

The first satellite system, Iridium, was promising in theory but had so many problems that it never became a popular consumer service. Iridium functioned with the analog technology so when the newer digital services came out, Iridium could not handle that service sector. In addition, Iridium handsets were large and cumbersome and the service was expensive. Before Iridium was even fully builtout with an estimated 80-90 satellites, it declared bankruptcy. Iridium was a consortium of the largest telecom providers. The U.S. military has reportedly taken over the system.

Globalstar — a newer satellite system — is still promising even though it, too, is in financial trouble. Globalstar offers global cellular digital PCS service even in remote areas where there is no ground-based system. The service is competitively priced, the handsets are reasonably small and they can trade off with other ground-based carriers. It is possible for a wireless customer to sign up with a major service provider in, say, New York City, and travel to remote areas outside the metropolitan area and still get coverage. In theory, there are no dropped calls. Anyone wanting wireless service but wishing to stop the rampant ground-based buildout, should consider signing on with Globalstar. Hopefully Globalstar will not go the way of Iridium.

Teledesic is another promising technology in the wings. Founded by Craig McCaw, one of the original U.S. wireless entrepreneurs from the Seattle area, Teledesic uses a combination of satellites that marry to fiber-optic cable. It is perhaps the safest technology from an ambient RF standpoint.

The power output from satellite handsets is higher than with other wireless phones. But the antenna design for satellite handsets is such that the transmission goes directly overhead, not through the user's brain tissue in a 360-degree radiation pattern the way it now does with the handsets for ground-based networks.

Ambient radiation is very much like the secondary smoke issue. Anyone making a cell phone call is creating radiation all around themselves. People rarely think of it that way. There is some environmental concern about the remote RF signals from satellite systems reaching the earth, even though the power density of the signals is very weak compared with ground-based networks. People with heightened sensitivity to electromagnetic fields report being affected. Called electromagnetic sensitivity syndrome, or "electric allergy" in Europe, such physical reactions are recognized in other countries but not in the U.S. And there is concern that we may be creating negative effects in other species; effects that are yet to be determined.

With the advent of Globalstar and Teledesic, one could make the argument that the purpose of the Telecom Act — to create a universal consumer wireless capability — has already been fulfilled. We have technologically accomplished what Congress set out to do. One could argue that it is now reasonable to reverse Section 704, and that it is unnecessary to preempt any local zoning. Those wanting wireless service can now have it anywhere; they just have to purchase a different calling plan. And those concerned about safety can have those worries addressed as well. Like the state of Vermont, all 911 calls should be handled by satellite systems since they are the most reliable in major weather calamities and for determining the location of the call.

What we need is the political will to make this transition happen. Because of cost, satellite systems will always be self-limiting, which is good from a RF-exposure standpoint. Exposures will automatically be limited as a factor of satellites' distance. Only those with enough capital will become players. This could lead to monopolies but with so many un-answered questions on the table about safety, perhaps this is an industry that argues for only a few participants.

Ground-based networks are cheap to build when compared with satellites or wired infrastructure. But as long as the telecom industry is only driven by the bottom line and has Congress on its side, nothing will change. Since direct legal challenges to Section 704 have yet to be suc-cessful in the highest courts — a subject to be discussed later — the rem-edy still remains in the legislative arena. Consumer pressure on legislators can be very effective and is the most important route to undoing Section 704.

Consumers need to know they have a purchasing choice with satellite systems that could make a tremendous difference. It is also important to understand that the public's airwaves are a finite natural resource. If, as cell phone users, we voluntarily decide to "recycle" the airwaves and "conserve" the resource by forgoing non-essential calls, that will reduce the need for more antennas and RF pollution.[21] As consumers we need to understand that we are part of the solution, as well as the problem. Until we comprehend this subject the way we do other aspects of energy conservation, we will continue to wrangle with the issue of cell towers at the local level.

The Science:
Energy As An Environmental Issue

In our rush to focus on specific technologies, it is easy to forget that energy is inherent to everything in the environment. The earth itself is a giant dipole magnet with a north and a south pole. There are constant emanations in the 10-Hertz (Hz) frequency range that come from the earth's core, and a natural static magnetic field of about 500 milligauss. This static field shifts subtly over a 24-hour period, and there are seasonal shifts as well.

All living things have evolved within this protective electromag-netic cradle. Scientists used to think that the earth's magnetic properties were interesting but not terribly important. Now it is understood that the earth's magnetic fields play a role in everything from numerous species' migrations and seasonal mating patterns, to our own circadian rhythms,

---

[21] See Jeffery Anzevino's presentation, Chapter 10.

among many other things. There is also the likelihood that the earth's magnetic fields are a hidden variable in all scientific research.[22]

It turns out that we — and all other species, including trees and plantlife — are fantastically sensitive to electromagnetic fields and the earth's micropulsations. Some think we are "entrained" by it. (Entrainment means 'to be subtly carried along,' like when a mother and child sleep together and their breathing rates synchronize.)

Electromagnetism truly is the forgotten environmental component.[23] Plantlife, for instance, depends on electromagnetism in marvelous ways. When a thunderstorm is approaching and the earth and ionosphere trade electrical polarities, the uptake of water increases in plants and trees hours before any raindrops fall. One can see pine trees, for instance, extending their branches straight up toward the sky, waiting for the rain.

Some lakes are known to have over 200 varieties of fish that use electromagnetism in one way or another — to find food, avoid danger, or swim in synchronous schools for example. Sharks have a vast array of electromagnetic tools, including eyes that are ten times more light-sensitive than our own. Their ability to detect minute electrical discharges, called neuronal firings, whenever living tissue is moved is what guides a shark's final attack. (Interestingly, if the voltages are increased, sharks will miss the signals altogether.) Electric eels can deliver a 200-volt zap, and this is not to mention the sound frequencies used by ocean mammals like whales and dolphins.

Living creatures are loaded with a magnetic material called magnetite — a natural mineral that is millions of times more sensitive to external magnetic fields than any other living material. Bird beaks and eye areas are loaded with it. It serves as a navigational device in nighttime migration and on cloudy days. Fish have lateral lines on both sides of their bodies that are pure magnetite crystal chains. That's what allows them to swim in schools without colliding with each other. Other creatures with magnetite include bees. Their bellies contain thick magnetite clusters. Bees are thought to use it as a magnetic compass to orient themselves with the angle of the sun and the center of the earth, which they use as a gravity vector. They then return to the hive, and "dance" elaborate descriptions of where the pollinating flowers are located for the rest of the hive. In 1973,

---

[22] See Carl Blackman's presentation, Chapter 2 for more discussion of this point.

[23] For a fuller discussion of environmental effects, see Raymond Kasevich's presentation, Chapter 11; and *Electromagnetic Fields, A Consumer's Guide to the Issues and How to Protect Ourselves,* by B. Blake Levitt (Harcourt Brace 1995).

Karl von Frisch won the Nobel Prize for his work in discovering the "honeybee dance."

In fact, whenever anyone tries to determine if a species has magnetite, that species invariably does. One of the things that is observed with magnetite clusters, is that there are often a multitude of rich nerve endings that are attached to it, indicating that magnetite performs a multi-system function in living organisms.

In the 1980's, Dr. Joseph Kirschvink at the University of California discovered that humans also manufacture magnetite in the meninges, which covers the brain.[24] This raised immediate concerns about the safety of Magnetic Resonance Imaging (MRI) scans of the brain. And it also raises questions about the safety of cell phones. Any of the standards currently in place presume that humans do not manufacture magnetite.

Bird Kills and Towers

One of the key environmental issues with towers today concerns bird deaths.[25] One estimate holds that a single cell tower below 200 feet in height may account for as many as 3,000 songbird deaths a year along major migratory routes. These are conservative estimates by the U.S. Fish & Wildlife Service. Actual deaths may be significantly higher when nighttime scavenging by other species is factored in near tower sites.

Songbird populations are plummeting in many areas of the country. With an estimated 96,000 cell towers alone in the U.S., and another 100,000 planned by 2003,[26] one can only imagine what this will do to avian numbers. Perhaps we really are in for a "Silent Spring" like Rachel Carson predicted. But this time it isn't from DDT.

Bird kills near towers is not a new subject but it has become a relatively new environmental issue. The lead federal organizations, as well as the industry, are working together to find solutions, but short of

---

[24] See "Magnetoreception and Electromagnetic Field Effects: Sensory Perception of the Geomagnetic Field in Animals and Humans," by Atsuko Kobayashi and Joseph L. Kirschvink, *Electromagnetic Fields; Biological Interactions and Mechanisms*, Edited by Martin Blank, p. 367-394, Advances in Chemistry Series 250, American Chemical Society, Washington, D.C., 1995.

[25] See Albert Manville's presentation, Chapter 4, for a full discussion of this subject.

[26] Figures from the Cellular Telecommunications & Internet Association, "Wireless tower boom creating local static," by Stacie Oulton, *Denver Post*, April 8, 2001, p. 33A.

building far fewer towers, and taking down many of the existing ones, the solutions can only be seen as half measures.

One solution concerns lighted towers over 200 feet. Birds are attracted to red light and by certain kinds of light pulsation. Industry is voluntarily changing to white strobe lights on towers and altering the timing patterns between strobes. And of course everyone is advocating stealth siting of antennas on/in preexisting buildings rather than the erection of new towers. But this brings up other exposure problems to the human population, as previously discussed.

Other questions come up with this subject, too. For instance, given the magnetite in avian physiology, might the RF signals be acting as an attractant, or in some way interfering with birds' navigational abilities? Several years ago, cell towers were thought to have interfered with homing pigeons when large numbers of them were thrown off course after towers were erected in their fly routes.[27] A recent theory by Dr. Jonathan Hagstrum of the U.S. Geological Survey in Menlo Park, CA., however, speculates that rather than cell towers being the culprit, low frequency sound waves from the Concorde SST are responsible.[28]

It has been presumed that towers act as structural obstacles in birds' flyways. But birds have often been observed frantically circling a tower before collision, especially towers with metal guy wire supports. Sometimes birds get vertigo near towers and fly full-force into the ground. Or they get tangled in guy wires. Metal is conductive and RF energy can form "hot spots" of standing waves along guy wires. The theory that RF acts as an attractant is discounted by key ornithologists — because avian magnetite is in such small crystals that a precise resonant match with RF is unlikely, they say. But there are many different kinds of resonance that have yet to be explored. The subject is in its infancy. That RF may be acting as an attractant still makes for an interesting area of research.

Other species, in particular frogs and salamanders, are known to be sensitive to RF, perhaps because water is a conductive medium. Reproductive problems, deformities and death have been observed in amphibian populations.

---

[27] *Microwave News*, November/December, 1998.

[28] Hagstrum's paper appears in the *Journal of Experimental Biology*, vol. 203, p. 1103-111, 2000.

The Body Electric

Everything about the human anatomy is electromagnetic — we just don't think of ourselves that way. Brain waves are electrical, the heartbeat is electrical, cell division itself is electrically influenced, how neurons communicate with each other is electrical (it's called "signal transduction") and all of our hormonal and enzymatic activities are electrically regulated. In fact, one could say that not much happens in the human anatomy that isn't electrically influenced in one way or another. Even the chemical-mechanistic model of the human anatomy at its core is an electromagnetic model because all chemical reactions involve the sharing, trading, or exchange of electrons at the elemental level. And every time we move a muscle, there is that small electrical discharge, previously mentioned in the environmental section.

Researchers call this electrical cacophony "background thermal noise" and it is the basis upon which specific absorption rates are determined in standards setting.

The different ways that the anatomy uses electromagnetic energy is extremely varied and complex. The human brain, for instance, makes use of a wide range of different electromagnetic frequencies. Delta waves between 1-3 Hz are associated with deep sleep; theta waves between 4-7 Hz are associated with emotions and mood; alpha waves between 8-12 Hz signify relaxation; and beta waves between 13-22 Hz are where conscious thought occurs. It is interesting to note that most human brain activity occurs around 10-15 Hz — right where the earth's micropulsations are.

Pulsing certain frequencies can have dramatic effects on humans. For instance 10 Hz is usually relaxing, but epileptic seizures can be induced with pulsed light in that frequency when the external stimulus synchronizes with the brain's alpha waves. There are reports of seizures being induced in tower repair personnel, and in children living near cell towers. The digital PCS systems are pulsed in the ultra high frequency (UHF) ranges.

It has been known for decades that the human anatomy is actually resonant, in the strict physics sense of the term, with the FM radio bands around 87 MHz, and that human brain tissue reaches peak absorption in the UHF bands — right where telecommunications technology functions.

In laymen's terms, resonance means we act as perfect receiving antennas for a particular frequency. We are resonant with the FM bands because those wavelengths are about six feet long — the size of the average human male. There are whole-body resonances but different body areas and organs will have different matches, too. What this means for us is that the UHF frequencies couple with brain tissue in a way that they don't with other areas of the body. It is possible, under certain circumstances, to develop standing wave phenomena — meaning that the energy doesn't rapidly dissipate, but rather forms a localized hot spot. Under some circumstances, standing waves may actually augment or become stronger than the original exposure. This is something to keep in mind with cell phones and cordless transmission products of all kinds when the antenna is next to the head.

There are also several forms of resonance. The subject is complicated and at any given time, there are numerous variables to be considered in energy research. Other species have resonant matches with certain frequencies too. We haven't even begun to explore this subject regarding the effects to other species from the massive amounts of energy we continuously infuse into the environment.

The human anatomy has also been found to react to the extremely low frequencies (ELF) around 50-60 Hz — the frequency band common to our electric utilities. Decades of research has produced data showing a generalized stress response from ELF-EMFs, suppression of melatonin and serotonin, changes in calcium ions in the cell,[29] effects on fertility in test animals, cancers of just about every type, associations with Alzheimer's disease and Amyotrophic Lateral Sclerosis (ALS) — commonly called Lou Gehrig's disease,[30] immune system suppression, autoimmune diseases and many other problems. Based on some popular press articles, people think the powerline frequencies have been found to be safe, but nothing could be farther from the truth.

Most of our RF technologies are "modulated" with ELFs, which means that a lower frequency is superimposed on a higher frequency carrier wave. Modulation is used in all telecommunications, TV, and radio transmission. If it's wireless, it's usually modulated. This means we are getting complex, multi-frequency exposures from all of our RF technologies. But the exposure standards in place throughout the world do not take modulation into consideration. Nor does most of the research that has been

---

[29] See Carl Blackman's presentation, Chapter 2.
[30] "Stronger ALS-EMF Connection: New Link to Epilepsy Observed," *Microwave News*, September/October, 2000, p. 8-9.

conducted. There is an enormous information gap in the way energy research has been done, and in the way it is therefore interpreted.

For engineering convenience, artificial categories have been created when dividing up the electromagnetic spectrum for scientific review.[31] Those setting standards for RF do not factor in any of the ELF research even though RF is modulated with the ELF bands. This means that a comprehensive scientific understanding never develops and therefore the standards for RF exposure cannot be considered reliable.

Despite what anyone says, no safe level of RF has ever been determined. What we need is a broader based examination to understand real biological effects, not just in humans but in other species as well.

Artificial Exposures

The question is, if we are as in tune with, and influenced by, the earth's natural electromagnetic background as many now think, what — if anything — are we doing to ourselves with a barrage of artificial exposures across a range of frequencies, especially in the non-ionizing bands?[32] Are we creating so much interference that we are cut adrift from our most basic moorings? And to what consequence?

Although energy is a part of the natural world, many of the artificial exposures we have created do not exist in nature. We have infused the environment with unusual waveforms such as sine and sawtooth waves, and we have created very high power intensities for some frequencies like the RF/UHF bands that are weak in their natural state. Plus, we have created propagation characteristics like digital signaling and modulation that simply do not exist in nature. These are all man-made artifacts with no clear understanding of the bioeffects, despite our ever-increasing EMF ambient background.

The buildout of the wireless infrastructure is creating a seamless blanket of microwave exposures for the first time in our evolutionary history in close proximity to the population. The use of cell phones is greatly increasing that exposure to millions of people worldwide. With wireless computer systems proposed for many schools, children — who are in a

---

[31] Blackman, *Loc.cit.*

[32] Robert O. Becker, M.D., in his seminal work *The Body Electric, Electromagnetism and The Foundation of Life*, written with Gary Selden (Quill/William Morrow, 1985) calls our electromagnetic attunement "breathing with the earth." Also see Robert Cleveland's presentation, Chapter 7, for illustrations of the electromagnetic spectrum.

higher state of cell division and who have thinner skull bones and are therefore more vulnerable — will be exposed to significant RF radiation for long periods of time. Long-term exposures are thought to be cumulative. We are, in effect, engaging in a massive biological experiment. With cell phones, one could argue that the exposures are somewhat voluntary. But with cell towers, these are involuntary exposures forced on people by the government.

Bioelectromagnetics

The area of science where this subject is most at home is called bioelectromagnetics, or biophysics. It is an arcane area that is not taught in most medical schools. Professionals wander into it from any number of other specialties like physics, biology, clinical medicine, psychology and others. There is no area of science, or medicine, or the law, or technology, or public policy or public health that is untouched by bioelectromagnetics, believe it or not. With communications and high-tech weaponry, it even intersects with national security issues.

Bioelectromagnetics is also the cutting edge for many therapeutic applications. In diagnostics, MRI scans use several non-ionizing frequencies. Genetics and cloning use low level current to jump start cell masts into life. Cancer treatments use microwaves to shrink prostate tumors. Orthopedics uses low-level electrical current to stimulate intractable bone breaks. Cardiologists use RF to stop abnormal heart rhythms. These are only a few.

The reason the non-ionizing bands are used is because they penetrate the human anatomy so deeply and are so biologically effective. It is important to keep in mind that, beyond simple thermal models of the human anatomy, no one really knows what the underlying mechanisms are that make for such effective therapies. And it is equally important to keep in mind that what has the ability to heal, also has the ability to harm.

The application of bioelectromagnetics breaks down into two camps: therapeutic uses, where the research is well funded because profits can be made there; and hazards research which is almost nonexistent in America today. Hazards research is a little like raining on someone's high-tech parade. No one in the therapeutics camp wants to think that there is more weight on the risk side than the benefits side of the risk/benefit ratio.

The hazards side is, of course, more problematic. It means we need to be a lot more judicious about the products we bring to market, and more careful with the processes by which they function.

Public Health Issue

Most public health officials and doctors are unaware of the body of research — both pro and con — that bioelectromagnetics encompasses, despite the fact that the primary issues on the table concerning ambient exposures are about the public health.

Urban "electrosmog" has increased dramatically over what it was twenty years ago. In 1978, after surveying twelve large American cities, the U.S. Environmental Protection Agency (EPA) issued a report on background radiation levels.[33] Median exposure of the population was very low at 0.005 microwatts per centimeter squared ($\mu W/cm^2$), with the major contributor being from FM radio. This was long before the advent of cellular technologies and a host of other RF-generating services like pagers, palm pilots, and the like.

No U.S. follow-up has been done since the late 1970's, but in 2000, a survey was conducted in Sweden by Dr. Yngve Hammerius of Chalmers University of Technology in Goteborg. Dr. Hammerius found radiation levels to be ten times higher than they were just two decades ago in that country. In the cities monitored, the median power density was 0.05 $\mu W/cm^2$, with 61% coming from cell tower base stations.[34]

Ambient increases in American urban areas are thought to be comparable or even higher, given the larger number of wireless service providers licensed by the FCC. It is time we pressured Congress to refund the EPA's research program, pressured the EPA to follow-up on the 1978 background RF levels, and in general took a far more cautious approach to this subject.

---

[33] *Radiofrequency Radiation Levels And Population Exposure in Urban Areas of the Eastern United States,* United States Environmental Protection Agency, Office of Radiation Programs, EPA-520/2-77-008, May 1978.

[34] "Urban Electrosmog Increasing," *Microwave News,* July/August, 2000, p.3.

Disconnect in the Sciences

One of the reasons we are in the situation of a burgeoning technology overtaking our understanding of the health consequences is because there is a major disconnect in the sciences with a stake in this subject. Whole branches of science can be completely out of touch with each other.

Bioelectromagnetics is the crash point between the living sciences like biology, and the non-living sciences like physics and engineering. Biologists rarely know anything about physics, and physicists rarely know anything about biology. But bioelectromagnetics is an integrative specialty where the two converge and it is one of the most contentious areas of science today. A certain amount of territoriality and professional bias comes into play in bioelectromagnetics circles.

Unfortunately, the non-living sciences have historically dominated the field of bioelectromagnetics, determining everything from how the intellectual debate is framed, who participates, what research is funded, and how — ultimately — the safety standards are set. This has created an inherent bias towards the needs/perspective of the physics community, which is concerned with how to make the technology work, when in fact the issues are biological in nature, meaning, what are the consequences of the technology? The physicists and biologists are often at each other's throats in the bioelectromagnetics community because of it.

The short course on the argument is that physicists and engineers — who create the technology — shouldn't be controlling anything when it comes to biological effects research. Scientists from the non-living branches shouldn't be making determinations on public health. That is the jurisdiction of our public health officials, clinicians and others from the biology branches of science.

On the subcommittee of the American National Standards Institute[35] that sets standards for frequencies used in telecommunications, there

---

[35] The American National Standards Institute (ANSI) is an organization comprised mainly of industries that set voluntary national standards for numerous industrial applications and processes. The industry subcommittee for radiofrequency radiation is the Institute of Electrical and Electronics Engineers (IEEE). The subcommittee title is C-95.1 for the microwave bands. The standards they recommend are titled ANSI/IEEE C.95.1. The last year of the revision is then added, i.e. ANSI/IEEE C.95.1-1992. Until 1996, the FCC had traditionally adopted the ANSI/IEEE recommendations. But in 1996, the EPA, which has final jurisdiction over ambient exposures but has failed to produce their own

are only about five M.D.s out of a review panel that numbers in the hundreds. Many committee members are military or industry researchers. Conflicts of interest abound. The standards are often determined less with biology in mind than with engineering requirements to make the systems work.[36]

But the problems on the table are not about physics and engineering. As a society, we already know what those branches can create through their incredible talent. Now we are concerned with biological questions, such as: What are the consequences to the living systems in the path of these technologies? Are some people more sensitive than others? Is it safe to allow ambient levels of RF to proliferate as long as they stay within a certain threshold? Do we know what that threshold is? Are the data reliable? If not, what data do we need? And should we be more cautious until we get it?

Heart of the Controversy: Thermal v. Non-Thermal Effects, The FCC Standards

The heart of the scientific controversy revolves around what are called thermal-effects — meaning certain frequencies' ability to heat tissue like what occurs in a microwave oven — versus non-thermal effects, meaning anything that occurs below that heating threshold.

No one disputes that there are biological effects from non-ionizing radiation in the radiofrequencies. The only issue is whether there are hazardous effects below heating. If so, what are they? And are they reversible? No one disputes the accuracy of the heating model. It is well established, and in fact is used as the jumping-off point for other biological understandings.

The non-thermal effects work, however, is far more interesting. It means that we don't understand something fundamental about the human anatomy, all the while we are increasing our exposures. Industry and the military like to pretend that this entire body of work either doesn't exist, or

---

standards, insisted that the FCC adopt the National Council On Radiation Protection and Measurements (NCRP) standards which were five times more stringent than IEEE's. In response, the FCC – after considerable pressure from the industry and the U.S. military, created a two-tier exposure limit. IEEE is used for "controlled" environments where professionals would be allowed higher exposures; and the NCRP standard was adopted for "uncontrolled" environments where civilians would likely be exposed.

[36] See Carl Blackman's presentation, Chapter 2.

is suspect. But non-thermal effects are established now too.[37] Only the old guard from the 1950's cold-war era in the military, and the industry, continue to try to hold the line on the non-existence of non-thermal effects. Their purpose is to make sure that nothing changes regarding public policy. It is to industry's advantage to keep saying, "nothing is proven" and have people believe it.[38]

But that is not true and hasn't been for a long time. Immune system suppression, increases in the permeability of the blood brain barrier, changes in calcium ions, DNA damage, and numerous cancers are well established in the scientific literature, among many other things. The problem is, no one knows quite how to interpret the data or what to do about it because the implications are enormous to modern life. Merely turning down the power intensities of RF generation may not be adequate.

The FCC standards currently in place are based on the thermal model of the human anatomy with safety factors built in. But is that enough? The last time the standards were revised by the IEEE C-95.1 committee was in 1991 and approved by ANSI in 1992.[39] The committee reviewed no studies past 1985. In 1996, the FCC adopted a combination of this standard, and the slightly more restrictive standard that was put out by the National Council of Radiation Protection and Measurements (NCRP) in 1986. This means that by the time the FCC created the standards currently in place, no new studies had been reviewed or included in the database for eleven years!

Since 1985, hundreds of new studies have been published — approximately 80% of which have found biological effects, some at very low power intensities comparable to cell tower exposures.[40] But none of these

---

[37] The U.S. military's traditional position has been that non-thermal effects do not exist. The U.S. Air Force Office of Scientific Research, and the research labs at Brooks Air Force Base in Texas, are the lead military agencies for non-ionizing biological research today. They help create non-lethal weapons using non-ionizing radiation, conduct research, and co-sponsor symposiums on therapeutic applications, among other things. There are contradictions in their position, however, as can be demonstrated in the co-sponsorship of two electromedicine conferences in 2000 and 2001 entitled "Nonthermal Medical/Biological Treatments Using Electromagnetic Fields and Ionized Gases."

[38] See Andrew Marino's presentation for a full discussion of standards of proof and how determinations are made.

[39] *IEEE Standard for Safety Levels with Respect to Human Exposure to Radio Frequency Electromagnetic Fields, 3 kHz to 300 GHz, IEEE C.95.1-1991.*

[40] See Henry Lai's presentation, Chapter 3, and Appendix B for a list of recent research abstracts provided by Dr. Lai.

studies are factored into the U.S. standards, which continue to be among the most lenient in the world. Other countries, however, are using the recent literature to adopt far more stringent standards, as well as recommending prudent avoidance when siting cell masts near the population.[41]

When telecommunications companies point out that they are in compliance with the FCC regulations and in some instances are well below the standard, it is supposed to make people feel more comfortable about the technology. But the standards that are in place are completely inadequate, given the new research, as well as a more complex understanding of how biological systems function. No one should be lulled into complacency with this argument.

Industry representatives who present information at the local level often blur important distinctions. They liken the antenna technology to baby monitors and to 25 and 100-watt light bulbs, in an attempt to assuage fears with common analogies for products we have long accepted. What they leave out is that the technology uses 100 watts of radiated power per channel, and there can be dozens of channels on one antenna, and dozens of antennas on one installation. Understood this way, telecom facilities are not so low-powered after all but are rather like having an AM radio station transmitter in the neighborhood. And since most towns try to co-locate many providers together — which they should — areas around towers can quickly become very complex electromagnetic environments that are difficult to assess and monitor.

Non-Linear Effects

One of the most fascinating, and baffling, observations across a breadth of energy research at different frequencies is something called non-linear effects.[42] In energy research, it is often observed that the most profound effects are observed at the lowest intensities, or that "windows" exist for some effects at low exposures but not for others at higher exposures.

This is the exact opposite of our standard toxins model where the highest exposures create the most dramatic effects. In a toxins model, adverse effects are determined at specific exposures and regulations are then

---

[41] For a discussion of "prudent avoidance" and the "precautionary principles" adopted by other countries, see Carl Blackman's presentation, Chapter 2.

[42] See Carl Blackman's presentation, Chapter 2, and Andrew Marino's presentation, Chapter 5, for more discussion of non-linear effects.

set where effects are no longer observed. Virtually all of our regulatory apparatus is built on this traditional model.

But non-linear effects stands the toxins model on its head. Again, it means we do not understand something fundamental about living biological systems, all the while we are increasing our energy exposures. Energy research is very different than toxins research. We are clearly dealing with a whole new model. With non-linear effects, some exposures may prove unsafe at any intensity. There is already some indication of this in some of the research. And if this is true for us, it is certainly true for other species.

Flaws in the Research

There is a serious design flaw in much of the research that has been used to reach conclusions about RF safety. Historically, because of economic constraints — and because scientists are impatient human beings like the rest of us — energy research has been designed with high-power exposures for short periods of time. Damage has been calculated, then downward extrapolations have been made to presumed safe levels. This has been effective for the thermal model of the human anatomy because heating effects can be readily observed. But with non-thermal effects, that approach is pure speculation, especially when non-linear effects are considered.

For the standard toxins model, the high-exposure-downward-extrapolation is the normal route. But in real life, energy exposures are not like that. Real life consists of long-term, low-level chronic exposures such as would be experienced by those living near telecommunications installations — and that kind of research, unfortunately, is sparse. In fact, there was only one major long-term, low-level study conducted back in the early 1980's and it found increases in cancer in test animals.[43] In the 1990's, a

---

[43] In the early 1980's, the U.S. Air Force commissioned a $5 million study into the biological effects of long-term, low-level exposures in test animals at the University of Washington's Bioelectromagnetics research lab, the oldest in the country. Nearly the entire first group of test animals died of an unidentified infection. Dr. Robert O. Becker, author of *The Body Electric* and *Cross Currents...* observed at the time that this was likely due to immune system suppression which made the test animals more susceptible – an observation that he and colleagues had made in research of their own. The tests had to begin again. Several generations of rats were exposed to pulsed microwaves in ranges that simulated the levels allowed by current standards for humans. Results found increases in adrenal medulla tumors, malignant endocrine and ectrocrine tumors, and increases in carcinomas and sarcomas. The authors of the study tried to downplay their own

handful of studies of multi-generational, low-level exposure studies of test animals also found adverse effects.[44][45]

Beyond these few studies, most energy research is of an inappropriate kind and it is being used to reach inappropriate conclusions about safety.

Research Manipulation

There is currently no unbiased, federal research program into this subject. The lead agencies have all been defunded. Industry completely controls the show and there are a number of ways to manipulate the research without actually tampering with the data itself.

One way is to make sure that the right research is never funded — to keep looking at, for instance, thermal effects rather than non-thermal effects; or to keep designing tests with high-power, short-term exposure parameters. Another way is to set up the research protocols so that no effects are likely to be found, such as setting the power densities at vanishingly small intensities. Or to not replicate studies that have found effects — that way industry can say "that study was not replicated," implying that someone tried and failed thereby casting doubt on the integrity of the original work, when in fact no attempt was made at all.

When major organizations like the National Research Council are asked to conduct meta studies to see if patterns are emerging in certain areas of the science, they often restrict their analysis to studies that have

---

findings and the study became controversial. (*Effects of Long-Term Low-Level Exposure on Rats*, by A.W. Guy *et al.*, University of Washington, Vol. 9, USAFSAM_TR-85, Aug. 1985.)

[44] In 1997, investigators in Greece exposed five generations of mice to RF in several places near an antenna farm. RF power densities were between 168 nW/cm^2 and 1053 nW/cm2. A progressive decline in fertility was observed which ended in irreversible infertility by the fifth generation. Prenatal development of newborns was altered. ("RF Radiation – Induced Changes in the Prenatal Development of Mice," by Ioannis N. Magras and Thomas D. Xenos, *Bioelectromagnetics* 18:455-461 1997.)

[45] Also in 1997, investigators in Australia exposed mice prone to develop lymphoma to pulsed 900 MHz EMFs at low intensities. After 18 months, lymphoma risk was found to be statistically higher in exposed animals. The significance of this study is that alterations were found in immune system B-cells. Changes in B-cells are implicated in 80-90% of all cancers. This formed a plausible theory about why so many different kinds of cancers have been observed with EMF exposures. ("Lymphomas in Eu-Pim1 Transgenic Mice Exposed to Pulsed 900 MHz Electromagnetic Fields," by Michael Repacholi *et al.*, *Radiation Research*, 147: 631-640, 1997.)

been peer reviewed and replicated. If replication has been blocked, such studies never make it into the overall research picture — which can then be skewed in favor of industry findings.

Sometimes studies are repeated by other researchers using different test parameters. When the same results aren't reached, it is said that the original study "wasn't replicated" which in the literal sense, it wasn't. The design was altered. But the phrase is again used to discredit the original work.

All of this would imply some massive collusion on the part of individual researchers to hoodwink the public, but that's not the case. Most researchers embody the utmost personal and professional integrity. The problem is that industry — and only industry — is footing the bill.

Some of the things the telecom industry routinely does cannot be considered in the best interest of the public. For instance, in their contracts, industry requires independent researchers to sign confidentiality clauses, agreeing not to speak about their work until it is published. There can be up to three-year lag times between when the research is done and professional publication. And sometimes the research just never sees the light of day — if it goes against industry desires.

Contrast that to the pharmaceutical industry where researchers have to pick up the phone and immediately call the FDA if adverse effects are found in test animals or in clinical trials with drugs. The telecommunications industry also gets final edit before research findings are made public. No other industry exercises this loophole and expects to get away with it. Some independent researchers have stated that they have been asked to change their interpretations of their work to suit industry spin. The problem is endemic to telecom research. This situation is clearly deplorable for all concerned. Independent, unbiased research must be funded as soon as possible.

The Bottom Line

The bottom line is this: our current presumptions about RF safety may be totally unreliable. Inappropriate research has been used to reach inappropriate conclusions. Inappropriate professions — physicists and engineers — are controlling the situation and making decisions for the public health that is far outside of their professional expertise. And our government regulatory agencies have been defunded to the point of inefficacy, as well as co-opted from the inside by the very industries they are supposed to regulate.

This shifts the burden onto citizens to make the decisions, and to insist that some clarity be brought to this issue. We are the ones taking the risks.

Case Law

Telecommunications law used to be confined to a few law firms in the Washington, D.C. area where a handful of attorneys helped various industry clients navigate the labyrinths of government and FCC regulation. Today, most municipal land-use attorneys have a passing knowledge of how telecommunications law intersects with planning and zoning issues, with varying degrees of legal accuracy and insight. The Telecom Act created a whole new area of case law and has spawned concentrations in legal expertise that did not exist at the local level prior to 1996. It is still very much of an evolving area of the law.

When the telecom buildout first started in earnest after 1996, the industry seemed to think they had all the power and legal right to swagger through communities, intimidating towns into giving them pretty much what they wanted. But gradually, towns stood up for themselves. Case law that protects the communities has more and more come into being as various suits, covering different issues, made their way through the courts and the appeals process.[46] One of the interesting things to ponder about this subject is the fact that Congress, in enacting Section 704, shifted the burden of ironing out the details onto the judiciary branches of government. That's what happens when ideology reigns over intelligent governance.

At the time of the BLEC Cell Towers Conference in December of 2000, a major legal effort had been launched at the U.S. Supreme Court to reverse Section 704 on constitutional grounds. A Petition for Writ of Certiorari had been filed by Whitney North Seymour, Jr., Esq., of Landy & Seymour in New York City in the Fall of 2000.[47] By December 2000, the Supreme Court had neither accepted nor rejected the petition for review. Since that time, the petition has been declined, leaving a lower court ruling in place.[48]

---

[46] For a full discussion of pertinent case law, see James Hobson's presentation, Chapter 9.
[47] See Appendix A for the full brief.
[48] The original suit was filed in the United States Court of Appeals for the Second Circuit in New York City. Petitioners were the Cellular Phone Task Force, the Ad-Hoc

Only one out of every 100 cases submitted to the Supreme Court are accepted. However, since the case was not tried on its merits, the legal points are still cogent and waiting to be heard in the proper venue, at another time.

Seymour's brief argues that although the federal government has the power to set health standards in areas relating to interstate commerce, that where it has defaulted on its obligations to protect public health, the federal government may not simultaneously prevent the states from taking action to do so. It further argues that with the FCC and the EPA hobbled by Congress in their respective regulatory roles, the power and responsibility to protect the public health reverts to the people of the states as part of their inviolable sovereignty. The legal arguments are a classic federal v. states rights case. Many other important points were also made in the brief, which go directly to the heart of the problem.

Numerous municipalities across the country, as well as several congressional offices filed amicus briefs in support of the petition, but the Supreme Court declined to hear the case. It was a big disappointment to

---

Association of Parties Concerned About The Federal Communications Commission Radio Frequency Health and Safety Rules, and the Communications Workers of America, AFL-CIO, CLC, *et al.* These had been three separate, but related suits that were combined for review by the Second Circuit. Each petitioner came at the subject from a different angle. The Cellular Phone Task Force, headed by Arthur Firstenberg and represented by attorneys John Schulz of Colorado and Edward Collins of Massachusetts, argued that the FCC was in violation of the Americans With Disabilities Act in not taking those with electrical sensitivities into consideration with RF exposures, among other points. The Ad-Hoc Association of Parties Concerned... headed by Libby Kelly of California (a former consultant in the U.S. Department of Health and Human Services and now President of the California Council On Wireless Technology Impacts in Novato, CA.), and David Fichtenberg, a public health statistician in Olympia, Washington, represented by James Hobson, Esq. of Washington, D.C., argued that the FCC was not enforcing its own National Environmental Protection Act (NEPA) regulations which it is required to do by law, among many other points. And the Communication Workers of America, represented by Howard Symons, Esq. of Washington, D.C., argued that in setting a two-tiered exposure standard, that communication workers were being discriminated against because they were subjected to higher exposures than non-professionals. Intervenors included most of the telecommunications and broadcast industries and adjunct others. There were hundreds of amicus briefs filed in support of the various petitions. The briefs and supporting materials were voluminous and the case complex. It is difficult to sue a federal agency but there was a narrow window of opportunity after the FCC adopted new regulations in 1996. The Second Circuit courtroom was packed during oral arguments. The ruling, which was finally handed down in April of 1999, went against all petitioners and in favor of the FCC.

the many people who had hoped for relief from the highest court. (In declining to hear the case, the Supreme Court essentially bounced the solution to the problem back onto the legislative branch that created it in the first place.) Three other Petitions for Certiorari were also filed at that time over other legal points originating from the Second Circuit case. All were declined.

There is now conflicting case law at the appellate level in the U.S. Fourth Circuit Court of Appeals concerning constitutional questions about the Telecom Act that have yet to be resolved. The Fourth Circuit is considered among the most conservative in the country and is often the last step before cases go to the Supreme Court. The issues raised in the Seymour brief are not over by any means. They are just waiting for another spoke of the wheel to ride.

Liability

Liability issues can be significant for municipalities and individual site owners alike. Keep in mind that the industry has been successfully shifting liability away from itself and onto others in numerous ways — including rigged science, controlling the standards-setting committees, buying influence at the political level, co-opting key regulatory agencies, and getting industry-friendly riders through the E-911 bill, to name a few.

Unbeknownst to most people at the local level, this liability has been shifted downward to those making land-use decisions. The federal preemptions against taking the environmental effects of RF into consideration do not necessarily protect local officials who can still be named individually in lawsuits for poor siting decisions. Despite the preemptions, it is still their legal obligation to do everything possible to protect the health, safety, and welfare of the community and its citizens.

The same is true of churches and private landowners that lease space to telecom providers. There is no statute of limitations on health claims for EMF damage. Everyone with a stake in siting decisions can be sued if adverse health effects turn up. With more and more science circling around the problem and coming up with significant data, such siting decisions near populated areas are lawsuits-waiting-to-happen.

Municipalities are increasingly seeing applications from independent tower companies like SBA and American Tower Corporation. These are not service providers but rather companies looking to establish towers wherever they can in order to lease space to RF industries. Towns can

legally disallow towers built on speculation. The Telecom Act only preempts for providers of the service, not independent speculators.

Such independent tower companies are invariably set up as limited
liability corporations (LLC). High-risk businesses always do this. SBA at
least acknowledges in its investment portfolios that RF may turn out to be
a risk for investors in company stock. American Tower Corporation has
been fined $212,000 by the FCC for antenna structure violations at various
sites around the country. The fines relate to 36 separate violations that include failure to notify the FCC of ownership changes; failure to register
towers with the FCC, and failure to properly light towers during construction, among other problems.

With a limited liability company, most of the financial assets are in
other holding companies and are therefore out of reach. If a town, or individual gets into trouble with a LLC, they may end up owning a tower, but
not much else. Many service providers are selling their own towers to such
companies. It is yet another way of shifting the liability away from themselves. No one wants to be responsible for damage at the local level for
property devaluation and for health claims. That puts the liability squarely
on individual planners and zoners, as well as the landowners where installations are sited, if citizens need legal redress.

A Note About The Precautionary Principle and Prudent Avoidance

Several European countries, having taken a look at the recent data,
are taking a different approach to the RF question. They are recommending prudent avoidance when siting antenna installations near schools, residences, hospitals or wherever people congregate. For cell phone use, they
are recommending that children below the age of 16 be advised not to use
cell phones for anything other than emergencies.[49]

This approach is part of what is referred to as the Precautionary
Principle, which has been adopted by many countries, including the U.S.,

---

[49] Thus far, groups making this recommendation include: the Independent Expert Group
On Mobile Phones and Health – commonly called "The Stewart Report" in the UK, The
Greater Glasgow Board of Health in Scotland, The German Pediatric Society, The Ecolog
Institute in Hanover Germany, The European Parliament Directorate General for Re-
search, the Italian government, and The Royal Society of Canada. Other countries have
instituted far more stringent RF regulations than the U.S. See Sage Associates chart, Carl
Blackman's presentation, Chapter 2.

for various applications in international treaties. It is not a radical or new way of going about situations that deal with environmental uncertainty.

The Precautionary Principle holds that when questions of safety are concerned, precautions should be taken to protect the public health even if scientific data is incomplete, or mechanisms of action are not understood. It is the only approach that makes sense given what we already know about RF, and given the situation in America with industry influence at all levels. Prudent avoidance should be the driving motivation for towns siting antenna installations near the population.

What Towns Can Do: Planning and Zoning Regulations

Something municipalities fail to keep in mind is the basic legal fact that it is up to the providers of a service or product to prove that their wares are safe. It is not up to us to prove that they are unsafe. The telecommunications industry has largely failed to do that. Just because they are within the FCC guidelines for RF emissions, does not prove safety.[50]

No town today should allow itself to be intimidated by telecom service providers or adjunct industries like tower companies. Despite the preemptions, there is still a lot of power reserved to the municipalities, and there is a growing volume of good case law to back up local decisions. But those in decision-making positions need to understand that this form of land use regulation is very different than traditional forms. Telecom regulation needs to be understood from a completely different vantage point. This is NOT just an aesthetic issue. It is a medical one.

Good zoning regulations are still the best protection but this kind of regulation can be complicated.[51] Here are some key provisions that should be included:

- Monitoring for RF emissions is essential, both before an installation goes on line, and afterward. It is the only way to determine what was changed in the environment, and to document the date of that change. Pre- and post testing will give a community a baseline of data in case problems turn up later. It will also assist with liability issues because it will demonstrate that the town was truly paying attention. Regular, annual monitoring should be instituted by

---

[50] See Andrew Marino's presentation for a fuller discussion of this point, Chapter 5.
[51] See Anthony Blair's presentation, Chapter 13, for sample regulations from Great Barrington, Mass. – the first community to write this kind of land-use by-law.

independent RF engineers — not industry engineers. This becomes particularly important as other RF industries co-locate on the same installation. The industries should pay for the monitoring, not the taxpayers. Monitoring protocols should be consistent from year to year, using the same equipment, etc.[52]

- Large setbacks should be established from homes, schools, hospitals, or wherever people congregate — at least 1500 feet. But individual topography counts a great deal.[53] In some circumstances, 1500 feet may not be enough if dwellings on nearby hillsides are on a lateral plane with antennas. Also other RF sources need to be factored in. Sometimes different frequencies can couple with each other in ways that engineering computer models cannot predict, creating significant exposures in unexpected places.

- Take metal objects into consideration because they are conductive materials that can create localized hot spots. Things to avoid siting antennas on, or near, include: metal water tanks, roofs, architectural girders, elevator cables, etc.

- Establish by-right zones where facilities can locate — but nowhere else.

- Discourage private entrepreneurs and churches from establishing sites. Such people and organizations rarely understand the complexities of the issue or what they are getting into.

- Only allow signal strengths that will provide for adequate coverage and adequate capacity, not blanket coverage. The right to determine signal strength at the local level has been upheld in federal case law in U.S. Sprint v. Willoth, and by the FCC. The FCC only requires approximately 75% coverage of an area — not 100% coverage. It has been understood from the beginning that there would be holes in coverage, especially in hilly topography. If towns have environmentally sensitive areas or historic landmarks to protect, they should acknowledge such sites in their master plans of development as off limits to this technology.

- Towns should require extensive engineering detail in their applications, otherwise companies do not have to prove that a facility is

---

[52] See Appendix D, Cabot, Vermont for a monitoring protocol.
[53] See William Curry's presentation, Chapter 6, for a full discussion of how topography can affect RF exposures at specific locations.

really needed. They may be speculating on a site without admitting it.

- Require independent engineering review of all applications and modifications to existing sites. Often applicants are sloppy and rote in their preparations, using cookie-cutter computer models from site-to-site. In requiring such detail, towns are establishing the facts of a case that may be needed after turning an installation down. Engineering detail is critical.[54]

- Encourage those who want cell service to switch to satellite-based systems such as Globalstar and Teledesic, which will reduce the number of ground-based facilities.

- Require the service provider, the tower owner, and the landowner, to all be part of the application. That will discourage towers being built on speculation.

- Write airtight liability protection into the regulations by all concerned, with proof of insurance annually submitted. This should transfer to any new owners of the facilities or properties. Failure to substantiate proof of liability protection should constitute a revocation of any permit.

- There are many other constructive things that towns can do . . .

Most importantly, contact your legislators and insist that they fund the appropriate, unbiased, government research into the long-term, low-level biological effects of RF radiation. That is the only way we will know what the risks actually are. Until then, it is a great global experiment, without the courtesy of citizens being asked to sign consent forms for their participation. It is equally important to refund the other agencies with a stake in this issue — the EPA, the FDA, and the FCC. Budget slashing zeal has gone too far. The agencies can no longer do their respective jobs. We are the ones paying the price in uncertain risks, and sleepless nights when our children are affected.

There are ways to remedy these problems. But as a society, we must put our shoulder to the task. It is still fundamentally up to us to enact good laws, make our wishes known to our legislators, and hold them accountable. It is also up to us to insist that industries be more responsible

---

[54] See Cabot, VT. regulations in Appendix D for engineering details contained in zoning regulations. These were also discussed in Mark Hutchin's presentation, Chapter 12, and in Tony Blair's presentation, Chapter 13.

when bringing new products and services to market. And finally, it is up to us, as consumers, to be more judicious in how we use new technologies. Increasing ambient RF exposures may prove to be environmentally unsafe for all living creatures. The price may indeed be steep for mere wireless "convenience."

B. Blake Levitt
P.O. Box 2014
New Preston, CT. 06777
Email: blakelevit@cs.com

Chapter 2

Is Caution Warranted in Cell Tower Siting?
Linking Science and Public Health.

By: Carl Blackman, Ph.D.[1]

Some of the topics I'll cover in my presentation include: why — in light of the proliferation of telecommunications technologies — the subject of EMF (electromagnetic fields) is important to us today; examples of pertinent data and its interpretation; what methodologies are used to evaluate public health exposures; some human exposure criteria; and directions we might take in the future to solve some of the questions at hand.

So that we all will have the same basic understanding of the principle terms used in discussing electromagnetic fields, let me start with some fundamental definitions. When it comes to radiofrequency radiation (RFR), one term often used is "intensity." Intensity is analogous to the brightness of a light bulb, or the loudness of a sound. As a general rule, the greater the intensity, the greater the effect.

With that definition, we can now look at exposure maximum values in use, or suggested for use, in various countries. Intensity limits vary widely around the world as seen below.[2]

From this table it is apparent there is over a 3-order of magnitude difference considered for allowable EMF exposures around the world. Those making standards recomendations are all looking at the same research data. The basic difference

International Standards for Radiofrequency Radiation (cell phone frequencies at 800-900 MHz)

Location	intensity, microwatts/cm^2
Saltzberg (pulsed RF)	0.1
Switzerland	4.2
China	6.6
Russia	10.0
Italy	10.0
Auckland, New Zealand	50.0
United States	~ 580.
Canada	~ 580.

Modified from SAGE Associate 2000

[1] Research Scientist, U.S. Environmental Protection Agency, MD-68, Research Triangle Park, NC 27711-2055. Phone: 919.541.2543. Please note the opinions I express are my own and not those of my employer.
[2] Table provided by Cindy Sage, Sage Associates, 2000.

between the standards is due to different approaches taken in evaluating those research results.

One approach is called "proof beyond a reasonable doubt" and is based on observations of how EMF energy affects tissue. It is universally accepted that a microwave oven heats food. The acceptance of this phenomenon, and an understanding of the mechanism that causes temperature rise in biological samples, is the underlying basis for current high-level EMF exposure limits.

The other approach is to use results that cannot be completely explained, and draw conclusions that could protect the public until more is known. This is called "proof on balance of probabilities." The classic example of this approach is John Snow's analyses and interpretation of the general cause of a cholera epidemic in London. It is used to mark the beginning of epidemiology studies.

There are extreme positions taken by proponents on both ends of a continuum of ideas, i.e., all industrial applications should be allowed until conclusive proof of harm is established; or conversely, nothing should be allowed until safety is established. These positions are not helpful to establish a dialogue. We don't need to turn off electricity and cause our modern society to disappear, nor should we ignore clues of possible health problems.

Some Complexities

The definition of intensity given before is deceptively simple. The subject is far more complex than that. The concept that more of a given agent will produce a greater effect in its simplest manifestation describes a linear effect. However, there are non-linear phenomena that occur, which do not follow that simple (intuitive) concept.

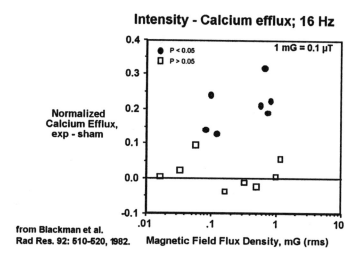

Intensity - Calcium efflux; 16 Hz

from Blackman et al.
Rad Res. 92: 510-520, 1982.

Here is some data we published in 1982 showing increased intensity of a magnetic field (at low frequency) going from left to right along the horizontal axis. The vertical axis shows greater amounts of calcium ions leaving — or "effluxing"— from animal brain tissue contained in a test tube. The increases that are statistically significant are in solid circles.

These results show that there are at least two intensity regions — or "windows"— that cause effects in the tissue specimens, but other intensities that do not cause effects.

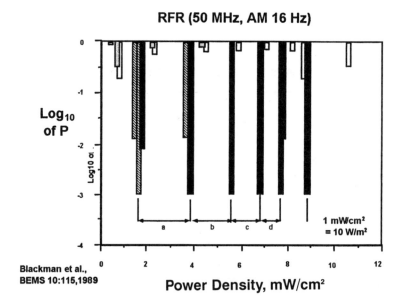

RFR (50 MHz, AM 16 Hz)

Blackman et al.,
BEMS 10:115,1989

Power Density, mW/cm²

This figure also shows changes in calcium ion efflux, but here the electromagnetic field is in the radiofrequency range and it carries the low frequency (16 Hz) as amplitude modulation, just like an AM radio does. Again, the horizontal axis shows increased intensity, going from left to right. The vertical axis is a function of the calcium efflux, and any bar that extends below the dashed line is an indication of a statistically significant finding. On this graph we see six intensity windows of effects.

From these studies of intensity, we can conclude that intensity windows exist for effects at extremely low frequencies (ELF) and at higher radiofrequencies (RFR); that the results of our observations were unusual, the results nontraditional; and that what we observed were non-linear effects. Such effects are mostly ignored in standards setting situations.

Our observations with calcium ions are important because cells use calcium for any number of critical functions. The efflux response observed indicates a possible change in the signaling processes at the cell outer membrane, which acts as a switchboard communicating information between the exterior environment and the intracellular activities that guide cell differentiation and control growth. The health implications are not fully understood but anything that alters basic cellular signaling processes warrants further investigation.

Frequency

Another critical concept to understand in this research area is frequency. Frequency is analogous to the various colors of visible light or the different pitches of sound. Usually different ranges have different effects, and results are not always expected. Often, these are non-linear responses. An example is that of growing plants indoors. With some light, the plants are a healthy green but never produce flowers. By changing the bulbs to "grow lights" which supply the plants with different colors of light, i.e. different frequencies, flowers will appear.

Gaussian fit by f_{ac} ($R^2 = 0.97$)

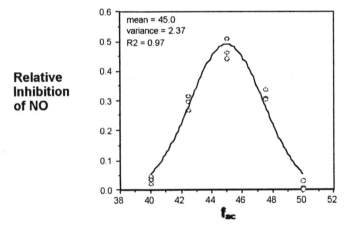

One of the examples of what different frequencies of magnetic fields can do is shown here in this figure. The horizontal axis shows different frequencies, and the vertical axis shows changes in the action of nerve growth factor to stimulate the growth of neurites (primitive neurons) from PC-12 cells (which have properties of cells in the peripheral nervous system). It is obvious there is a frequency range "window" within which magnetic fields inhibited neurite outgrowth (NO).

Frequency @ 0.69 mGrms - calcium efflux

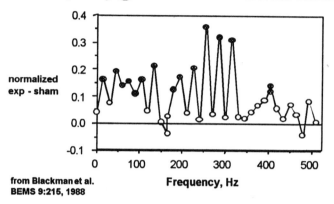

from Blackman et al.
BEMS 9:215, 1988

This figure shows calcium ion release from brain tissue (vertical axis), with the solid circles showing statistically significant differences between exposed and sham-exposed samples, as a function of frequency on the horizontal axis. Again, multiple windows of frequency are shown to be effects.

The important information from the results we have observed is that there are two major features of EMF exposure: intensity and frequency; the responses were non-linear; and that the mechanism responsible for the observed changes is unknown.

Keep in mind that some review committees who set exposure standards only use data that has an understood mechanism of action. Thus, those committees ignore the results shown above.

Other Factors

There are other factors that influence whether exposure to certain frequencies and intensities of electromagnetic fields will cause biological changes. Some of these factors include:

- One's physiological state, including age at either end of the spectrum (young or old), pregnancy, susceptibility to other illnesses, genetic polymorphisms, or additional exposures (co-insults) from chemicals or diseases.

- The earth's own static magnetic field. While this magnetic field is essentially "everywhere," its value varies over the surface of the earth because of different rock formations, and because of anthropogenic activity, e.g., use of steel support structures in buildings, etc.

This following figure is an example of one of these factors — the static magnetic field of the earth.

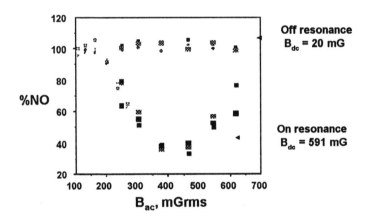

The horizontal axis shows increased intensities of the 45-Hz magnetic field from left to right, and the vertical axis shows changes in the ability of nerve growth factor to stimulate neurite outgrowth in PC-12 cells. There are two data sets: one with the static magnetic field at 591 milligauss, and the other when that field is altered by artificial means to 20 milligauss. It is obvious that changing the value of the static magnetic field, as can occur when you move around inside buildings containing steel support beams, can influence the effects of oscillating fields.

The overall summary of these data shows that EMF does not necessarily act like a single agent. EMF can act more like a chemical cocktail, in which the various components can affect different biochemical systems *within* a biological system. The consequence of this more complex action is that caution must be used in evaluating the significance of such exposures for public health.

Much additional research is needed to explore EMF interactions with biological systems. Dr. Andrew Marino recently provided new insight that diverges from standard analyses and has the potential to alter analytical approaches.[3] Most studies compare the averages of exposed groups' responses with those of control groups. There were a few reports noting changes in the variability of data points around a mean value, but no one had directly investigated such an observation until recently. Dr. Marino and colleagues used special mathematical techniques to show that in some cases EMF exposure may not cause changes in the averages of a biological endpoint, but that it can impart instability to biological processes. This observation may be particularly important, if the biological system is also being stressed by other agents that have it balanced at an irreversible threshold. Additional research must be done to determine how widespread this phenomenon is, and whether it can have health consequences. There is still much that remains unexplained in EMF biological effects research.

Current Evaluation Practices of EMF Data: The Engineering Model

It is useful to consider how EMF is currently evaluated for biological effects and their health implications.

Traditionally, committees that are established to do these evaluations break up the data into frequency bands (e.g. ELF, VHF, radiofrequency, microwave, etc.) and only look at data within certain specified bands. Why is this done? Because developments in engineering technology allowed higher and higher frequencies of EMF to be generated, the bands have been established for engineering convenience of notation, not for health considerations, and that notation still is used as convention. The consequence of this approach is an engineering-based clustering of data that reduces evidence for coordinated experiments performed across several frequency bands. This approach to evaluation drastically reduces the impact of basic science results because the weight of complete evidence is itself reduced.

---

[3] *Am J Physiol Regul Integ Comp Physiol;* 279:R761-8, 2000.

Biologically-based Model

In contrast to the engineering-based segmentation of biological results, another approach may be more productive when addressing public
health concerns — that is, biologically-based clustering of data. This is the
way it is done in other areas of science concerned with public health issues. In EMF research, we should group experimental results that show
similar EMF features such as intensity and frequency-exposures; cofactors
such as the influence of the earth's magnetic field, and/or chemical coinci-
dent exposures; and physiological similarities such as age, or selected sensitive populations.

An example that would illustrate the relaxation of the engineering-
based rules would include combining data from several frequency bands
such as the ELF band with the RFR band, especially when the RFR is
"complexed" or modulated with ELF. A common example of this real-life
combination is radio transmission when the human voice or other sound is
heard directly through a radio. This is accomplished by modulating a RF
"carrier" signal with an ELF signal. There are several types of modulation,
i.e., ways to encode ELF signals on RFR. They include amplitude modulation (AM), frequency modulation (FM) and pulsed modulation, among
other complex forms.

Why a New Model is Important

When this clustering of ELF and RFR effects are viewed together,
a powerful, comprehensive set of studies emerges that has present day
relevance, but which is normally left out of some review processes because they don't all fit into the bands studied by one committee, i.e., the
engineering model. Here is an example.

In 1968, it was reported that human response times changed under
exposure to ELF fields. In 1970-76, monkeys were shown to exhibit
changed response times during exposure to ELF, and that EEG patterns
also changed. Additional work exposing cats to either ELF or RFR amplitude modulated with ELF produced EEG changes and changes in the
release at the surface of the brain of the neurotransmitter GABA, and of a
surrogate chemical, calcium ions. In the latter 1970's and in the 1980's,
calcium ion changes were observed in brain tissues from newly hatched
chickens exposed to ELF and to RFR. Also in the 1980's, calcium efflux
changes were observed when RFR-exposed human brain cells in culture,

and when frog hearts were exposed in vitro. More than ten years after these studies were reported, two theoretical papers were published (in the late 1990s) that may lead to improved understanding, because the papers provide some basis to examine the underlying mechanisms responsible for the results reported in these earlier papers. This series of reports represents a remarkable collection of coordinated studies but they have been essentially ignored because no evaluation group has the mandate to study them together.

There are different types of modulation that occur in our environment. I've mentioned effects from amplitude modulated (AM). Very few studies have been done using frequency modulation (FM), which is among the most prevalent type of exposure today. Similarly, few studies have been reported for pulsed modulation, which is used in the newer digital PCS telecommunications systems, although there is some indication this type of modulation might have effects similar to AM.

Influence of frequency on DNA synthesis

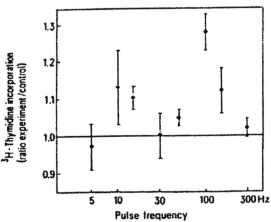

Takahashi et al., Experientia 42: 185-6, 1986

This figure is an example of the effects of different rates of EMF pulses (along the horizontal axis) on the incorporation of thymidine into DNA (vertical axis). Higher incorporation is interpreted as an increased synthesis of DNA, and thus faster growth of cells. The authors have shown that the intensity and width of the pulses also have non-linear effects. It is useful to remember that some cell phones use radiofrequency carrier waves mixed with low frequency analog signals, and in other types of transmissions, pulsed signals are mixed with the carrier waves.

Human Responses to Cell Phone Frequencies (1998-2000)

- **Preece et al.**
  - 915 MHz (IJRB 75:447, 1999)
  - Reduced reaction time during exposure
  - 50 Hz (IJRB 74:463, 1998)
  - Temporary deterioration in attention
- **Koivisto et al.**
  - 902 MHz (Neuroreport 11:414 & 761, 2000)
  - Reduced response time to simple tasks
  - Altered EEG during a memory task
- **Freude et al.**
  - Cell phone frequency (Eur J Appl Physiol 81:18, 2000)
  - Decrease in slow brain potential during a visual monitoring task

On the basis of the information I've just reviewed, it is interesting to revisit some recent reports of human exposures to cell phones. There are three publications since 1998 listed above from different countries in Europe (United Kingdom, Finland and Germany). They all show changes in brain function associated with changed reaction times. Could the previous thirty years of research publications (examining numerous frequency bands) help guide further study of these cell-phone induced effects? There is a low probability that these reports from different frequency bands will be examined together unless a biologically based evaluation practice is established.

What is the current exposure situation in cell phone communications? Because of the complicated modulation signal in the cell-phone technology, there is the possibility that effects could occur that are caused by unknown mechanisms of action. At the base stations — even though they produce intensities to humans that are substantially lower than those received from handheld devices — there are typically up to four independent companies per site, giving off simultaneous RFR signals, and the exposures to nearby neighborhoods are continuous – often 24-hours a day. This combination of factors has not been tested in a laboratory environment for biological consequences.

Open, neutral-body guided discussions with all the stakeholders present and contributing would be very helpful for regulators who must evaluate the escalation of new types of EMF exposure scenarios. For example, if the RFR intensity of telecommunications base stations is reduced because of public concern, more antennas will be needed so that signals will be of sufficient strength to allow the technology to function. Micro antennas are already being placed in the interior of buildings to fill in "shadows" where cell phones won't work well. Further, wireless Internet connections (to replace wired computers) pose a potential major new source of exposure to the population.

A Recent Unbiased Review

Some of the concerns expressed by a British physicist, G. J. Hayland,[4] who took an unbiased look at the science, raised questions about the adequacy of the current exposure guidelines. He observed that there are limitations in the reports and conclusions of various review panels and that some of the evidence used to conclude safety is "less solid" than normally stated by government agencies and the telecommunications industry. He concluded that scientific justifications exist for non-thermal effects and that research into thermal effects will always be more robust than that of non-thermal effects, which are more subtle. He also concluded that non-linear systems need to be factored in because no one is effected in the same way by exposure to the same radiation; and that more care should be taken when siting base stations near schools, or allowing children to use cell phones.

Possible Regulatory Approaches

There are three possible regulatory approaches:
1. Accept only proof beyond reasonable doubt. This approach requires theory to support any premise. Therefore there are inherent problems because theoretical models may fail due to inaccurate assumptions. This is the current approach.

---

[4] "Physics and biology of mobile telephony," *The Lancet*, 356:1833-36, Nov 25, 2000.

2. Accept proof based on the balance of probabilities. This approach proved to be the avenue for most of our industrial progress. But for RFR exposures, more information is needed to ensure the protection of the public health.

3. *Caution.* One major caveat that should guide all evaluations is that EMF may act more like a chemical mixture than a single agent. (Agent Orange is an example where the minor chemical contaminant — dioxin — caused the problems.) Adoption of this view would require a much more complex balancing of effects, theory, and awareness of the potential public health issues than is currently done, in that we are using exclusively the thermal model. We need to provide a sufficient measure of safety (in light of uncertainties), while still allowing technological advances.

The Current Research Situation

The data indicate more research is needed because EMF cannot be considered to act like a single chemical. In the past, civilian agencies both competed and coordinated research efforts under the Electromagnetic Radiation Management Council (ERMAC). At the present time, there is very little funding for research other than that provided by industry. In future research efforts, long-term funding should not come from a single agency. We do not need a "czar" to dispense EMF research funds focused on one agency because this could lead to only a few individuals guiding decision making. This situation has gotten the research area into trouble in the past. The best situation to advance research most efficiently is to employ the benefits of "marketplace competition;" to have managers from different agencies — each with their own independent processes to select projects submitted to them — compete to fund the best research. A coordinating council with an advisory role only (similar to the former ERMAC) could be established to ensure that there is no unproductive duplication of research efforts.

Approach to Regulation for Public Health: The Precautionary Principle

What have other knowledgeable sources urged to protect public health regarding EMF exposures? The concept of "prudent avoidance" was first proposed by Granger Morgan in an Office of Technology report, as well as in a science editorial in the late 1980s. It essentially calls for reducing exposures with uncertain health outcomes, as much as possible, without undue inconvenience or unreasonable expense.

Another similar concept that has been emerging from the European Union since the late 1990's is called the "Precautionary Principle." It has been embodied in numerous international treaties, including many signed by the U.S.

The Precautionary Principle holds that when an activity raises threats of harm to human health or the environment, precautionary measures should be taken even if some cause-and-effect relationships are not fully established scientifically. In the context of cellular phone technology, the proponent of the activity, rather than the public, should bear the burden of proof.

Both of these approaches require more publicly-funded research to resolve issues of concern.

Summary on Cell Towers Exposures

How does all of this information affect the siting of cell phone towers? Although the power output of a base station is considerably higher than for a cell-phone handset, as a general rule (depending on one's proximity), the exposure received by individuals from cell towers or other telecommunications antenna arrays, are relatively low when compared to a cell-phone antenna held directly against the head. Distance from the radiating source counts. But some experimental and theoretical work questions the common assumptions that hazards from such exposures only come from radiofrequency-induced heating. Other effects may occur below that heating threshold.

Blanket safety statements about tower exposures cannot be made because exposure conditions can be different for each tower. While biological effects do not "prove" public health problems, they help guide the planning of future research into the most product areas.

Advocates of a prudent approach are concerned about the uncertainties still remaining and wish to apply the precautionary principle to tower siting — maintaining a reasonable distance from schools, people's homes, workplaces, or wherever people congregate.

Lastly, such advocates believe it is important to support independent, multi-source funding of research on EMF effects. They believe it is the only way to better understand what these ubiquitous exposures may mean to us all.

Carl Blackman, Ph.D.
3413 Horton Street
Raleigh, NC 27607-3414
Email: CFB705@compuserve.co

Chapter 3

Biological Effects of Radiofrequency Radiation from Wireless Transmission Towers

By: Henry Lai, Ph.D.

Definitions

Wireless transmission towers for radio, TV, telecommunications, radar and many other applications, emit radiofrequency radiation (RFR). Once emitted, the radiation travels through space at the speed of light and oscillates during propagation (like waves in the ocean). How many times the wave oscillates in one second determines its frequency.

Radiofrequency radiation covers a large segment of the electromagnetic spectrum and falls within the non-ionizing bands. Its frequency ranges between 10 kilohertz (KHz) to 300 gigahertz (GHz). [One hertz (Hz) is one oscillation per second. One kilohertz (KHz) is 1000 Hz; one megahertz (MHz) is 1,000,000 Hz; and 1 gigahertz (GHz) is 1,000,000,000 Hz.]

Different frequencies of RFR are used in different applications. For example, the frequency range of 5.4 to 16 KHz is used in AM radio transmission, while 76 to 108 MHz is used for FM radio. Cell-phone technology uses frequencies between 800 MHz and 3 GHz. And RFR of 2,450 MHz is used in microwave cooking. These are just a few examples.

The intensity of RFR is called the power density. Generally, it is measured in milliwatts per square centimeter (mW/cm^2), which is an energy relationship that exists in space. However, biological effects depend on how much of the energy is absorbed in the body of a living organism, not just what exists in space.

Absorption of RFR depends on many factors including the transmission frequency and the intensity, the duration of exposure, and one's distance from the source. Other factors include an organism's size, shape, water content, and orientation toward the radiating source. Children, for instance, absorb energy differently than adults.

The term used to describe the absorption of radiofrequency radiation is "specific absorption rate" or SAR, which is the rate of energy that is actually absorbed. Specific absorption rates are measured in watts per kilogram (W/kg) of tissue. Specific absorption rates are a more reliable determinant and index of RFR biological effects than are power densities because SARs reflect what is actually being absorbed rather than the energy in space.

There are some indications that biological effects may also depend on how energy is deposited and distributed in the body. In addition, different propagation characteristics such as "modulation," or different wave forms and shapes, may have different effects on a living system. For example, the same amount of energy can be delivered to tissue "continuously" or "in short pulses." Different biological effects may result depending on the type and duration of the exposure.

Transmission Facilities

The intensity of RFR decreases with the distance from the generating source, therefore exposure to RFR from transmission towers is usually of low intensity depending on one's proximity. But intensity is not the only factor. Living near a facility means the exposure will be of a long duration because a person will be exposed to radiation for many hours in the day.

Thus, the relevant questions are:
- Do biological/health effects occur after exposure to low-intensity RFR?
- Do effects accumulate over time, since the exposure is of a long duration and is usually intermittent?
- What precisely is low-intensity RFR and what might its biological effects be?
- What does the science tell us about such exposures?

RFR Government Guidelines:
How Spatial Energy Translates to the Body's Absorption

The U.S. Federal Communications Commission (FCC) has issued guidelines for both power density and specific absorption rates. For power density, the U.S. guidelines are between 0.2-1 mW/cm^2. At 100-200 ft. from a cell phone base station, a person can be exposed to a power density of 0.001 mW/cm^2 (i.e., 1 microwatt/cm^2). The Specific Absorption Rate (SAR) at such a distance can be 0.001 W/kg (i.e., 1 milliwatt/kg). The U.S. guidelines for SARs are between 0.08-0.4 W/kg. Thus, lets define low-intensity exposure to RFR of power density of 0.001 mW/cm^2, or a SAR of 0.001 W/kg.

Biological Effects at Low Intensities

Do biological effects occur at such low intensities? Many have been documented. Here are some examples of biological effects that occurred in studies of cell cultures and animals after exposures to low-intensity RFR:

- De Pomerai *et al.* (2000) reported an increase in a molecular stress response in cells after exposure to RFR at a SAR of 0.001 W/kg. This stress response is a basic biological process that is present in almost all animals — including humans.
- Dutta *et al.* (1989) reported an increase in calcium efflux in cells after exposure to RFR at 0.005 W/kg. Calcium is an important component of normal cellular functions.
- Fesenko *et al.* (1999) reported a change in immunological functions in mice after exposure to RFR at a power density of 0.001 mW/cm^2.
- Magras and Xenos (1999) reported a decrease in reproductive function in mice exposed to RFR at power densities of 0.000168 - 0.001053 mW/cm^2.
- Persson *et al.* (1997) reported an increase in the permeability of the blood-brain barrier in mice exposed to RFR at 0.0004 - 0.008 W/kg. The blood-brain barrier envelops the brain and protects it from toxic substances.
- Phillips *et al.* (1998) reported DNA damage in cells exposed to RFR at SAR of 0.0024 - 0.024 W/kg.
- Velizarov *et al.* (1999) showed a decrease in cell proliferation (division) after exposure to RFR of 0.000021 - 0.0021 W/kg.

These are important findings at such low-intensity exposures. There are many other reports in the recent research literature showing biological effects in cell cultures and animals after exposure to low-intensity RFR. But we don't know if these effects occur in humans exposed to low-intensity RFR, or whether the reported effects are health hazards. Biological effects do not automatically mean adverse health effects. Many biological effects are reversible. However, it is very clear that low-intensity RFR is not biologically inert. Much more needs to be learned, however, before a presumption of safety can be made.

Long-Term Exposures and Cumulative Effects

There are flaws and important gaps in the RFR research. The majority of the studies on RFR have been conducted with short-term exposures, i.e. a few minutes to several hours. Little is known about the effects of long-term exposure such as would be experienced by people living near telecommunications installations, especially with exposures spanning months or years in duration. What are the effects of long-term exposure? Does long-term exposure produce different effects from short-term exposure? Do effects accumulate over time?

There is some evidence that effects of RFR do accumulate over time. Here are some examples:
- Phillips *et al.* (1998) reported DNA damage in cells after 24 hours of exposure to low intensity RFR. DNA damage can lead to gene mutation, which accumulates over time.
- Magras and Xenos (1999) reported that mice exposed to low-intensity RFR became less reproductive. After five generations of exposure, the mice were not able to produce offspring. This shows that the effects of RFR can pass from one generation to another.
- Persson *et al.* (1997) reported an increase in permeability of the blood-brain barrier in mice when the energy deposited in the body exceeded 1.5 J/kg (joule per kilogram) — a measurement of the total amount of energy deposited. This suggests that a short-term/high intensity exposure can produce the same effect as a long-term/low intensity exposure. This is another indication that RFR effects can accumulate over time.

There is some indication that an animal becomes more sensitive to the radiation after long-term exposure. Let us consider two of the critical experiments that contributed to the present U.S. RFR-exposure standards — the "Behavior-Disruption Experiments" carried out in the 1980s.

In the first experiment, de Lorge and Ezell (1980) trained rats on an "auditory observing-response task." In the task, an animal was presented with two bars. Pressing the right bar would produce either a low-pitch or a high-pitch tone for half a second. The low-pitch tone signaled an "unrewarded" situation and the animal was expected to do nothing. However, when the high-pitch tone was on, pressing the left bar would produce a food reward. Thus, the task required continuous vigilance in which an animal had to coordinate its motor responses according to the stimulus presented in order to get a reward by choosing between a high-pitch or low-pitch tone. After learning the task, rats were then irradiated with 1280 MHz or 5620 MHz RFR during performance. Disruption of behavior (i.e., the rats couldn't perform very well) was observed at a SAR of 3.75 W/kg for 1280 MHz and 4.9 W/kg for 5620 MHz. Disruption occurred within 30-60 minutes of exposure.

In another experiment, de Lorge (1984) trained monkeys on a similar "auditory observing-response task". Monkeys were exposed to RFR of 225, 1300, and 5800 MHz. Disruption of performance was observed at 8.1 mW/cm^2 (SAR 3.2 W/kg) for 225 MHz, 57 mW/cm^2 (SAR 7.4 W/kg) for 1300 MHz, and 140 mW/cm^2 (SAR 4.3 W/kg) for 5800 MHz. The disruption occurred when body temperature was increased by 1°C.

The conclusion from these experiments is that "disruption of behavior occurred when an animal was exposed at a SAR of approximately 4 W/kg, and disruption occurred after 30-60 minutes of exposure and when body temperature increased by 1°C." Thus, the 4 W/kg figure is used in the setting of the present U.S. RFR exposure guidelines for humans with theoretical margins of safety added. With this, the limit for occupational exposure was set at 0.4 W/kg (i.e. 1/10 of the SAR where effects were observed) and for public exposure 0.08 W/kg (i.e. 1/5 of that of occupational exposure). But is this standard adequate?

The studies described above are effects of short-term exposure (less than one hour). Are they comparable to long-term exposure? The same investigators of the above short-term exposure experiments reported two series of experiments in 1986 on the effects of long-term exposure.

Here are the results:
- D'Andrea et al. (1986a) exposed rats to 2450 MHz RFR for 7 hours a day, 7 days a week for 14 weeks. They reported a disruption of behavior at an SAR of 0.7 W/kg.
- D'Andrea et al. (1986b) also exposed rats to 2450 MHz RFR for 7 hours a day, 7 days a /week, for 90 days at an SAR of 0.14 W/kg and found a small but significant disruption in behavior.

The experimenters concluded, "the threshold for behavioral and physiological effects of chronic *(long-term)* RFR exposure in the rat occurs between 0.5 mW/cm^2 (0.14 W/kg) and 2.5 mW/cm^2 (0.7 W/kg)."

Thus, RFR can produce an effect at much lower intensities after an animal is chronically exposed. This can have very significant implications for people exposed to RFR from transmission towers.

Other Observations

Other biological outcomes also have been reported after long-term exposure to RFR:

- Effects were observed after prolonged, repeated exposure but not after short-term exposure (Baranski, 1972; Takashima *et al.*, 1979).
- Effects that were observed after short-term exposure, disappeared after prolonged, repeated exposure, i.e., an indication of habituation (Johnson *et al.*, 1983; Lai *et al.*, 1987, 1992).
- Different effects were observed after different durations of exposure (Dumanski and Shandala, 1974; Lai *et al.*, 1989).

The conclusion from this body of work is that effects of long-term exposure can be quite different from those of short-term exposure.

Effects Below 4 W/kg: Thermal v. Non-Thermal

There are many studies that show biological effects at SARs less than 4 W/kg after short-term exposures to RFR. For example, effects on behavior have been observed at SARs less than 4 W/kg. [D'Andrea *et al.* (1986a, b) at 0.14-to-0.7 W/kg; DeWitt *et al.* (1987) at 0.14 W/kg; Gage (1979) at 3 W/kg; King *et al.* (1971) at 2.4 W/kg; Lai *et al.* (1989) at 0.6 W/kg; Mitchell *et al.* (1977) at 2.3 W/kg; Navakatikian and Tomashevskaya (1994) at 0.027 W/kg; Schrot *et al.* (1980) at 0.7 W/kg; Thomas *et al.* (1975) at 1.5 to 2.7 W/kg; Wang and Lai (2000) at 1.2 W/kg.]

For decades, there have been questions about whether an effect is thermal (i.e., a significant change in temperature) or non-thermal (i.e., no significant change in temperature). The present guidelines, as mentioned before, are presumably based on thermal effects (e.g., a change of body temperature of 1°C). However, this distinction is now obsolete. We actually don't need to know whether RFR effects are thermal or non-thermal to set exposure guidelines for RFR exposure. However, most of the studies on biological effects of RFR carried out since the 1980's were under 'non-thermal' conditions. In studies using isolated cells, the ambient temperature during exposure was generally well controlled. In most animal studies, the RFR intensity used usually did not cause a significant increase in body temperature of the animals exposed. But scientists continue to wonder about non-thermal effects. Some scientists recognize that non-thermal effects are established, even as the implications are not fully understood.

There are several arguments for the existence of non-thermal effects:
1. There are reports that RFRs of the same frequency and intensity, but with different modulations and wave forms, produce different effects (Arber and Lin, 1985; Baranski, 1972; Frey *et al.*, 1975; Oscar and Hawkins, 1977; Sanders *et al.*, 1985).
2. RFR triggers effects different from an increase in temperature (D'Inzeo *et al.*, 1988; Seaman and Wachtel, 1978; Wachtel *et al.*, 1975).
3. Effects are observed with RFR of very low intensities, when temperature increase is unlikely (dePomerai *et al.*, 2000).

Conclusion

- Biological effects do occur after a short-term exposure to low-intensity RFR. However, potential hazardous health effects of such exposure to humans are not clear.
- Not much is known about the biological effects of long-term exposure. The effects of long-term exposure can be quite different from those of short-term exposure.
- The present U.S. guidelines for RFR exposure are not up-to-date. The most recent IEEE Guidelines only included research data up to 1985. In addition, effects of long-term exposure, modulation, and other propagation characteristics are not considered. Therefore, the current guidelines are questionable in protecting the public from possible harmful effects of RFR exposure.

- Exposure of the general population to RFR from wireless communication devices and transmission towers should be kept to a minimum and should follow the ALAR principle — "As Low As Reasonably Achievable."

Henry Lai
Bioelectromagnetics Research Laboratory
Department of Bioengineering, Box 357962
University of Washington, Seattle, WA 98195-7962
Email: hlai@u.washington.edu

Literature cited:

1. Arber, S.L., and Lin, J.C., 1985, "Microwave-induced changes in nerve cells: effects of modulation and temperature," *Bioelectromagnetics* 6:257-270.
2. Baranski, S., 1972, "Histological and histochemical effects of microwave irradiation on the central nervous system of rabbits and guinea pigs," *Am J Physiol Med* 51:182-190.
3. D'Andrea, J.A., DeWitt, J.R., Emmerson, R.Y., Bailey, C., Stensaas, S., and Gandhi, O. P., 1986a, "Intermittent exposure of rats to 2450 MHz microwaves at 2.5 mW/cm^2: behavioral and physiological effects," *Bioelectromagnetics* 7:315-328.
4. D'Andrea, J.A., DeWitt, J.R., Gandhi, O. P., Stensaas, S., Lords, J.L., and Nielson, H.C., 1986b, "Behavioral and physiological effects of chronic 2450 MHz microwave irradiation of the rat at 0.5 mW/cm^2," *Bioelectromagnetics* 7:45-56.
5. de Lorge, J.O. , 1984, "Operant behavior and colonic temperature of Macaca mulatta exposed to radiofrequency fields at and above resonant frequencies," *Bioelectromagnetics* 5:233-246.
6. de Lorge, J., and Ezell, C.S., 1980, "Observing-responses of rats exposed to 1.28- and 5.62 GHz microwaves," *Bioelectromagnetics* 1:183-198.
7. de Pomerai, D., Daniells, C., David, H., Allan, J., Duce, I., Mutwakil, M., Thomas, D., Sewell, P., Tattersall, J., Jones, D., and Candido, P., 2000, "Non-thermal heat-shock response to microwaves," *Nature* 405:417-418.

8. DeWitt, J.R., D'Andrea, J.A., Emmerson, R.Y., and Gandhi, O.P., 1987, "Behavioral effects of chronic exposure to 0.5 mW/cm^2 of 2450 MHz microwaves," *Bioelectromagnetics* 8:149-157.

9. D'Inzeo, G., Bernardi, P., Eusebi, F., Grassi, F., Tamburello, C., and Zani, B.M., 1988, "Microwave effects on acetylcholine-induced channels in cultured chick myotubes," *Bioelectromagnetics* 9:363-372.

10. Dumansky, J.D., and Shandala, M.G., 1974, "The biologic action and hygienic significance of electromagnetic fields of super high and ultra high frequencies in densely populated areas," *Biologic Effects and Health Hazards of Microwave Radiation: Proceedings of an International Symposium,*" P. Czerski, *et al.,* eds., Polish Medical Publishers, Warsaw.

11. Dutta, S.K., Ghosh, B., and Blackman, C.F., 1989, "Radiofrequency radiation-induced calcium ion efflux enhancement from human and other neuroblastoma cells in culture," *Bioelectromagnetics* 10:197-202.

12. Fesenko, E.E., Makar, V.R., Novoselova, E.G., and Sadovnikov, V.B., 1999, "Microwaves and cellular immunity. I. Effect of whole body microwave irradiation on tumor necrosis factor production in mouse cells," *Bioelectrochem Bioenerg* 49:29-35.

13. Frey, A.H., Feld, S.R., and Frey, B., 1975, "Neural function and behavior: defining the relationship," *Ann N Y Acad Sci* 247:433-439.

14. Gage, M.I., 1979, "Behavior in rats after exposure to various power densities of 2450 MHz microwaves," *Neurobehav Toxicol* 1:137-143.

15. Johnson, R.B., Spackman, D., Crowley, J., Thompson, D., Chou, C.K., Kunz, L.L., and Guy, A.W., 1983, *Effects of long-term low-level radiofrequency radiation exposure on rats, vol. 4, Open field behavior and corticosterone,* USAF SAM-TR83-42, Report of USAF School of Aerospace Medicine, Brooks AFB, San Antonio, TX.

16. King, N.W., Justesen, D.R., and Clarke, R.L., 1971, "Behavioral sensitivity to microwave irradiation," *Science* 172:398-401.

17. Lai, H., Horita, A., Chou, C.K., and Guy, A.W., 1987, "Effects of low-level microwave irradiation on hippocampal and frontal cortical choline uptake are classically conditionable," *Pharmac Biochem Behav* 27:635-639.

18. Lai, H., Carino, M.A., and Guy, A.W., 1989, "Low-level microwave irradiation and central cholinergic systems," *Pharmac Biochem Behav* 33:131-138.

19. Lai, H., Carino, M.A., Horita, A., and Guy, A.W., 1992, "Single vs. repeated microwave exposure: effects on benzodiazepine receptors in the brain of the rat," *Bioelectromagnetics* 13:57-66.

20. Lai, H., Carino, M.A., and Guy, A.W., 1989, "Low-level microwave irradiation and central cholinergic systems," *Pharmac Biochem Behav* 33:131-138.

21. Magras, I.N., and Xenos, T.D., 1997, "RF radiation-induced changes in the prenatal development of mice," *Bioelectromagnetics* 18:455-461.
22. Mitchell, D.S., Switzer, W.G., and Bronaugh, E.L., 1977, "Hyperactivity a disruption of operant behavior in rats after multiple exposure to microwave radiation," *Radio Sci* 12:263-271.
23. Navakatikian, M.A., and Tomashevskaya, L.A., 1994, "Phasic behavioral and endocrine effects of microwaves of nonthermal intensity," *Biological Effects of Electric and Magnetic Fields,* vol. 1, D.O. Carpenter, ed., Academic Press, San Diego, CA.
24. Oscar, K.J. and Hawkins, T.D., 1977, "Microwave alteration of the blood-brain barrier system of rats," *Brain Res* 126:281-293.
25. Persson B.R.R., Salford L.G., and Brun, A., 1997, "Blood-brain barrier permeability in rats exposed to electromagnetic fields used in wireless communication," *Wireless Network* 3:455-461.
26. Phillips, J.L., Ivaschuk, O., Ishida-Jones, T., Jones, R.A., Campbell-Beachler, M., and Haggren, W., 1998, "DNA damage in Molt-4 T-lymphoblastoid cells exposed to cellular telephone radiofrequency fields in vitro," *Bioelectrochem Bioenerg* 45:103-110.
27. Sanders, A.P., Joines, W.T., and Allis, J.W., 1985, "Effect of continuous-wave, pulsed, and sinusoidal-amplitude-modulated microwaves on brain energy metabolism," *Bioelectromagnetics* 6:89-97.
28. Schrot, J., Thomas, J.R., and Banvard, R.A., 1980, "Modification of the repeated acquisition of response sequences in rats by low-level microwave exposure," *Bioelectromagnetics* 1:89-99.
29. Seaman, R.L., and Wachtel, H., 1978, "Slow and rapid responses to CW and pulsed microwave radiation by individual Aplysia pacemakers," *J Microwave Power* 13:77-86.
30. Takashima, S., Onaral, B., and Schwan, H.P., 1979, "Effects of modulated RF energy on the EEG of mammalian brain," *Rad Environ Biophys* 16:15- 27.
31. Thomas, J.R., Finch, E.D., Fulk, D.W., and Burch, L.S., 1975, "Effects of low-level microwave radiation on behavioral baselines," *Ann NY Acad Sci* 247:425-432.
32. Velizarov, S., Raskmark, P., and Kwee, S., 1999, "The effects of radiofrequency fields on cell proliferation are non-thermal," *Bioelectrochem Bioenerg* 48:177-180.
33. Wachtel, H., Seaman, R., and Joines, W., 1975, "Effects of low-intensity microwaves on isolated neurons," *Ann NY Acad Sci* 247:46-62.
34. Wang, B.M., and Lai, H., 2000, "Acute exposure to pulsed 2450-MHz microwaves affects water-maze performance of rats," *Bioelectromagnetics* 21:52-56.

Chapter 4

Avian Mortality at Communication Towers: Steps to Alleviate a Growing Problem

By: Albert M. Manville, II, Ph.D.

The issue of bird strikes at communication towers is an issue with which the U.S. Fish and Wildlife Service (FWS) is very much involved. Migratory birds are a trust responsibility for the FWS. We are responsible for the conservation and management of 836 species of migratory birds: 778 are so-called nongame species (such as the Eastern bluebird), and 58 species are legally hunted as game (such as the wood duck). All are protected under the Migratory Bird Treaty Act of 1918, as amended.

While populations of some species are doing well (some too well — e.g. snow geese, urban Canada geese, cowbirds, and cormorants), many others are not. We are seeing the continued decline of over 200 avian species. For example, there are only approximately 180 endangered whooping cranes in the wild; 77 bird species are listed as endangered; and 15 are listed as threatened under the federal Endangered Species Act (ESA). One hundred and twenty-four species are currently on the list of nongame species of management concern — meaning birds whose populations are declining, some precipitously. The next step could be the ESA — a train wreck we prefer to avoid. One species of management concern is the cerulean warbler.

For approximately one-third of the 836 species of migratory birds, we have essentially no population data. Thus, the individual factors that kill birds — including collisions with towers, wind generators, electric power lines, glass windows, oil spills, aircraft, cars, electrocutions, predators such as cats, pesticides, and other causes—are all of growing concern. The loss and/or degradation of habitat are the greatest threats to all wildlife. Of even greater concern are the cumulative and combined impacts of these mortality factors, including those impacts to bird populations.

Bird-watching is Big Business

Birds are big business in North America. More than seventy-one million adult Americans — 1 in 4 — feed, photograph, and watch birds. More than $28 billion dollars are spent pursuing these activities each year by bird enthusiasts. Bird-watching, has become America's fastest growing outdoor activity, increasing 150 percent in the past decade. More Americans reportedly go on vacations to watch birds today than to play golf.

Birds have environmental significance far beyond our visual enjoyment. Birds pollinate flowers, disperse tree seeds, and eat weed seeds. They remove insect pests that have an impact on commercial food crops and forest species, thus making possible multi-billion-dollar industries extremely dependent upon birds.

The global reduction of pollinators — including birds — raises alarm. Fully two-thirds of our flowering plants are pollinated by birds, insects, and bats, which produce a global economic benefit estimated at $117 billion per year. In short, birds are extremely important to us all.

Role of FWS

The FWS plays several roles in dealing with communication towers:

- Tower permitting and placement are coordinated through our Division of Federal Program Activities (formerly Division of Habitat Conservation) and Ecological Services field offices around the country.
- Avian management, monitoring and research are coordinated through my office — the Division of Migratory Bird Management.
- Enforcement is handled through our Division of Law Enforcement in our 7 regions and Washington, D.C. (Arlington, VA) offices.

Our offices of Federal Program Activities and Ecological Services use Federal Communications Commission regulations — specifically 47 Code of Federal Regulations (CFR) Chap. 1, Sect.1.1307 — to implement National Environmental Policy Act (NEPA) and Section 7 ESA issues.

Unfortunately, migratory birds are not specifically mentioned within this regulation, even though FWS feels towers are having a significant cumulative impact upon birds. Birds are categorically excluded from

NEPA analysis under this regulation, except where towers are <u>proposed</u> to be built on National Wildlife Refuges, or where threatened and endangered species, and/or their critical habitats, may be affected.

However, even under Sect. 7 of the ESA, there is no actual requirement for the tower licensee to contact us. Even when a "may affect" determination is required, there is *no consistent guidance and no standardized way* of conducting it. We've attempted to get at this through a tower site evaluation form now available publicly.

Early in 1998, the Division of Migratory Bird Management became actively involved in the tower-collision issue. A large kill of up to 10,000 Lapland longspurs, a migratory songbird, occurred on January 22, 1998, at three towers and a natural gas pumping station in western Kansas on a snowy, foggy night. The issue was almost immediately brought to our attention by the environmental community. In April 1998, I was asked to brief the Policy Council of the American Bird Conservancy on, among other things, bird mortality from tower strikes. At that time, I provided a partial — but certainly *not* complete — literature review, as well as abstracts, put together by Migratory Bird staff member John Trapp.

Following that meeting, informal discussions continued with representatives from the Federal Communications Commission, the FWS offices of Federal Program Activities, and the Division of Migratory Bird Management. In November 1998, representatives of the FWS's regional, field and Washington, D.C., offices met in Panama City, Florida, to discuss, "Migratory Bird Conservation and Communication Towers: Avoiding and Minimizing Conflicts." A tower risk model was developed at this meeting and the document was made available to the public.

In late December 1998, I met with representatives of the environmental dispute resolution group, RESOLVE. We discussed the need for a facilitated meeting with various stakeholders in order to review research needs and gaps; put concerns on the table; and begin a dialogue with various players interested in — and concerned about — the issue.

That meeting took place in Washington, D.C., on June 29, 1999. Forty-two stakeholders were present representing government agencies, including the Federal Communications Commission, the Federal Aviation Administration, the Federal Highway Administration, the USDA's National Wildlife Research Center, the U.S. Fish & Wildlife Service, and the Wisconsin Department of Natural Resources. The research community was also represented, including the Illinois Natural History Survey, the Buffalo Museum of Science, Geo-Marine, the State University of New

York (SUNY) at Geneseo, and Cornell and Clemson universities. Industry was also represented, including the Personal Communications Industry Association, the Cellular Telecommunications and Internet Association, Motorola, SBC Wireless, and Environmental Resources Management; as well as a broad-based representation from the environmental community.

On August 11th, 1999, the first-ever public workshop on "Avian Mortality at Communication Towers" took place at Cornell University in conjunction with the 117th meeting of the American Ornithologists Union. The workshop was co-sponsored by the FWS, the Ornithological Council, and the American Bird Conservancy.[1] I had the privilege of co-chairing and facilitating the meeting, which included presentations by seventeen speakers, as well as a discussion of research and funding needs with a focus on where the gaps were located. Future directions to fill in those gaps were discussed by a panel of twenty-three experts.

Birds and Communications Towers

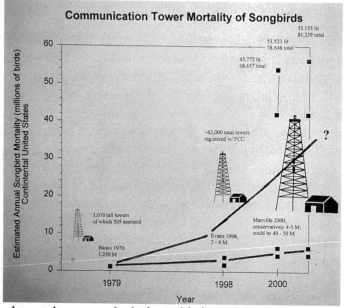

We learned a great deal about birds and communication towers at this workshop. Published accounts of birds striking tall, lighted structures

---

[1] The complete transcripts of that meeting are available on our web site at http://migratorybirds.fws.gov/issues/towers/agenda.html.

such as lighthouses, although often anecdotal, have appeared in the literature since as far back as 1874. The earliest report of birds dying from a tower collision in the U.S. was published in 1949 after a radio-tower strike incident in Baltimore, Maryland.

The first long-term study of birds striking towers was begun by Tall Timbers Research Station in 1955, at a television station in northern Florida. Over the 25-year study, 42,384 bird carcasses representing 189 species were collected and identified from collisions with this tower, its guy wires, other birds, or the ground.

To date, the longest study of bird mortality has been conducted by physician Dr. Charles Kemper, in Eau Clair, Wisconsin. Beginning in 1957, the 38-year study has collected 121,560 bird carcasses representing 123 species. Dr. Kemper's all-time, one-night record kill occurred in 1963 when he collected and identified over 12,000 birds, not accounting for the almost certain scavenging by cats, dogs, foxes, raccoons, skunks, owls, crows, and others species then present. Similar avian fatality studies are continuing today by ornithologists Todd Engstrom, Art Clark, Bill Evans, and others.

Today the FWS conservatively estimates that four to five million birds are killed per year in the U.S. by colliding with towers, guy wires, other birds, or the ground. Mortality could range to a high end of 40-50 million. Only a cumulative impacts study will ascertain the true magnitude of this problem.

Much other information about bird strikes with communication towers, including radio, television, cellular, microwave, paging, messaging, open video, public safety, wireless data, government dispatch, and emergency broadcast, has been published since the 1970's.

Unfortunately, most materials only review carcass counts and species variability, *not* the presumed or suspected causes of bird collisions. Research into this area is sorely lacking. Published accounts do, however, answer one question. Birds vulnerable to communication towers comprise nearly 350 species of so-called neotropical migratory songbirds — thrushes, vireos, and warblers are the species that seem to be most vulnerable. These are birds that breed in North America in the spring and summer and migrate to the southern United States, the Caribbean, or Latin America during the fall and winter. These species generally migrate at night and appear to be most susceptible to collisions with lighted towers on foggy, misty, rainy, low-cloud-ceiling nights during their migrations. Lights seem to be key.

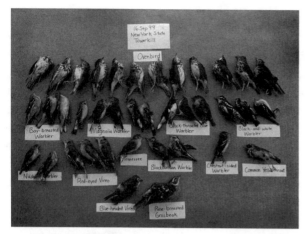

Bill Evans New York Study, 1999

Federal Aviation Administration (FAA) regulations currently require towers taller than 199 feet above ground level to contain pilot warning light(s). Towers within 3.8 statute miles of an airport, and towers along major highway travel corridors, must also be lighted. According to the FCC's October 2000 Antenna Structure Registry database, there were 79,000 registered towers, nearly 52,000 lighted — most exceeding 199 feet above ground level. The January 2001 database contains over 81,000 registered towers, of which more than 53,000 are lighted.

While some argue that the database understates the number of lighted towers, suggesting that upwards of 80,000 are currently lighted, we do know tower construction has increased exponentially in the past four years and continues to grow at six to eight percent per year. Six to ten thousand new towers are constructed each year.[2]

Different Aspects of Bird Mortality and Towers

What is it specifically about the towers that seem to attract the birds? Lighting again is critical. We know, for example, that the bird's eye contains from four to six different types of cones, whereas the human eye has only three. We also know that light can affect bird behavior both visually and electromagnetically. While the retina of the bird's eye is far more sensitive to the red and ultraviolet spectra, current scientific thinking indicates that light duration — the "off" phase of lights between the blink or flash phases of light pulses — is far more critical in altering bird behavior than is color.

---

[2] See the website www.towerkill.com for additional information.

In addition, solid or blinking red lights *seem* to attract birds on foggy, misty nights far more than do white strobes, which may flash once every three seconds — the currently allowable maximum "off" phase between flashes. While some preliminary research supports this premise, we will need further testing to validate this hypothesis. Simply put, the longer the off phase, the less likely the attraction. Thanks to cooperation from the FAA, I've managed to help convince that agency to allow a very controlled experiment by ornithologist Bill Evans to test this hypothesis in New York State. The FAA agreed to allow lights to be turned off for very brief periods of time under extremely strict, controlled conditions. The study will hopefully begin in 2001.

The taller the tower, the more likely it will kill birds. Guy wires and lights are critical. The more guy wires there are supporting a tower, the greater the risk for bird strikes. Lights seem to draw birds in especially during inclement nights. The birds appear to shut off their normal "nocturnal" migratory cues of star and magnetic compass orientation, and appear to switch on "diurnal" cues. Attracted to the lights, they fly around and around in a "tornado" of birds, striking the guy wires, the tower, themselves, or the ground — and frequently die.

Jenny Nehring, University of Tennessee tower study.

A Worse-case Tower Scenario

A worse-case scenario would be:

- A tower with a height greater than one-thousand feet, with multiple guy wires
- A tower with multiple solid or pulsating red lights
- Towers located in a bird migratory corridor, near or next to a wetland, with federally listed endangered or threatened bird species also present. (In fact, this real-life situation already exists.)

Unfortunately, the Telecommunications Act of 1996 only exacerbated this problem. All television stations must be digitized by 2003, adding (by some estimates) 1,000 new "mega-towers" over 1,000 feet tall. The literature strongly supports the hypothesis that the taller the tower, the more birds are likely to be killed.

The Migratory Bird Treaty Act of 1918, as amended — our "marching orders" for the Division of Migratory Bird Management — is a strict liability law. The killing of any bird is not technically allowed under the law unless permitted. The Service does not allow the "incidental taking" of migratory birds except under permit and we do not issue "incidental" or "unintentional take" permits.

What about the impacts of electromagnetic radiation and radio waves? With the possible exception of pulsed microwave radiation such as is used in the newer digital PCS telecommunications systems, research indicates that most radiofrequency radiation has not been shown to be a problem. Possible radiation impacts to avian physiology, however, still need further research and review. The body of research on this issue is sparse.

FWS Efforts With the Bird-Strike Problem

While the FWS recognizes that research into the actual causes of bird collisions with towers is scant, some preliminary but promising findings provide insight into minimizing bird collisions with towers. A list of interim guidelines, *voluntary and nonbinding* both to the industry and to our Service personnel were approved this past September by our director.

We strongly encourage the following for companies planning to site and construct towers:

- Regardless of the type of communications being considered, we *always* recommend co-location onto an existing structure — a tower, church steeple, monopole, spire, water tower, or billboard — as the first option in siting a communications array. Depending, for example, on tower load factors, from six to ten providers may co-locate on an existing tower. Crown Castle USA has some towers with 120 clients co-located on a single tower; they average nine tenants per tower.

- If co-location is not practical, we suggest keeping towers under 200 feet, unguyed, and unlit. If at all possible, new towers should be located in existing "antenna farms" preferably in areas not used by migratory birds, or species federally or state-listed as endangered or threatened, or listed as nongame species of management concern.

- We encourage the review of local meteorological conditions, especially where there is a high incidence of fog, mist, and low ceilings during spring and fall migrations, as well as avoiding siting towers in such areas.

- If towers must be over 199 feet in height (the FAA's threshold for pilot warning lighting), we strongly suggest keeping them unguyed, using lattice or monopole structures with no supporting wires. Where permissible by FAA and local zoning regulations, only white strobe lights should be used at night. These should be up-shielded to minimize disruption to local residents. They should have the minimum number of lights, with minimum intensity and number of flashes per minute allowed by the FAA — currently twenty per minute. The use of solid red or pulsating red warning lights should be avoided at night.

- Guyed towers constructed in known raptor or waterbird concentration areas should use daytime visual markers — bird diverter devices — on guy wires to prevent collisions by these day-active species. Guidance from the electric utility industry is available for bird diverters.

Lattice construction for towers over 750'

- Towers should be constructed in a way that limits or minimizes habitat loss within the tower "footprint." If significant populations of breeding birds are known to occur within the proposed tower footprint, construction should be limited to those months when birds are not nesting — times other than spring and summer.
- If a tower is constructed or proposed for construction, FWS designated researchers should be allowed access to the site after construction is completed in order to: conduct searches for dead birds — both large (cranes, swans, and geese), and small (thrushes, warblers); to place above-ground catchment nets below towers; to position radar, Global Positioning System, infrared, thermal imagery, and acoustical monitoring equipment, as necessary, to assess and verify bird migrations and habitat use; and to assess the impact of various tower sizes, configurations, and lighting schemes.
- Lastly, we encourage the removal of towers no longer in use or when determined to be obsolete, within twelve months of cessation of use.

In addition to the voluntary tower-siting guidelines just mentioned, we also distribute a tower site evaluation form to help in our review of applications — including NEPA and Section 7 ESA issues.

Next Steps

On June 29, 1999, forty-two stakeholders attended the RESOLVE meeting. The Communication Tower Working Group (CTWG) was created — initially with 15 representatives from federal and state agencies, the research community, industry, and the conservation community. I have the privilege of chairing the CTWG for the Service. Today, the Working Group is represented by over 50 stakeholders. The task of the Working Group is simple: develop and implement a research protocol that will determine what causes bird collisions with towers, and what can be done to avoid them.

In November 1999, the first meeting of the Working Group occurred with thirty-three different representatives attending. Subcommittees were created to deal with research, funding and legal issues. The Research Subcommittee met in April 2000. The Subcommittee agreed on a protocol to conduct a nationwide study that will:

- Quantify, with statistical certainty, the cause and effects of color and duration of lighting, and the correlation between bird kills and weather.
- Determine the critical tower height and a height threshold.
- Assess and quantify the most dangerous tower situations.
- Assess radar, acoustic, and ground survey techniques that could be used to determine major migratory corridors/flyways, or routes, and stopover areas, in order to avoid tower sitings in these areas.
- Develop an effective monitoring protocol — borrowing heavily from the wind generation and power distribution industries.
- Assess cumulative impacts of towers on bird populations in North America.

In 1979, Dick Banks published a special scientific report for the FWS estimating annual bird mortality. Banks estimated *annual tower-kill mortality at nearly 1.3 million birds per year* based on 500 of the then-existing 1,010 tall towers. Today, we conservatively estimate mortality at four to five million birds per year. This could range to a high end of 40-50 million per year. Only systematic monitoring will provide us a better figure.

The Research Subcommittee finalized the framework for a nationwide study. A detailed literature review and synthesis of the bird-strike issue was also provided at this meeting. In June 2000, the full Communication Tower Working Group met, and approved the framework for the study.[3] SW Bell Wireless solicited research proposals for pilot studies to look at these problems. Several have been successfully peer-reviewed and are being submitted for possible industry funding.

The Cellular Telecommunications and Internet Association solicited a nationwide research proposal for the framework approved by the Working Group, but acknowledged that the Working Group would be competing with two other existing cell-phone health safety studies that CTIA is currently funding. The nationwide research will likely cost in excess of $15 million for a three- to- five-year study.

I have also met with a representative of White House Office of Science and Technology Policy to begin fine-tuning our nationwide re-search proposal — next to be reviewed by the Research Subcommittee.

Crown Castle USA is looking to provide researcher access to their tower sites. I am working with them on the access issue. Funding will need to come from the federal government as well as from industry. We're working on that and are hopeful that some seed money can be appropriated.

Meanwhile, the media and the public have shown considerable interest in this issue. We believe it to be a serious environmental problem, especially as more towers proliferate to support the infrastructure for advanced telecommunications services.

Albert M. Manville, II, Ph.D.
Division of Migratory Bird Management, U.S. Fish & Wildlife Service
4401 N. Fairfax Dr., Suite 634
Arlington, VA 22203
Email: Albert_Manville@fws.gov

---

[3] The Personal Communications Industry Association (PCIA) provided $10,000 in funding to hold the two meetings.

Chapter 5

Assessing Health Risks of Cell Towers

By: Andrew A. Marino, Ph.D., J.D.

I'm going to discuss the health consequences of being exposed to electromagnetic fields from cell towers. Are they safe, or is there a risk? I'm not going to answer the question. This is not the time or place for me to do that. I want to be very clear about what I mean by "risk." People who live beside the cell towers are going to get sick, just like anybody else. They may get cancer; they may have heart attacks; or get other kinds of diseases, because that's what can happen to people — eventually. If it were the case that we could take even one such sick person, and make no change whatsoever in his life except to erase exposure to the electromagnetic field, and it turned out that this change delayed the onset of his disease — then that is what it means to say that exposure to the fields is a risk.

Safe?   Risk?

- Risk?/Safe? Is <u>not</u> purely or even mostly a scientific question.
- It is impossible to get an answer from science, and it is unwise to accept <u>any</u> answer from scientists.

I'm going to make two basic points. The first is that the question of whether something is a risk, or is it safe, is not a scientific question. Second, I'm going to conclude that it is exceedingly unwise for you to put your faith in scientists because they're no better than you. They're no worse than you. They're just like you. It makes no sense for you to let scientists do your thinking for you.

This question that I intend to talk about —"risk? or safe?"— is a complex one, but we can group the issues into three separate areas. I will talk about all three pieces of the puzzle.

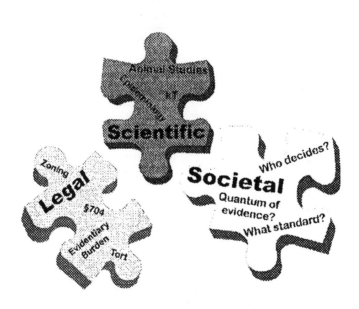

Let's suppose the answer to the question — "risk? or safe?" — is actually scientific. Consider two questions. First, what would the answer look like? It's clear that we have to have some concept of what it would look like because that's the only way we're going to know it when we see it. So, what would it look like? Second, how would we get the answer? Bear in mind that if there is no agreeable and acceptable way to do that, then the situation would be truly hopeless.

Suppose ⟶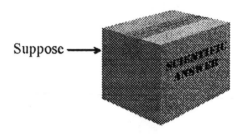

Q1: What would it look like?

Q2: How would we get it?

The orthodox answer to the first question is that the facts answer the question, and that when we have enough of the facts the answer will be obvious. Is that true? Well, let's see.

Orthodox Answer to Q1

If you're educated as a physicist or engineer in this country you are taught that there are three kinds of facts that you will use in your career. We can find something, we can measure something, and — because of the intellectual achievements of our forefathers, we have all of the deep, deep laws of nature in the form of mathematical equations — we can deduce things.

There are four sets of laws. From those laws we can deduce things. What things? Everything you can think of. For example, one of those four laws, in conjunction with measurement facts, completely explains how cell phones work. There's no mystery about them. Their behavior is entirely predictable — that is, it can be deduced.

OK - Then What's a Fact?

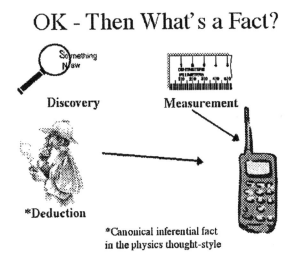

Discovery Measurement

*Deduction

*Canonical inferential fact
in the physics thought-style

The simple truth is that there are no deductive facts that can be summed to answer the question of risk — not even one. Thus, all of the special expertise of the physicists is simply unavailing. It doesn't matter. Physicists can give no more of an authoritative answer to the question than Groucho can.

*Risk?/Safe? = Nonquestion
in Physics

*Don't confuse this question with the
relatively trivial kind of question that
can be answered by a measurement

Well how are we going to get a scientific answer to the question — "risk? or safe?" This task begins with recognition that there is plainly and obviously another kind of inferential fact, and it is obtained by a reasoning process that is totally different from the deductive reasoning process.

*Abduction
(the other kind of inferential fact)

 "The evidence suggests that the beans came from the bag."

*The canonical reasoning form in biology and medicine

Now, in a sense, the abductive fact is a poor country cousin of a deductive fact. A deductive fact pounds the table. It says, "This is the way it is. Exactly. Certainly." It's the nearest thing to infallibility that you'll ever see on earth. The abductive fact, in contrast, says, "It looks like this is the case. The data suggests that such-and-such is true. But of course, I could be wrong."

Subjectivity in Abductive Facts

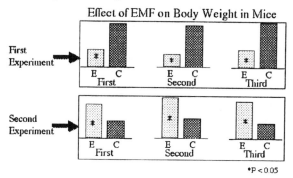

Okay? So let's decide the question using abductive facts since that's the only kind of fact open to us. Well, it turns out there are basic problems with that approach to answering the question. This illustration depicts one of the more fundamental difficulties, namely, that abductive facts are at least partially subjective. I want to illustrate this point using real data. I've shown it in qualitative form because the numbers themselves aren't important. These experiments were performed at a private research institute in Richland, Washington, on behalf of the electric power industry. These are folks who are keen for you to understand that the electromagnetic field from powerlines are safe.

The investigators exposed three successive generations of mice to electromagnetic fields, and then repeated the entire experiment. The first time they did it they found that the mice in the exposed group were always smaller than the controls, and the second time they did the experiment they found that the mice were always larger than the controls.

What is the overall conclusion of this work? Incidentally, when I present this question to my students, a fair number of them say that no conclusion is possible, and that it's necessary to repeat the experiment. Well, that's an unacceptable answer. That's simply not an option. Why? Because, these two experiments cost several million dollars. Not even the power companies can continue to fund studies of that magnitude without an answer. This is the real world, imperfect as it is, and we need an answer.

Well, there are two possibilities. The investigators argued this way: They said in the first experiment the mice were smaller than the controls and in the second experiment they were larger than the controls. Therefore, on average, they were identical to the controls, suggesting there was no effect due to the EMF. The alternative view is this: Both experiments clearly showed that fields could affect the growth rate of mice, but the direction of the effect was affected by factors that were not controlled in the experiments. Note that depending on the interpretation one accepts or adopts, the experiment is or is not evidence that being exposed to power-line fields is a health risk. The point of this example is to show you that abductive facts have a significant subjective component.

Abductive Generalizations are More Subjective

I think that you can easily see that because individual studies in biology do not speak for themselves but rather must be interpreted, for an even greater reason generalizations based on biological studies also depend on human interpretation. This is an important illustration. If you understand my point here, then you'll understand my further and deeper point, which is that I really don't care what either one of these guys says is the conclusion. What I really want to know is *why* they are saying what they are saying, and how they got to that conclusion.

Why is there subjectivity in biological facts? For the reason that I mentioned earlier, namely — that scientists are no better than you. Their brains are no better than your brains. Brains of some scientists are robust and work well. Other scientists have teeny little brains. Some brains work only in response to financial inducements, irrespective of facts. Other brains have big wormholes. They used to work well, but worms got in there. Finally, there are a lot of present-day scientists

Why Biomedical Facts Are Subjective to the Extent That They Are

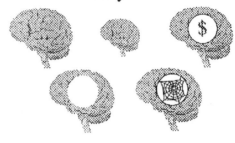

who put a lot of stuff in their brains and then walled it all off a generation ago. Nothing new has entered since Gerald Ford was President.

Because of the properties of abductive reasoning, which I mentioned previously, use of a blue-ribbon panel to decide the question of — risk? or safe? — never works. It can't. The best it can ever do is give you a consensus of the people who the guy who picked the panel liked. It would be far more honest intel-

The Blue-Ribbon Panel Process Doesn't Work

lectually to skip the blue-ribbon panel and go directly to the guy who appointed it and ask for a ruling.

For the rest of this chapter, I would like to do two things. First, I want to revisit the domain of physical science to show you that a judgment that cell tower fields are a health risk is entirely consistent with physical reasoning. Then I will say some things about the legal issues associated with cell towers and their fields. First, the

Man-Made Linear Systems

Simple Linear Systems

matter of physical reasoning... A "linear system" is a system that has the following property: when the input is small, the output is small. But if the input is large, then the output is large. It's that simple. If the wind is blowing at a certain velocity, then the windmill turns at a certain rate. If the wind goes up a little, or down a little, then the speed of the windmill changes accordingly. In proportion to how much you turn the screw, that's how far it advances. In proportion to how fast you pedal the bike, that's how fast you go.

Man-Made Linear Systems

Complex Linear Systems

There are many linear systems that are quite complex. A cell phone is a good example. A cell phone follows simple linear laws — that is the reason it is so dependable. Linearity is a codeword for reliability or predictability. All of man's machines, essentially, are linear in nature because man has little use for machines that aren't predictable. Having a cell phone that might work sometimes, but might not work other times is hardly a desirable situation.

Man-Made Nonlinear System

Man sometimes makes nonlinear systems — like this Lava Lamp — for fun, but they're not predictable, so they're generally not useful.

Nature, on the other hand, is loaded with nonlinear systems. That is, systems that do not have the property that I mentioned earlier that defines a linear system. The weather is a classic example. Because weather systems are nonlinear, it is impossible now — and will forever remain impossible — to have long-range weather predictions. It's the nonlinearity that is the source of the long-range unpredictability.

Natural Nonlinear System

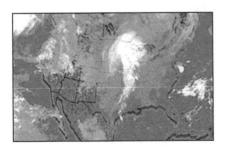

I want to illustrate for you the dimension or significance of this unpredictability in nonlinear systems. To do that I have taken some equations that are used to mathematically model the weather. They are nonlinear equations and I used them to calculate, in this model, how the temperature would evolve over time. As you can see in the illustration to the left, beginning at 30°, the temperature bounces around between 28° and 32° over four seconds.

Sensitivity to Initial Conditions

Sensitivity to Initial Conditions

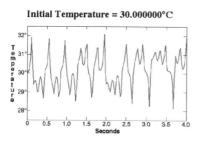

Initial Temperature = 30.000000°C

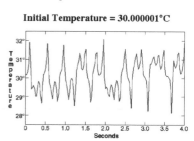

Initial Temperature = 30.000001°C

In the illustration to the right, I have used exactly the same equations, made no changes whatsoever except that the initial temperature was now immeasurably and imperceptibly greater than was the temperature that started the previous pattern that I showed. One millionth of a degree different. A difference so small that for all practical purposes it is unmeasurable and not able to be regulated. This is the pattern of evolution of the system starting with this initial condition.

Sensitivity to Initial Conditions

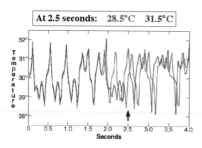

At 2.5 seconds: 28.5°C 31.5°C

Here I have superimposed the two patterns on one another. What you see is that the patterns were, initially, identical. But after a few seconds, the evolution of the two systems differing by a millionth of a degree, differed markedly. For example, after 2.5 seconds, there was a difference of about 3° in the two cases.

Remember that initially the systems differed only by a millionth of a degree and after a few seconds they now differ by 3°. This phenomenon is called sensitivity to initial conditions. It is exhibited only by nonlinear systems. And it is inconsistent with the idea of trying to predict the exact behavior of the system. You could say some things about the future behavior, but you can't predict things in anything like the way you can in linear systems.

Chaos
is
Sensitivity to Initial Conditions

Butterfly Effect

Another name for this phenomenon is 'deterministic chaos', also called the 'butterfly effect', based on an observation that a butterfly flapping its wings in the southern hemisphere could affect the weather in the northern hemisphere. As counter-intuitive as that notion may be, it is true. Small changes can be amplified enormously in nonlinear systems.

So what? Well, the human brain is a nonlinear system. Here is some evidence... In the top panel, I show you 600 sections of a human EEG recording. In the middle panel I've taken a small slice of the top panel and expanded it so that now I show sixty seconds of data. The bottom panel shows the further expansion so that only six seconds of data can be seen. The thing to notice here is that the pattern of the EEG looks the same across all the time scales. This is a signature

Human EEG

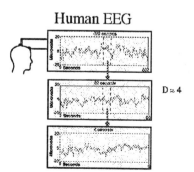

property of a geometrical entity known as a fractal. Fractal behavior suggests that the underlying electrical activity was nonlinear in nature.

So what? Here's what. If a living thing is governed by nonlinear laws, and you take a collection of those things — say, five mice — and you expose them all to the same environment, the expected behavior if —

Nonlinear Model

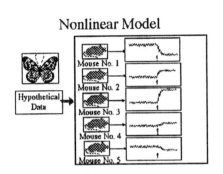

and only if — the environmental stimulus can affect the mouse, is that every parameter you're measuring will change differently in different mice. In a linear model, all the changes would be of about the same amount and would go in the same direction. In a nonlinear model this is what happens... Now you can see what would happen if you averaged the results. If you had a linear effect then the more animals you averaged, the clearer the result would appear. If the underlying law is nonlinear in nature, however, when you average the results you wind up concluding that there is no effect. The 'ups' balance out the 'downs'. The choice to approach the data by invoking the statistical process of averaging is equivalent to the choice of ignoring the stimulus-response relationship which, given the assumptions in this slide, actually exists.

What direct evidence is there that cell phones cause changes in the human EEG? Published right now? None. Coming in the future? Stay tuned.

Cell Phones Cause Nonlinear Change in EEG

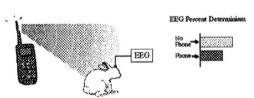

I now want to make a series of legal points. First, it is a basic principle of statutory and common law that the burden of showing safety for a new device or technology is on the proponent of the device or technology, and not on the potential victims. Nothing, absolutely nothing about Section 704 of the Telecommunications Act, in my opinion, changed that burden. If a particular litigant or zoning board decided to conduct itself as if that were the case, then that's their mistake.

Terminology

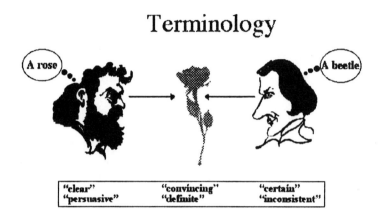

- It is essential to understand what particular words mean

In trying to ferret out who is saying what, and on what basis, as banal as it may sound, pay attention to what the words may mean in the assertion of claimed fact. It is my experience that the only way a proponent of safety succeeds is if the words in which his argument is cast are undefined, and you fill the need for him with your own idiosyncratic notion of what they mean. I have listed several examples on this illustration. Ask yourself when you see these terms in cell-phone literature, what exactly do they mean? I think this much is true: If there is no clear meaning assigned, then it is impossible to answer the question.

<u>All</u> Industry Research is Dubious

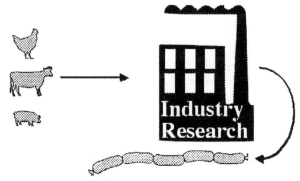

- Unless you know what goes on inside
the factory, you can't trust the product

One of the most foolish things someone who suspects that cell phone towers might be health risks could do is accept evidence provided by the industry. Everything it says must be challenged. The industry isn't going to shoot itself in its foot. Don't you know that from your own experience in life?

If I had available to me the amount of money available to pro-industry spinners, I could fill an auditorium room with medical school department chairmen who would swear on a stack of Bibles that there is no substantial evidence that there isn't green cheese on the far side of the moon. I return to the point I made earlier. You don't want a conclusionary statement from any expert. You want to regard him as a paid spokesman for the company. What you want to ask is why he says that, and how he reaches that conclusion.

Scientists Are Only People

- All industry spokesmen (especially M.D.'s and Ph.D.'s) should be regarded as compensated endorsers

Examination of Witness

"May I remind the witness that he is under oath."

- Effective cross-examination is as rare as it is important

The greatest vehicle for finding truth is cross-examination. I have been cross-examined for hundreds of hours, and I can tell you it is never a comfortable position. The rules are all in favor of the cross-examiner. Never believe anybody who hasn't been thoroughly cross-examined.

"It doesn't look to me like it could do any chromosomal damage."

Decide beforehand what acceptable evidence IS.

Before you go into a contest aimed at assessing whether cell tower fields are safe or a health risk, you must decide in advance what you consider to be acceptable evidence of one or the other inference. If you can't do that, you're wasting everybody's time.

Finally, I want to make it clear that I do not want to be understood as somehow advocating some kind of massive governmental rule-making intervention in the cell phone area. I think that would be the worst possible thing that could happen. It would be a disaster. The EPA and the FCC are woefully inadequate to deal with this issue. So is,

Risk?/Safe?
A Basic Societal Issue

▪ Should you or the government decide?

in my view, the NIH and the World Health Organization. All these groups are hamstrung by traditions, constituencies, rules and laws. Perhaps the best you can hope for is that research is done, that it is not rigged, that all the results are made available to you if you want them, that all the issues are evaluated on a level playing field where both sides have equal resources and are able to confront the experts on the other side. That's as good as it gets.

Then, you have to make a choice...

Andrew A. Marino, Ph.D., J.D.
Louisiana State University Health Sciences Center
Department of Orthopaedic Surgery
Department of Cellular Biology and Anatomy
1501 Kings Highway / Post Office Box 33932
Shreveport, LA 71130-3932
E-mail: amarino@lsuhsc.edu

Chapter 6

Some Unexpected Health Hazards Associated with Cell Tower Siting

By: Bill P. Curry, Ph.D.

This chapter presents four types of hazards to health that are often not recognized by those organizations responsible for citing cellular and PCS phone base station antennas. People living in these conditions are sometimes subjected to higher radiation density than is predicted by the simple analyses that are used to justify the safety of a proposed antenna installation.

The main hazards identified here are:
1. Omnidirectional antennas located very close to residences.
2. Directional antennas that focus radiation toward residences located on hills whose heights are comparable to the height of the antennas.
3. A less well-known hazard is the coupling of microwave radiation from cell phone antennas with the ground wave of a powerful low frequency broadcast station.
4. The effect of varying ground conditions and weather conditions on the strength of the microwave radiation near the ground — a factor that is not adequately considered when siting cell phone antennas in regions with high mineral content in the soil. In fact, the standard equations used to estimate compliance with FCC rules simply assume that the ground reflectivity is always sixty percent, and the same assumption is used near structures above the ground. But, the enhancement of the radiation density near the ground and near structures depends in a complicated way on the frequency of the radiation, the electrical properties of the ground (which are strongly dependent on weather conditions) or of the structure, and the angle at which the emitting antenna element can be seen from the ground or from a structure.

The first type of hazard is depicted in Figure 1. This is a consequence of inadequately informed city planning.

Figure 1.   A residential street in South Bend, Indiana

The antenna tower in this picture is 153 feet high. It is behind (and part of the property of) the house just to the right of the large two-story house in the center of the picture. The tower owner bought the house and put the tower in the backyard. He rents space to an elderly woman. A young family owns the house in the center, and they have been afflicted by mysterious maladies, such as superficial skin tumors. They had no such trouble until the tower was erected only about twenty-five feet away from their house.

I have measured the radiation density in the center house and on a second floor porch shown below.[1]

Figure 2.   Second floor porch of the center house in Figure 1

The young woman in the foreground is one of the homeowners. She is also the mother of two small children, and she is quite concerned about the dangers for her children. I am standing nearest the RF radiation meter, and my upstretched arm is pointing to one of the antennas that is not visible in the photograph. At this location, I measured among the largest radiation density I have ever measured at a residence — above 65 microwatts per square centimeter RMS average radiation density. Table 1 lists biological effects reported in peer-reviewed literature at radiation density at or below 100 $\mu W/cm^2$.

---

[1] Since preparation of this manuscript, the author was advised that the manufacturer of his RF meter is reevaluating the instrument's calibration. After completion of this procedure, the reported radiation measurements will be corrected, if necessary.

Published RF/MW Bioeffects and Adverse Health Effects:

- Sleep disorders and insomnia; decrease in REM sleep
- Slowed motor skills and reaction time in school children
- Altered white blood cell activity in school children
- Decreased sperm count and reduced insulin production
- Headaches, tinnitus, and spatial disorientation
- Blood-brain barrier changes and altered brain activity
- Impaired nervous system activity
- Increased heart rate and blood pressure
- Loss of concentration and "fuzzy thinking"
- Decreased immune function
- DNA damage in human white blood cells[2]

During the course of preparing this paper, I compiled a list of questions that perhaps should be included in cell tower siting decisions, but usually are not. Some of these are the following:

- Cell phone base stations must have environmental evaluation if Effective Radiated Power of <u>all channels</u> (ERP) >1000 watts and antenna height <10 meters (32.8 feet) above prevailing terrain. Should this not mean total power from all providers at a given location as well?
- PCS phone base stations require environmental evaluation if ERP >2000 watts and height <10 m. Shouldn't all providers be included?
- In hilly areas, how should "prevailing terrain" be defined?
- The FCC document OET Bulletin-65 says, "When performing an evaluation for compliance with the FCC's RF guidelines, all significant contributors to the ambient RF environment should be considered..." Why not require this on cell tower applications, also?
- Shouldn't effects of unlevel terrain, other RF sources, and soil properties on the radiation density in areas near cell phone base stations be included in application reviews?

---

[2]Adapted from C. Sage, *An Overview of RF / MW Radiation Studies Relevant to Wireless Communications & Data,* in Proceedings, International Conference on Cell Tower Siting, Salzburg, AT, June 2000).

A case in point that illustrates the combined hazard of siting cell towers (or other microwave sources) in a region of undulating terrain over soil with significant reflective properties and in the presence of additional strong RF sources, is the situation that exists on a ridge at Duanesburg, NY. Residents of this ridge are less than four miles from a 50,000 watt AM broadcast station (WGY) in Schenectady. The ridge is approximately 180 feet (54.9 meters) high.

In early 1997, a cell phone base station tower was erected near the base of the ridge. The tower rises 250 feet (76.2 meters) above the valley floor, and the antennas mounted at the top of the tower extend to a height of 253 feet. Later that same year a different service provider successfully sued the town of Duanesburg and won the right to install another set of antennas 50 feet below the original set of antennas. Thus, the lower set of antennas rises only 20 feet (6.1 meters) above the top of the ridge. Does this not violate FCC requirements for exclusion from environmental evaluation? In addition, there are microwave dishes that communicate only with a distant tower.

Forty residents (members of fifteen families) on this ridge have suffered various illnesses that may be related to RF radiation, since the operation of the cell tower commenced in 1997.

During 1999, I measured the radiation density at several locations along the ridge. Figures 3 and 4 show a summary of these measurements and the health circumstances of the residents.

**Figure 3.   Radiation Density Measurements at two locations
on the ridge near Duanesburg, New York**

This house is 500 feet horizontally from the tower. Power density varied from a few to nearly $70\mu W/cm^2$. Here, a 42 year-old lady has recently been diagnosed with bleeding at the outer edges of her brain.

This location was between horizontal antenna lobes.
Power density varied from 2-7.3 μW/cm^2.

Figure 4.   **Radiation Density Measurements near the top of the ridge**

This is the home of Mr. and Mrs. Lawrence Stankavich, who asked my wife and me to make RF measurements. The antennas are visible to the right of the house. The house elevation is higher than in the previous pictures. The tower is 1700 feet horizontal distance from the house. Measurements were made in a field between the house and the tower. Power densities varied from a few μW/cm^2 to about 25μW/cm^2 on a "light" radiation day. Residents endure severe headaches, sleep disorders, tinnitus, pressure in ears, etc.

In Figure 3, the antennas are seen in full perspective, and it is apparent that the residents are well below the antennas. In Figure 4, however, the antennas are almost on eye level with the residents. The Stankavich's have told me that there are times when they cannot even enter their upstairs office, because the pain in their heads is so great. In addition, they have the worst problems when the soil is wet. Under bad radiation conditions, they often have to drive miles away from home and sleep in their car to get any relief.

Their problems are usually worse at night when, they suspect, the lower set of antennas are broadcasting pulsed data transmissions (such as fax). However, during the day and a half (including night) that my wife and I made measurements, the night radiation level was down to background, and there was no apparent indication that pulsed radiation was being detected. This apparent lack of pulsed radiation may be why they reported less discomfort than usual. We also found that the highest radiation level occurred around 3 P.M. to 5 P.M., and this observation correlates with heavy traffic on a nearby expressway between Albany and Schenectady. Presumably, cell phone usage increases as expressway traffic increases, and the antennas were positioned to accommodate cell phone users traveling along the expressway.

The characteristics of the radiation environment of the ridge can be better understood by looking at the antenna patterns of the antennas on the cell tower. The top set of antennas were manufactured by Sinclair of Canada. From them I obtained the antenna patterns shown in Figure 5. I gratefully acknowledge their cooperation.

Figure 5.   **Antenna patterns for the upper antennas on the cell tower near Duanesburg, New York**

Maximum gain is 13.7 dBi,   23 times isotropic power

Horizontal beamwidth is 128 degrees

Vertical beamwidth is 7.9 deg. with 6 deg. mech. downtilt

Manufacturer's radiation patterns are shown below:

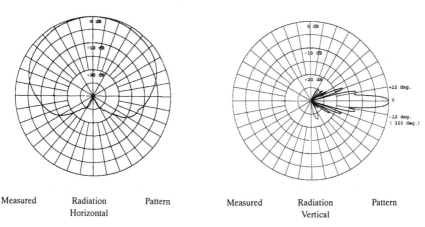

Measured	Radiation	Pattern	Measured	Radiation	Pattern
	Horizontal			Vertical	

The left graph in Fig. 5 shows the antenna gain in the horizontal plane. Gain (expressed in dBi) is a logarithmic measure of the radiation at any location divided by the radiation that would have been emitted had the source radiated equally in all directions. On the tower, there are three horizontal directions toward which antennas are oriented, so that the combination of horizontal patterns for all three sectors resembles a three-leaf clover. The polar graph on the right shows the radiation lobes in the vertical plane. The highest gain region is denoted the "main beam." A person standing at the height of the antenna would intercept the main beam, if the antenna were not tilted downward. In this installation, the antennas pointing toward the Stankavich residence were mechanically downtilted six degrees. This means that at approximately 400 feet horizontal distance from the tower, the radiation level at the Stankavich's elevation will be at least one-half the strength of the main beam, and the main beam is twenty-three times stronger than the radiation from an equivalent isotropic source.

The antennas mounted below the top antennas were manufactured by Swedcom in San Francisco. Not only were they so gracious as to send me the antenna patterns, but I would also like to acknowledge many helpful discussions with Mr. Jack Mackenzie of Swedcom.

Figure 6.   **Antenna patterns for the lower antennas on the cell tower near Duanesburg, New York**

Maximum gain is 14.2 dBi - 26 times isotropic power

Horizontal beamwidth is 86 degrees

Vertical beamwidth is 16 deg. - 0 deg. downtilt

Manufacturer's radiation patterns are shown below:

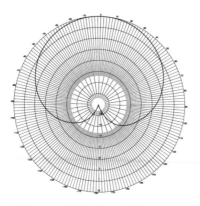 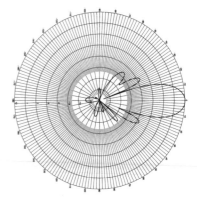

Measured Horizontal Pattern   **Measured Vertical Pattern**

The lower set of antennas was mounted without downtilt. However the vertical angular beam width of these antennas is almost twice that of the upper set of antennas. Consequently, at only 263 feet horizontal distance from the tower, the beam at the Stankavich's elevation will have one-half the radiation level of the main beam, and the main beam is 26 times stronger than the radiation from an equivalent isotropic source. Since the Stankavich's live 1700 feet (horizontal distance) from the tower, the main beams from the two sets of antennas will fully merge before the radiation reaches their location.

I presented a model of microwave sources embedded in the ground wave of a strong, nearby low frequency broadcast source at the International Conference on Cell Tower Siting in Salzburg, Austria, June 7-8, 2000. (This paper is available in the published proceedings of that conference.) This model is based on notions of early 20th century physicists that have been somewhat neglected in the heady environment of the wireless revolution. The early radio scientists found that low radio frequency waves can follow the contours of a surface. These ground waves die off with distance more slowly than waves radiated through the air. The ground wave from WGY in Schenectady is ubiquitous and strong. Its wavelength is 1214 feet (370 m), so the wave submerges the ridge, the residents, and the cell tower completely. This means that the microwave emissions from the cell tower occur in the presence of the WGY electric field. Under such conditions, the electric fields of the microwave and low frequency sources must be added vectorially to get the field of the composite wave.

Using a mathematical treatment developed initially by Arnold Sommerfeld during the years 1909-1925, I computed the electric field of the WGY ground wave, allowing for the electrical properties of the ground. This field is almost completely vertically polarized, as are the electric fields from the microwave antennas. Thus, the WGY field and the microwave fields can be added directly. The result is then squared and divided by the impedance of free space to get the radiation power density associated with the composite field. It should be noted that this is the instantaneous radiation density. The frequency of this composite radiation field is essentially the same as the original microwave frequency radiated by each of the antennas on the cell tower, so the human body will perceive the biological effect of the composite radiation field as that of an enhanced microwave source. While the condition of the ground does not significantly affect the strength of the microwave radiation in the absence of the

WGY ground wave, it materially affects the strength of the WGY ground wave, as shown in Figure 7 below.

Figure 7.   Electric field strength of the ubiquitous WGY ground wave
(The ridge is around 6.2 km from WGY.)

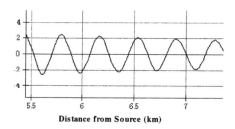

Distance from Source (km)

• Dry conditions, t = 0

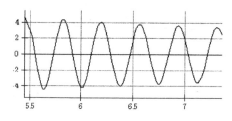

• Wet conditions, t = 0

The ground wave shown in Figure 7 is both position and time dependent. The graphs correspond to time = 0. As time progresses, the spatial wave shown moves from left to right, so that any fixed location will see the full variation of the WGY field strength as time passes. The calculation shown in Figure 7 was "calibrated" by comparing the electric field strength at 1 km from WGY with the values stated in the FCC's broadcast source database (at dry soil conditions). The calculated field was about 20 V/m, and the actual field in the FCC files was 19.15 V/m.

Figure 8 shows the computed amplification factor by which the ordinary radiation density of the microwave sources should be multiplied to obtain the radiation density of the composite field representing the coupling of the microwave sources with the WGY ground wave electric field. The extent of amplification depends on the electric field strength of the microwave sources and on the soil condition.

Figure 8:   **Microwave Radiation Density Amplification by ground wave of powerful Low Frequency Broadcast Station**

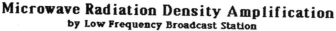

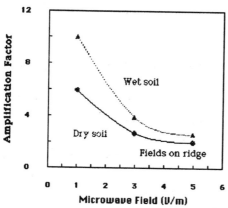

In the paper presented at the Salzburg conference, the field strength of the microwave sources on the ridge was not known and was estimated to be 1.0 V/m. The magnification factor under those conditions ranges from 6 to 10. However, the electric field strength for a folded dipole antenna was later evaluated from equations in C.A. Balanis, *Antenna Theory: Analysis and Design*, Second Edition, John Wiley and Sons, Inc., New York (1997). On that basis, the field strength of each of the antennas on the ridge is estimated to be 3-5 V/m, so the amplification factor on the ridge is probably in the range of 2-4 for each source. The radiation density of these sources alone is proportional to the square of their electric field strength. Thus, even though the magnification factor is lower for the sources on the ridge than was previously thought, the overall effect is significantly larger.

For example, for a microwave source field strength of 1 V/m, the composite radiation density is in the range 1.6-2.6 μW/cm^2 for each microwave source. In contrast, for a source field strength of 3 V/m, the composite radiation density is in the range of 4.8 μW/cm^2-9.5 μW/cm^2 for each microwave source. Finally, for a source strength of 5 V/m, the composite radiation density is 13 μW/cm^2-26 μW/cm^2 for each microwave source. Approximately, then, the composite radiation density when the ridge is dry can vary from about 5-13 μW/cm^2 for each microwave source, and when the ridge is wet the radiation density can range from 10-26 μW/cm^2 for each microwave source. Thus, since each microwave source has about the same strength (when both are operating), these estimates are roughly in accord with the measurements taken under dry conditions at the Stankavich residence. And they suggest at least one reason why the ridge residents' symptoms are so much worse when the weather is bad than when it is dry.

Concluding Remarks: Recommendations to Avoid Unexpected Hazards.

The analysis presented in this paper clearly suggests some considerations to reduce the likelihood of damaging the health of humans, pets, and other animals when siting cell towers. Currently, there is usually inadequate consideration given to these measures by both government regulators and industry representatives. Nevertheless, one can hope that the following precautions may someday be adopted:

1. Towers with omnidirectional antennas should never be placed in close proximity to residences.
2. Towers with directional antennas should never be at the same, or nearly the same, elevation as nearby residences.
3. Before siting any microwave tower, the existing RF environment should be thoroughly analyzed to avoid the possibility of microwave amplification by vector addition of RF fields.

Bill P. Curry, Ph.D.
22W101 McCarron Rd.
Glen Ellyn, IL 60137
Email: BPCurry@MCS.com

Chapter 7

Human Exposure to Radiofrequency Electromagnetic Fields: FCC Guidelines; Global Standards; Evaluating Compliance; Federal and Local Jurisdiction

By: Robert F. Cleveland, Jr., Ph.D.[1]

I'll try to give you an overview of what the Federal Communications Commission (FCC) is doing — or not doing, as the case may be — in this area of radiofrequency exposure safety.

The FCC licenses or authorizes most of the telecommunications services in the United States except for those actually operated by the Federal Government. We have regulatory authority over commercial broadcast stations, wireless facilities, satellite communications services, amateur radio and most other communications services.

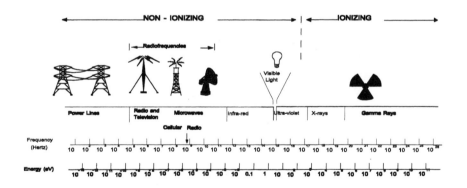

Diagram of the Electromagnetic Spectrum

This is a diagram of the electromagnetic spectrum to show the area of responsibility that we have jurisdiction over, starting at 100 kilohertz

---

[1] The views expressed in this chapter are those of the author and do not necessarily reflect the views of the Federal Communications Commission.

(kHz) and going up to the far microwave bands in the non-ionizing section of the spectrum.

FCC Policy

The FCC is not a health and safety agency. That's important to understand. We have to rely on other expert organizations and agencies for advice and guidance. The FCC does, however, have legal responsibilities under an act of Congress — the National Environmental Policy Act (NEPA) enacted in 1969 — to evaluate the impacts of any of the FCC's actions on the environment and on health.

FCC Guidelines for RF Exposure

In 1996, the FCC adopted new guidelines for evaluating human exposure to radiofrequency electromagnetic fields. This was a multi-year undertaking that we began in 1993 with a Notice of Proposed Rule Making. During the rule-making process, comments were made by the public, the industry, and other federal agencies.

The rule citation is: 47CFR1.1307(b). For those who want to see the text, it is available at www.fcc.gov/oet/rfsafety. This final action was required by the Telecommunications Act of 1996.

At the website listed above, we have information on our RF safety program, on FCC actions, and on FCC decision documents. You can download any of the publications. We have also set up a phone number, 202-418-2464, for public information. There is one person dedicated to responding to the public and any concerns you may have with respect to transmitters. If you have any questions of an environmental nature, you can call that number.

The FCC exposure limits are based on recommendations from two expert organizations: the National Council on Radiation Protection and Measurements (NCRP), and the American National Standards Institute (ANSI) in connection with the Institute of Electrical and Electronics Engineers (IEEE) — which developed a joint standard.[2]

---

[2] The NCRP is a nonprofit corporation chartered by the U.S. Congress to develop information and recommendations on radiation protection. The ANSI is a nonprofit, privately funded, membership organization that coordinates development of voluntary U.S. national standards. The IEEE is a nonprofit technical and professional society with a membership of over 300,000 engineers and scientists worldwide.

The FCC guidelines are also based on recommendations from various federal agencies involved with health and safety regulation including: the Environmental Protection Agency (EPA), the Food and Drug Administration (FDA), the National Institute for Occupational Safety and Health (NIOSH), and the Occupational Safety and Health Administration (OSHA).

In connection with this, the FCC is a member of a federal Radiofrequency Interagency Working Group (RFIAWG) that was established in 1995 by the EPA, which chairs the group. We have periodic teleconferences and meetings and we communicate almost daily by email on issues relating to radiofrequency safety and health.

The members of the interagency working group are the EPA, FDA, NIOSH, OSHA, FCC, and the National Telecommunications and Information Administration (NTIA). The purpose of the interagency working group is to coordinate and exchange information related to RF exposure issues. It was through the interagency group that the federal agencies made their original recommendations in the mid-1990's on the guidelines we ultimately adopted. And in June of 1999, the working group sent a letter to the IEEE committee responsible for developing the RF safety guidelines listing about fourteen topics or areas of concern related to any future revision of the IEEE standard.[3]

Exposure Limits, Not Emission Limits

It's important to remember that the FCC's RF limits are exposure limits, not emission limits. A lot of people become confused and think that we are talking about the levels from a source no matter whether people are present or not. But actually the standard is an exposure limit and that means that accessibility, either by the public or by workers, is the most important factor.

However, there is a provision in the guidelines, where time-averaging may be used under certain very well-defined circumstances — such as a worker who might be going into a high-field exposure situation. For members of the public, though, we normally do not allow time-averaging; we normally consider that to be continuous exposure.

---

[3] See Appendix G.

Specific Absorption Rates

Most of the current guidelines in the Western countries are based on the concept of the specific absorption rate (SAR). The SAR is the rate of energy absorbed per unit mass of biological tissue. The units are usually expressed in watts per kilogram (W/kg), or milliwatts per gram (mW/kg), of tissue.

The whole-body SAR is related to various factors including size, shape, and the orientation of the body being irradiated, among other things. There are also resonant SAR peaks, or maximum absorption rates. For example, for whole-body irradiation, we find the SAR peak in the bands between 70-100 Megahertz (MHz), which is in the middle of the FM radio band.

Most of the RF safety guidelines in Western countries are based on the SAR level for so-called harmful effects. The level chosen by standards-setting groups, including ANSI/IEEE, NCRP and ICNIRP — the International Commission on Non-Ionizing Radiation Protection, a standard used in Europe and elsewhere — is 4 watts per kilogram (4 W/kg). That is based on animal studies in which disruption of behavior was observed in some laboratory experiments. That's the threshold adopted by the various groups.

The groups took the threshold for hazard that was defined for unfavorable effects, and incorporated various safety factors to arrive at the actual numbers. The controlled or occupational limit that we use, for example, is 0.4 watts per kilogram (W/kg) which is obtained by dividing 4 W/kg by 10 = 0.4 W/kg. So a safety factor of 10 is incorporated for occupational exposures.

For the public, there is a safety factor of 50 that is used as a divisor to get from 4 W/kg to 0.08 W/kg. So the number for public exposure is 0.08 W/kg. For partial body exposure such as you would receive from a cell phone, the limit is different. The limit is derived by fairly complicated methods of scaling from the whole body exposure. The organizations came up with the number 1.6 W/kg. In order to be marketed in the United States, all the cell phones have to meet this level of 1.6 W/kg, which is stricter than the number being used in Europe recommended by the ICNIRP guidelines.

Two-Tiered Guidelines

Another important feature of the U.S. guidelines is the fact that they have two exposure tiers — one for the public, and one for workers. These are the legal definitions we use for defining the applications of the two tiers:

- Occupational/Controlled Limits... apply in situations in which persons are exposed as a consequence of their employment, provided they are fully aware of their exposure and can exercise control over their exposure.

- General Population/Uncontrolled Limits... apply to situations in which the general public may be exposed, or in which persons that are exposed as a consequence of their employment may not be fully aware of the potential for exposure, or cannot exercise control over their exposure.

The frequency range for our limits cover from 300 kHz to 100 GHz. The exposure limits depend on the frequency, and we define them in MPE's — or maximum permissible exposures. MPE's can be given in terms of power density [milliwatts per centimeter squared (mW/cm^2)] or in field strength [volts per meter (V/m) or amperes per meter (A/m)].

<u>Table 1</u>. FCC Limits for Maximum Permissible Exposure (MPE)

(A) *Limits for Occupational/Controlled Exposure*

Frequency Range (MHz)	Electric Field Strength (V/m)	Magnetic Field Strength (A/m)	Power Density (mW/cm^2)	Averaging Time (minutes)
0.3-3.0	614	1.63	(100)*	6
3.0-30	1842/f	4.89/f	(900/f^2)*	6
30-300	61.4	0.163	1.0	6
300-1500	--	--	f/300	6
1500-100,000	--	--	5	6

(B) *Limits for General Population/Uncontrolled Exposure*

Frequency Range (MHz)	Electric Field Strength (V/m)	Magnetic Field Strength (A/m)	Power Density (mW/cm^2)	Averaging Time (minutes)
0.3-1.34	614	1.63	(100)*	30
1.34-30	824/f	2.19/f	(180/f^2)*	30
30-300	27.5	0.073	0.2	30
300-1500	--	--	f/1500	30
1500-100,000	--	--	1.0	30

f = frequency in MHz   * = Plane-wave equivalent power density

FCC Limits for Maximum Permissible Exposure

These are the exposure limits. It's fairly complicated. They are also posted on the FCC's website.

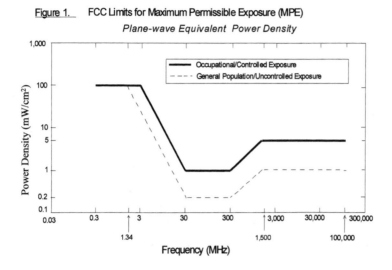

Figure 1.   FCC Limits for Maximum Permissible Exposure (MPE)

Plane-wave Equivalent Power Density

FCC limits for MPE's – graph

Graphically, you can look at the power density unit, based on frequency, for both the worker limit — which is the solid line; and the general public limit — which is the dotted line. Notice that the strictest limit is in the 30–300 MHz range. That's because the whole-body resonance occurs in this region. Standards-setting organizations have all made the guidelines strictest in that region.

Global Standards

In the U.S., standards are put forth by NCRP, IEEE, and the American Council of Governmental Industrial Hygienists (ACGIH) — which is exclusively used for worker exposures. In Europe and other countries, the ICNIRP standard is used. Some countries, such as a few in Eastern Europe and China, have been using other limits, and some of them are fairly complicated. For some frequencies, they are generally stricter than ICNIRP. Each country is a little different. It cannot be said that all of the Eastern European countries, for example, are using the same limits.

A couple of years ago, the World Health Organization (WHO) initiated the EMF Project — a multi-year effort to review EMF health effects data, and to promote international standards development, or "harmonization," of the various standards. The EMF Project website is www.whoch/peh-emf. There is quite a bit of information on bioeffects studies, and a compendium of the standards from all the different countries.

The FCC has several publications available at its "RF Safety" website. FCC Bulletin 56 contains general information for the public. Bulletin 65 and its supplements are more technical in nature and are used to evaluate compliance for different segments of the industry.

Another important FCC publication is the Local Government Guide, which was compiled under the sponsorship of the Local and State Government Advisory Committee (LSGAC) that has been set up to work with the FCC, trying to bring to the attention of the FCC concerns that local and state governments have. There is a summary in the guide of federal policy which describes what local and state governments can do, and what their jurisdictional responsibilities are. There are also graphs to evaluate wireless sites. It's a useful guide.

Evaluating Compliance with the RF Guidelines

There are four general methods for evaluating compliance — all of which are discussed in OET Bulletin 65. They include:

- Calculations and experimental methods.
- Computer modeling that can be used in some cases.
- Field measurements that can be taken. (Field measurements are usually the last word in what is actually being produced in a given area.)
- For portable and mobile devices, specialized procedures are used such as laboratory measurements for evaluating cell phone exposures.

Methods to Control RF Exposures

Once a site has been evaluated for compliance, and it has been determined that there is a need to control the exposure, or to change the exposure so the site will meet the guidelines, there are various ways to accomplish this:

- Restricting access by fencing or other means is the simplest way to control public exposure.
- Warning signs can be used to prevent access to restricted areas.

- Antenna heights can be increased to reduce RF levels at ground level. (Note! This brings up an interesting conflict with the migratory bird problem. Reducing tower heights to lessen bird-kills increases RF ground-level exposures to humans. Those two issues could be working against each other.)
- Relocation of antennas to another site is a rather drastic option. We've only had a few situations in which stations have had to relocate because of an RF problem.

For occupational exposures, more options are available for bringing a site into compliance, including:
- Educating and training personnel
- Developing safe RF work practices
- Limiting the time of exposure (time-averaging)
- Using alerting signs and restricting access
- Shielding RF sources
- Reducing the transmission power as necessary
- Using auxiliary/temporary transmitters
- Using protective clothing and personal RF monitors
- Elevating rooftop antennas above roof level
- Locating directional antennas near the edge of the rooftop so that no one can pass in front of the beam

Portable/Mobile Devices Such As Cell Phones

The limits we use for portable devices, such as handheld cellular telephones and handheld radios include:
- Limits for partial-body (localized) SAR in the 100 kHz – 6 GHz range for occupational/controlled exposure is 8 W/kg averaged over 1 gram of tissue
- For public/uncontrolled exposure the limit is 1.6 W/kg averaged over 1 gram of tissue

Our policy on mobile phones was adopted in 1996. The greatest exposure to the public is by far from mobile phones — there's no question about it. We have categorized mobile/portable devices in two ways: portable devices such as cell phones that are used within 20 centimeters of the body; and mobile devices that are not used within 20 centimeters of the body but are still able to be moved around.

In evaluating portable devices, the SAR limits apply. For consumer devices such as cell phones, the limit is 1.6 W/kg averaged over 1 gram of tissue. For mobile devices, field strength or power density limits apply, since the device is not held right up against the body.

Wireless Facility Siting: Federal v. Local Control

Section 704 of the Telecommunications Act of 1996 amended Section 332(c) of the Communications Act of 1934. The Act limited local authority to the placement, construction, and modification of wireless facilities. It also restricted local regulation of wireless facilities based on the safety of RF emissions, which, prior to the Act, could be considered by local jurisdictions.

For more information on this, see the LSGAC Guide at the FCC's website. As mentioned before, after the Telecommunications Act was passed, the LSGAC was established to provide advice and information to the FCC on local and state concerns. The LSGAC is an active group which meets every few months at the FCC. Members come from all over the country. Information particular to federal versus local control issues are posted on the FCC's website — www.fcc.gov/wtb/siting. (Go to the main page — www.fcc.gov — click on the Wireless Telecommunications Bureau, go to the siting home page, and the fact sheets are listed there.)

More recently, on November 17, 2000, Report and Order number FCC 00-408 was released. (It is also posted on the website.) This order was the result of a 1997 Notice of Proposed Rule Making regarding specifically how far a local government can go in requesting demonstration of compliance with the standards, and to clarify dispute resolutions.

This Order establishes procedures for requesting relief for the service providers from impermissible state or local regulation. It also directs local and state officials to the LSGAC Guide for help in ensuring compliance, and it outlines proper procedures when initiating FCC compliance investigations.

There is a provision in the report whereby, if a locality thinks there is a facility that might be out of compliance, even if the facility might be categorically excluded from doing a routine evaluation, the locality can still come to the FCC and request an investigation. The FCC is currently looking into such situations. In the report, there is specific information given about that possibility.

Recommended Power Density Limits at US Cellular Radio Transmitting Frequencies (calculated at 870 MHz)

	Occupational (controlled) (μW/cm^2)	General Public (uncontrolled)
IEEE (1991)	2900	580
NCRP (1986)	2900	580
ICNIRP (1998)	2175	435

Typical ground-level reading: < 1 μW/cm^2

Recommended Power Density Limits... 870 MHz

The above table shows the allowed limits for both occupational and public exposures for the 870 MHz range used by cellular radio systems. Typically, most ground-level readings around cell towers of at least 100 feet above ground level are in the range of less than 1 microwatt per centimeter squared (1μW/cm^2). As you can see from the table, the standards for safe exposure are considerably higher than ground-level exposures.

Recommended Power Density Limits at US PCS Transmitting Frequencies (calculated at 1900 MHz)

	Occupational (controlled) (μW/cm^2)	General Public (uncontrolled)
IEEE (1991)	6333	1267
NCRP (1986)	5000	1000
ICNIRP (1998)	4750	950

Typical ground-level reading: < 1 μW/cm^2

Recommended Power Density Limits at PCS... 1900 MHz

The above table shows that for the digital PCS frequencies, the limits are higher. We use the NCRP limits at 1900 MHz which are 1000 microwatts per centimeter squared (1000 μW/cm^2). However, ground-level exposures are still typically well below 1 mW/cm^2.

Other Concerns

- At some of the more complex sites, especially high-powered broadcast facilities, terrain differences may have to be considered.

- The FCC also has worked with OSHA to determine what workers are being exposed to when they have to climb towers, or do any kind of maintenance work on a tower. For example, when a person climbs a transmitting AM broadcast tower, radiofrequency energy flows through the body in the form of induced currents. So there's an issue of what the magnitude of the current is that flows through the body. Information is available in our bulletins to help ensure that workers are protected and that exposures do not exceed the guidelines.

- We are seeing more applications for satellite technology. This is an area we are going to be more involved with in the future.

- Roof-mounted antennas for wireless technologies can be a concern. With wireless tower-mounted antennas, most of the energy goes out in a donut-shaped or directional pattern. A person has to get up close to the antennas to get a high level of RF. But with roof-mounted antennas, people can often get close to the radiation source. High-powered paging antennas can sometimes create significant potential exposure. That's one reason the FCC recommends that wireless service providers consider mounting antennas at the roof's edge, so that people cannot walk in front of them.

Conclusion

The FCC is not a health and safety agency. It does not develop actual safety limits but rather implements the limits that have been recommended by expert agencies and organizations. Our job is to go out and assess the exposures as best as we can, and to make sure that the service providers and cell phone manufacturers are complying with the limits.

Robert F. Cleveland, Jr., Ph.D.,
Office of Engineering & Technology,
Federal Communications Commission, Room 7-A266, 445 12th Street, SW
Washington, D.C. 20554
Email: rclevela@fcc.gov   or
        rfsafety@fcc.gov

Chapter 8

State Centralized Siting of Telecommunications Facilities and Cooperative Efforts With Connecticut Towns

By: Joel M. Rinebold

What I will discuss in this presentation are telecommunication facilities: what they are, what the demand for services include, what the technology is, and some of the siting issues that the Connecticut Siting Council addresses.

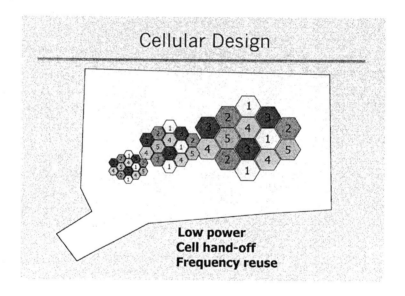

The cellular system design is based on a grid. The grid becomes divided as more and more users participate in the system. The cells in the initial system may ultimately be subdivided into parts of other cells, which then will be made up of several more cells.

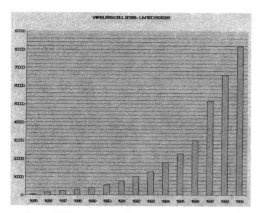

This dividing of initial systems is a function of demand, and the demand for cellular is significant. The last count in the U.S. was over 106 million subscribers with over 95,000 towers in place to support the infrastructure. That translates to over 46,000 new subscribers in the U.S. per day. These numbers are expected to double in approximately two years. So this problem we are facing is not "the industry," it's not "the government" — it's all of us.

Connecticut Siting Council Goals

The goals of the Connecticut Siting Council, not unlike other government entities and community groups, is to protect the public health, safety, and welfare, as well as our environmental resources. But we recognize the need for superior telecommunications systems in order to provide for economic development, public safety, and personal convenience. Connecticut is a service-oriented state now and we want to make sure we have high-quality telecommunications services that are being developed on a competitive basis.

A Question of Balance

All decisions involving site approval or regulation of telecommunications facilities are based on a simple standard that balances the need for a proposed facility with the effects on the environment and the community. If there is an insufficient need, or if there are substantial environmental effects that outweigh the need, the facility is not approved.

How Council Decisions Are Made

Decisions are always in writing, based on factual evidence, and substantiated at a public hearing where all submittals and testimony are available for cross-examination. In assessing environmental effects, we look at the environmental analysis, and the ecology at both the facility and the site.

Many people are also concerned about the scenic resources. I'll go into that shortly, but we do assess scenic impacts with profile analysis and balloon simulation.

We are also concerned with RF compliance and health effects. We use worst-case radiofrequency power-density modeling to make sure facilities are consistent with federal guidelines. We also solicit input from municipalities and local community groups to make sure that whatever we do is consistent with local land-use plans.

Scenic Evaluation

To assess scenic effects, we'll use maps in conjunction with land use and topography. We'll determine visibility through sight-line graphics and, if necessary, we'll perform computer-simulated photography showing a site with — and without — a tower.

Existing View   *Simulated Tower*

We model the visual effects before we approve any kind of a proposal.

RF Compliance

```
                    POWER DENSITY ANALYSIS
                    ========================
            AT THE TOWER BASE, FOR EACH RADIO/ANTENNA SYSTEM
            ------------------------------------------------
```

```
        SITE NAME:      TROOP I            PREPARED BY:  D.P.S.
        TOWER HEIGHT:   180 FEET           ON DATE:      02-23-1998
```

	OPERATING FREQUENCY	EIRP	DISTANCE TO BASE OF TOWER	MAXIMUM PERMISSIBLE EXPOSURE	AT THE BASE OF THE TOWER	
No	(MHz)	(WATTS)	(FEET)	(MW/SQ-CM)	POWER DENSITY (MW/SQ-CM)	PERCENT OF MAX. EXPOSURE
1	2136.4000	2798	142	1.424	0.0000163	0.0011
2	2130.8000	2783	138	1.420	0.0000172	0.0012
3	42.4800	492	184	0.200	0.0005006	0.2503
4	465.1500	820	170	0.310	0.0009721	0.3136
5	154.6650	4311	160	0.200	0.0057666	2.8833
6	460.1500	0	120	0.306	0.0000000	0.0000
7	6700.0000	9172	148	4.466	0.0000045	0.0001
8	867.5000	1641	187	0.578	0.0016153	0.2795
9	867.5000	1641	187	0.578	0.0016153	0.2795
10	822.5000	0	187	0.548	0.0000000	0.0000
11	822.5000	0	187	0.548	0.0000000	0.0000
12	148.1500	718	131	0.200	0.0014337	0.7169
13	149.9250	294	106	0.200	0.0008958	0.4479
14	1937.5000	4397	143	1.291	0.0073637	0.5704
15	1937.5000	4397	143	1.291	0.0073637	0.5704
16	1937.5000	4397	143	1.291	0.0073637	0.5704

```
            TOTAL PERCENT OF MAXIMUM PERMISSIBLE EXPOSURE FOR
            UNCONTROLLED ENVIRONMENTS FOR ALL 16 RADIO SYSTEMS   =   6.8845
```

NOTES: 1. THE POWER DENSITIES REPRESENTING THE 'MAXIMUM PERMISSIBLE EXPOSURE
           FOR UNCONTROLLED ENVIRONMENTS' ARE CALCULATED IN ACCORDANCE WITH
           IEEE C95.1-1991 (REVISION OF ANSI C95.1-1982).
        2. POWER DENSITIES ARE CALCULATED IN ACCORDANCE WITH THE METHODS
           DEFINED IN FCC DOCUMENT 'OST BULLETIN NO. 65', OCTOBER 1985.
        3. EIRP (EFFECTIVE ISOTROPICALLY RADIATED POWER) REFERENCES THE
           RADIATED POWER TO A POINT SOURCE, WHICH YIELDS POWERS 1.6406
           TIMES HIGHER THAN ERP.

Tower Base for Each Radio/Antenna System

With regard to RF analysis, we are in agreement that there should be a national standard where the best scientists in the country have considered the evidence; the public has had the opportunity to weigh in; and the best minds are put to the task of developing a standard. What the Siting Council insists upon is the ability to confirm compliance with those standards, if need be.

Our compliance determination process uses OET Bulletin 65, which is the methodology recommended by the FCC, to determine what the power density level will be for each antenna, at a particular frequency. We then assess that as a percentage. We repeat this process for each antenna with each frequency being used. We then add up the percentages so we have a cumulative number — or worst-case exposure figure. If it's over 100%, we go back and take a look at what can be done.

Solutions include providing some sort of protective fencing to reduce public access; reducing the power output from the antennas; or actually removing antennas. One way or the other, we insist upon compliance using worst-case modeling techniques.

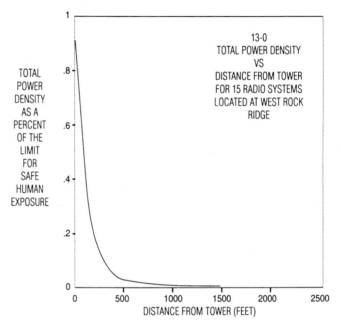

Total Power Density v. Density From Tower

We'll often graph the results so that we can be more responsive to public concerns, rather than simply saying "Don't worry, trust us, it's safe, it's within the standard." We'll plot the exposure as a function of distance so that people can then determine what exposures would be for them in proximity to where they live.

Determining The Need For A New Site

How do we determine the need for a site? Primarily, we look at the coverage, capacity, and signal strength through propagation analysis; the potential use of alternatives through site selection analysis; and the multiple use of all facilities through antenna separation analysis.

The heart of this whole process is developing propagation models — that is, determining what coverage already exists from facilities, or what would exist from potential facilities. We assess where some of the coverage holes are in proximity to a key area in a service region, such as along roads.

We try to come up with alternatives on how to fill the coverage holes. We've read the Telecom Act carefully and there is a determination that the facilities are needed, so we cannot deny a carrier the right to provide service to coverage holes. However, through careful regulation, we can guide the placement of these facilities in a safe manner and to locations that we find desirable. We can steer them away from locations that are undesirable. Toward that end, we look very carefully at applications, and go through a number of scenarios on where — and how — to develop telecommunications facilities. We work with communities to try to determine if the facilities can be put on existing towers, on water tanks, or developed on high-voltage transmission lines. But the first thing we look at is the use of existing structures.

We work long and hard to determine what combination of facilities will work to provide complete coverage in a way that the public will get services, but in a way that the public will not be burdened with unnecessary, or unsafe, or poorly sited facilities.

Let me emphasize that all of our regulatory work is done as contested-case proceedings. We not only subscribe to evidentiary proceedings, we engage in meaningful cross-examination. Our record is documented and in writing.

A decision by the council typically determines existing coverage for a particular carrier, and signal strength, using roads to estimate coverage. We then compare that with the proposed propagation for the carrier. We do this for any carrier that could go on the facility.

The idea behind this is to find the best location for as many telecom providers as possible so we don't have to be burdened with unnecessary towers in the future.

Another aspect of siting involves the analysis of a direct microwave path that can affect how tall a facility is. We try to identify point-to-point paths after considering all topographic and vegetative constraints, as well as alternative links.

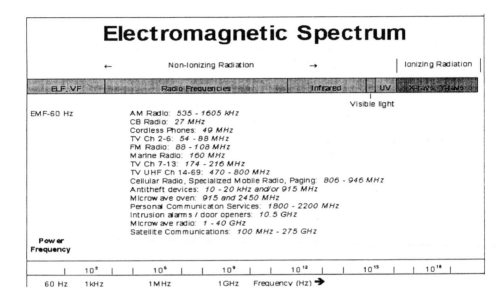

Electromagnetic Spectrum

←   Non-Ionizing Radiation   → | Ionizing Radiation |

| ELF, VF | Radio Frequencies | Infrared | UV | X-rays, γ-rays |

Visible light

EMF-60 Hz

AM Radio: 535 - 1605 kHz
CB Radio: 27 MHz
Cordless Phones: 49 MHz
TV Ch 2-6: 54 - 88 MHz
FM Radio: 88 - 108 MHz
Marine Radio: 160 MHz
TV Ch 7-13: 174 - 216 MHz
TV UHF Ch 14-69: 470 - 800 MHz
Cellular Radio, Specialized Mobile Radio, Paging: 806 - 946 MHz
Antitheft devices: 10 - 20 kHz and/or 915 MHz
Microwave oven: 915 and 2450 MHz
Personal Communication Services: 1800 - 2200 MHz
Intrusion alarms / door openers: 10.5 GHz
Microwave radio: 1 - 40 GHz
Satellite Communications: 100 MHz - 275 GHz

Power
Frequency

10^3 10^6 10^9 10^{12} 10^{15} 10^{18}

60 Hz   1kHz   1MHz   1GHz   Frequency (Hz) →

This chart of the electromagnetic spectrum shows the various technologies and what frequencies they use.

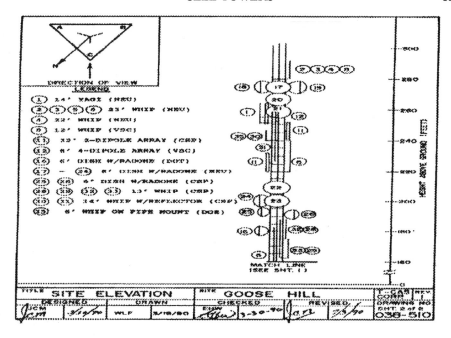

Site Elevation

As a function of wavelength and frequency, we determine minimum separation distances of antennas on a particular tower. This determines how high the tower has to be and what arrangement is necessary to keep that tower as low as possible, yet still provide the necessary services.

This is Meriden, Connecticut. These are broadcast antennas; not the requests we generally receive for wireless facility siting.

View of Tower Farm

We deal with monopoles in some places and we are pleased to see that some of the taller facilities that have become obsolete are being removed

Two Towers

Two Other Towers

On the illustration to the left, note that there is only one platform of carriers on that tower, yet a second tower is being built. There is no reason for this second tower.

Nonetheless, we are increasingly concerned and frustrated... The bifurcation of jurisdiction in the state[1] resulted in monopole farms — the exact thing we try to avoid with careful siting decisions. We try to avoid tower farms in general because they evolve, grow, and get out of control. The bifurcation of jurisdiction has been difficult for us to accept after some of our work efforts.

---

[1] Until a court decision in January, 2001 awarded control of the PCS frequencies to the Siting Council, towns had a 4-year window in which to site telecom facilities. The Siting Council controlled siting for the cellular systems, but not for the digital PCS sytems. The court decision was rendered in November, 2000 — the week of the Cell Towers Forum, with a written order in January 2001, from the Federal District Court. Since that time, various bills have been introduced at the state legislatures that would allocate different degrees of control and cooperation between the Siting Council and the municipalities. As of this writing, the Siting Council controls all telecom siting for the state of Connecticut but that was not the recent history. There had been a bifurcation of jurisdiction.

Stealth Siting

We are pleased to see the use of existing structures:

Antennas on water tanks

Antennas on high-voltage
transmission structures

Antennas on existing signage   Antennas on smokestacks

The development of a barn silo and equipment building to try to mask the visibility of the facility. This 100' silo is lower than the height of agricultural silos being produced for commercial grain storage.

Antennas hidden in a "Flagpole" tower

Antennas on a "Pine Tree" tower

Below is a map of some of the telecommunications facilities in Connecticut. Note that there are many areas where there isn't coverage. As the industry grows as a function of consumer demand, expect to see more facilities — whether they are towers, or antennas on buildings, or stealth towers like silos. We believe that there will be a need for very careful and considerate planning to develop these structures.

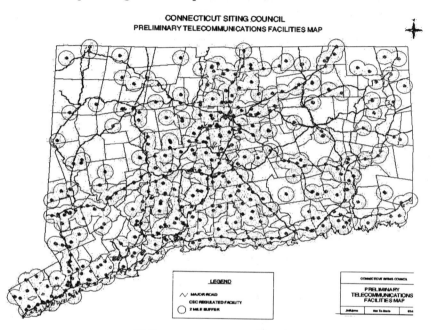

Telecomunications Facility Map

Conclusion

The elements of the decision-making process that are important and that the Connecticut Siting Council subscribes to are:

- A detailed analysis of alternative sites, structures, access and antennas.
- Worst-case cumulative modeling of radiofrequency power densities.
- Detailed propagation and antenna separation analysis to determine and limit facility height.
- Tower sharing wherever possible to minimize the need to build new towers, but still provide service.

- Assessment of the structure type, using antennas mounted on rooftops, monopoles, or lattice towers—as appropriate.
- Consideration of the future use of the site with provisions for site restoration and facility removal.
- And lastly, a comprehensive site development and management plan to protect sensitive environmental resources, erosion and sedimentation control, architectural treatment, and environmental monitoring.

Joel M. Rinebold
Executive Director
Connecticut Siting Council
10 Franklin Square,
New Britain, CT 06051

Chapter 9

Wireless Antenna Siting Issues: Substantial Evidence and Prohibition: The Two-sided Coin of Local Antenna Siting

By: James R. Hobson

Writing for the U.S. Court of Appeals for the First Circuit, Judge Michael Boudin cautioned both the PCS carrier, Omnipoint, and the zoning authority, Town of Amherst, New Hampshire, as follows:

> The substantial evidence test applies to the locality's own zoning requirements, and Amherst has framed those requirements so that they may be hard to fulfill unless the Board exercises its judgment favorably to the applicant. But this in turn makes Amherst more vulnerable to a claim, based on experience, that its regime is an effective ban. Thus, the two federal limitations — one dealing with bans and the other with substantial evidence — complement one another by ensuring that local law is both fair and is fairly administered.

Judge Boudin went on to emphasize the constraints faced by both wireless carriers and zoning authorities under Section 704 of the Telecommunications Act of 1996, 47 U.S.C. §332(c)(7) and hoped they would find a way to settle their differences:

> Before any further litigation, Omnipoint might find it prudent to discuss with the Board an amicable resolution or an agreed upon procedure to achieve one. The Board must also face reality. If the Board's position is that it can just sit back and deny all applications, that position in the end could, if maintained, prove fatal to the Board rather than Omnipoint. Under federal law, the town can control the siting of facilities but—as several Board members admitted—it cannot preclude wireless service altogether. Nor, in the face of a vigilant district court, can the town exhaust applicants by requiring successive applications without giving any clue of what will do the trick.[n.8] Thus, it is in the common interest of the Board and Omnipoint to find ways

to permit the siting of towers in a way most congenial to local zoning.

The statute's balance of local autonomy subject to federal limitations does not offer a single "cookie cutter" solution for diverse local situations, and it imposes an unusual burden on the courts. But Congress conceived that this course would produce (albeit at some cost and delay for the carriers) individual solutions best adapted to the needs and desires of particular communities. If this refreshing experiment in federalism does not work, Congress can always alter the law.

Issues

Has the tradeoff of local particularity for speed of wireless entry produced a legal standoff in which neither the local government nor the carrier has a clear advantage? If so, the cases that we don't see — the ones that are worked out in the local application or hearing process — may be more important than the disputes that make their way to federal appellate courts.

To help us answer the above question, I have taken a look at all the decisions on tower siting that I could find in the U.S. Courts of Appeal. I searched www.findlaw.com "All Circuits" using the terms "Telecommunications Act of 1996 *and zoning*." I'm sure I've missed some cases, but I found enough to begin to see useful messages.

The federal and state trial court decisions are more diverse in their reasoning and not so easy to catalog. In U.S. District Courts, the cases tend to be disposed on cross-motions for summary judgment, and a fair number of lower court decisions have been overturned or remanded. Attached is a recent listing I found on a law school web site. It should be used with care because some of the opinions have been reversed on appeal. Naturally, you'll find many of the trial court orders discussed in the appellate decisions.

Of the 12 federal circuits — not counting the Federal Circuit tribunal which hears Court of Claims, patent and veterans appeals — I found decisions on antenna siting under the 1996 Act in Circuits 1-4, 6-7 and 10-11, nothing in 5, 8-9 or the D.C. Circuit. Following is a brief review by Circuit:

First Circuit (MA, ME, NH, RI, P.R.)

Town of Amherst, New Hampshire v. Omnipoint Communications Enterprises, 98-2061, March 30, 1999

The flavor of the opinion appears in the earlier quotes from Judge Boudin, who practiced communications law in Washington for many years with the firm of Covington & Burling.

Omnipoint proposed a conventional multi-tower PCS system with towers tall enough to accommodate co-location by other radio users. Three of the sites were public and would generate revenue for the Town. The Town Selectmen endorsed the carrier's plan to the Board of Zoning Adjustment, but the Board denied the applications on grounds Omnipoint claimed were so vague as to amount to an effective prohibition. The applicant also asserted the denial was without substantial evidence and had been too long delayed. The U.S. District Court, on cross-motions for summary judgment, ordered the Board to grant the applications because of prohibitory effect. It did not reach the insubstantial evidence claim.

Noting that "Omnipoint did not present serious alternatives to the Town," the First Circuit found that:

> At least on the summary judgment record, it has not been shown that the Board will inevitably reject an alternative Omnipoint proposal with lower towers.

The Court described the burden on a carrier claiming "effective prohibition" under 47 U.S.C. §332(c)(7)(B)(i) as follows:

> To show from the language or circumstances not just that this application has been rejected but that further reasonable efforts are so likely to be fruitless that it is a waste of time even to try.

The District Court decision was vacated and the case remanded back to the Board of Zoning Adjustment, with a caveat that the Town act quickly.

Bethia Brehmer, et al. v. Planning Board of Town of Wellfleet, et al., 99-2185, February 6, 2001.

The Court upheld the Planning Board's decision to settle with the affected carrier, Omnipoint, on the grounds that compromise was the fastest way to resolve the Board's admitted error with respect to the federally preemptive RF radiation rules and that settlement did not violate local or state zoning law.

Southwestern Bell Mobile Systems v. Todd, 00-1164, March 30, 2001.

The Court followed *Town of Amherst* in placing on the carrier the burden of showing, with respect to alternative sites which might replace the denied location, that "further reasonable efforts . . . are so likely to be fruitless that it is a waste of time even to try." It found that Southwestern Bell Mobile had not met that burden.

The Court also came closer to the Fourth Circuit's view, in *Virginia Beach* (*infra*), than to the views of such cases as *Oyster Bay*, *Telespectrum* and *Aegerter* (*infra*), concerning the format and substance of the federally required written opinion and its basis in a written record. It refused to hold the volunteers who serve on zoning boards to the same standards as judges, and declared that if persuasive evidence could be found in the written record, it could be credited even if not expressly referenced in the written opinion.

The Court was particularly strong in recognizing the subjectivity of aesthetic judgments, and said that a Town's denial based on such judgments was not necessarily discredited simply because the same facts had been viewed differently by others.

Second Circuit (CT, NY, VT)

Cellular Telephone Co. v. Town of Oyster Bay, 98-9009, January 29, 1999

In denying tower permits, the Town did not present evidence formally at hearing but simply let citizens speak. The bulk of the public comment opposing the towers was vague and inexpert, and much of the concern was related to the asserted health threat of RF emissions from the towers.

The Court found the "volume and specificity" of the citizen commentary inadequate to satisfy Section 332(c)(7)(B)(iii), as against the expert witnesses put on by AT&T. The Court's finding was not against lay evidence *per se*, but the quality of it in this case, where the burden was on the speech involving property values and aesthetics to overcome the suspicion that the Town's denial turned improperly on RF emissions concerns.

The Court did not reach the controverted question of whether the applicant or the Town has the burden of proof on substantial evidence questions. It concluded, however, that injunctive relief, ordering the Town to grant the cellular tower permits, was the superior remedy to remand in view of Congress' evident desire for prompt rollout of personal wireless services.

Sprint Spectrum v. Willoth, 98-7442, May 24, 1999

This case shows what happens when a carrier says, in effect: "My way or no way." The Court upheld the U.S. District Court's affirmance of a local zoning decision denying Sprint its request to build three tall towers when the local government had suggested that one tower might fulfill the needs.

Cellular Phone Taskforce, et al. v. FCC, 97-4328 and associated cases, February 18, 2000

The Court upheld the FCC's rules at 47 C.F.R.§1.1301 *et seq.* controlling human exposure to radio frequency emissions from federally-licensed antennas. Among the issues in the challenge were the agency's interpretation of the scope of the preemptive language at Section 332(c)(7)(B)(iv) as well as the constitutionality of the statute, especially under the Tenth Amendment.

An unusual aspect of the rules is that the FCC admits to incompetence in evaluating the biohazards of RF emissions and thus depends on sister agencies such as EPA, FDA and OSHA. Although these agencies only participated in the initial round of the 1993-97 rulemaking, and not in the extended reconsideration round, the Court concluded, among other findings, that the FCC was entitled to assume that if the expert agencies had been troubled by new evidence introduced in the reconsideration round, they would have intervened.

The Supreme Court has denied petitions for certiorari (review) filed by Taskforce and by Citizens for the Appropriate Placement of Telecommunications Facilities. Thus the FCC's rules stand until they are revised.

Of course, those rules will continue to be interpreted by the judiciary. The U.S. District Court for the Southern District of New York has held, in *New York SMSA Limited Partnership and Crown Atlantic Company v. Town of Clarkstown*, 00 Civ. 3029 (CM), May 26, 2000, that it was acceptable for the Town to choose one site over another on the basis of superior RF hazard protection because no carrier was prohibited from providing service by that choice.

Freeman v. Burlington Broadcasters, 97-9141, February 23, 2000

This case is about the intersection between federal authority over radio licensing and radio interference, on the one hand, and local zoning powers on the other hand. But it does not specifically involve Section 332(c)(7).

The Town of Charlotte, Vermont, conditioned the approval of a radio tower supporting FM radio, public safety radio and cellular telephone antennas on the antennas' noninterference with appliances and devices in the homes of nearby residents. The Zoning Board of Adjustment found the condition unenforceable and this ruling effectively was upheld by the U.S.

District Court for Vermont, which dismissed the complaint of Charlotte citizens for lack of subject matter jurisdiction.

The Second Circuit panel agreed with the outcome disfavoring the interference condition, but based its substantive decision on Congress' grant of plenary power to the FCC to control broadcast interference to RF-vulnerable appliances and equipment. The U.S. Supreme Court denied a petition for certiorari.

Third Circuit (DE, NJ, PA)

Omnipoint v. Zoning Hearing Board, 98-1962, June 25, 1999 (Op. # 99-2186)

This finding of insubstantial evidence for denial of a tower zoning application is notable, chiefly, for its citation of legislative history (page 208 of the Congressional conference report on the Telecommunications Act of 1996) for the intent that zoning orders be addressed under the same standard applied to federal administrative decisions. This appears to put the decision squarely at odds with the Fourth Circuit view in *Virginia Beach* (see below) that zoning in all its facets, including the actual granting of permits, is a legislative activity where the law of the Commonwealth's looser standard is to be allowed.

APT Pittsburgh v. Penn Township, Nos. 98-3519, 98-3546, November 8, 1999.

The Court reversed a U.S. District Court judgment that the Township's ordinance was impermissibly exclusionary under Pennsylvania law. It held that the question was one of law to be reviewed de novo and not to be subject to the substantial evidence test of Section 332(c)7(B)(iii) of the Communications Act. The Court said that even though the ordinance restricted personal wireless service towers to light industrial zones, and even though most of the available land in that category was controlled by a single individual who allegedly refused to lease it to the provider, APT, the provider had not met its heavy burden. The Court said:

> In sum, the relevant inquiry here is not whether Ordinance 109 precludes APT from filling its service gap the way it would like at a price it would like to pay. The relevant issue is whether, despite the extensive amount of [light industrial] land where towers are permitted in the Township, Ordinance 109 effectively precludes *any* service provider from building a functional tower in the Township. (text following note 6, emphasis added)

The Court seems to be adding to previous judicial reasoning that any single denial usually does not create an effective prohibition unless alternatives are entirely absent. It seems to be saying that if any carrier other than APT could find a way to serve the area at issue, then service has not been prohibited. If that is what the Court is saying, we should expect carriers in the future to litigate whether service prohibition means the service of all carriers, or of the applicant only.

Cellular Telephone Co. v. Zoning Board of Adjustment, No. 98-6484, November 19, 1999.
Over the vigorous objections of the carrier in this case, the Court held that it is permissible for a local zoning authority to consider "quality" of wireless service, up to a point. The opinion defines a "gap" in service, but it does not define the critical term "significant gap" whose continuation might represent an effective prohibition of service. Instead, the Court remanded the case for further consideration of whether the Borough of Ho-ho-kus, New Jersey's denial of zoning permits amounted to effective prohibition of service by refusing the only means to fill a significant gap in cellular service.

Also notable in the panel opinion is the holding that the federal bar on "prohibition" in Section 332(c)(7)(B)(i) runs to "service" not "facilities," meaning that it may be entirely possible to "serve" a locality with facilities placed outside the jurisdictional boundaries.

Remanding the case back through the District Court to the Board on whether the Board's denial would perpetuate "significant gaps" in service amounting to effective prohibition, the Court nevertheless reminded the carrier that:

> Providers still bear the burden of proving that the proposed facility is the least intrusive means of filling these gaps with a reasonable level of service.

Omnipoint Communications Enterprises v. Newtown Township and consolidated cases, Nos. 99-1453, 99-1455, 99-1458, July 13, 2000
Here the carrier took to the U.S. Supreme Court the issue highlighted in *APT Pittsburgh* above — whether the concept of effective prohibition is to be applied provider by provider, or whether it is to be measured by the total service of all providers. On November 6, 2000, the high court denied Omnipoint's petition for certiorari, leaving in place the Court's conclusion that an applicant must show "that the area the new facility will serve is not already served by another provider."

Fourth Circuit (MD, NC, SC, VA, WVA)

AT&T Wireless v. City Council of Virginia Beach, No. 97-2389, September 1, 1998

This decision is well known for its deference to local zoning authorities. The panel noted that under Virginia law, zoning in all its aspects is a legislative activity in which legislators are permitted, and expected, to be influenced by the strongly held views of their constituents. The law of the Third Circuit may be different, as reflected in the Omnipoint decision discussed above.

The Court acknowledged that some of the citizen opponents had raised the issue of health risks from RF radiation, but found this too small a part of the overall discussion to be disabling. The decision is replete with citations to U.S. District Court cases from all over the country and thus makes a good research vehicle.

AT&T Wireless v. Winston-Salem Zoning Board, 98-195 (1999)

This decision generally follows the *Virginia Beach* reasoning with respect to the requirement of Section 332(c)(7)(B)(iii) that local zoning decisions be in writing and supported by substantial evidence. The panel opined that:

> The simple requirement of a decision in writing cannot reasonably be inflated into a requirement of a statement of findings and conclusions, and the reasons or basis therefore.

In a passing remark, however, the Court spoke of the "municipal board acting in a quasi-judicial capacity," a distinction that the *Virginia Beach* panel did not appear to make. The difference between a city council "legislating" a zoning ordinance and "adjudicating" an application under the ordinance is also drawn in a Seventh Circuit decision discussed below.

Petersburg Cellular Partnership v. Board of Supervisors of Nottoway County, 99-1055 (2000).

This split decision is notable chiefly for the singular opinion of the author, Judge Niemeyer, that Section 332(c)(7)(B) intrudes too much on the preserve of state and local governments in violation of the Tenth Amendment. Although Judge Niemeyer did not get a second vote for that conclusion, and the decision therefore rests on other grounds, we can expect that he will be cited by other appellants arguing Tenth Amendment protections against federal preemption.[1]

360° Communications v. Board of Supervisors of Albemarle County, 99-1816, January 24, 2000

The same Judge Niemeyer, writing the panel's reversal of a U.S. District Court finding of prohibitory effect from the County's denial of zoning, reinforced the *Virginia Beach* panel's discussion of zoning as a legislative activity:

> In Virginia, the grant of denial of a conditional-use permit is a legislative act, as is the adoption of a zoning regulation.

Sixth Circuit (KY, MI, OH, TN)

Telespectrum v. Public Service Commission of Kentucky, et al., 98-5822/5871/5919, September 8, 2000

After disposing of defenses that the KPSC Commissioners were immune from Telespectrum's suit under the Eleventh Amendment, and that an individual dissenting Commissioner should be immune, the panel upheld the District Court's summary ruling for Telespectrum on the ground that evidence was insubstantial for the denial of a permit to erect a 199-foot tower on rural land. The judges said the testimony of nearby landholders concerning loss of property value, health threats from RF radiation and availability of alternate sites "was no more than unsupported opinion." With respect to siting alternatives, the panel said that KPSC's order "that Telespectrum should continue this case and seek other locations" was not enough to keep the order from being final and reviewable.

Seventh Circuit (IL, IN, WI)

Aegerter v. City of Delafield, 98-2422, April 19, 1999

The panel here, implying that *Virginia Beach* was too sweeping, drew a distinction between the legislating of a zoning ordinance and the application of that ordinance to the facts of a particular application. And the distinction has consequences for the use of the substantial evidence test.

---

[1] See Appendix A for such a citation.

Tenth Circuit (CO, KS, NM, OK, UT, WY)

*Southwestern Bell Wireless v. Johnson County Board of County Commissioners,*98-3264, December 27, 1999

As in the *Freeman v. Burlington Broadcasters* case discussed earlier, this case is more about plenary federal authority preempting local regulation of interference caused by FCC-licensed radio transmitters than about zoning for towers as such. Johnson County sought to defend, however, by citing the ample zoning deference contained in Section 332(c)(7)(A), which the Court rebuffed by noting that subsection's limitation to "placement, construction and modification" of personal wireless facilities. In contrast, Johnson County had sought to empower its zoning administrator to shut down commercial wireless facilities interfering with public safety radio.

Eleventh Circuit (AL, FL, GA)

AT&T Wireless v. City of Atlanta, 99-12261, 4/26/2000

In a case of first impression in the federal circuits, the panel here overturned the lower court's ruling that the Communications Act remedies for denials of personal wireless facilities siting were intended to preclude use of the "civil rights" relief in 42 U.S.C.§§1983 and 1988, compensatory damages and attorneys fees.

On August 25, 2000, the Court vacated its own decision after discovering that the trial judge had failed to rule on AT&T's substantive due process claims, thus making the appeal unripe and depriving the Eleventh Circuit of jurisdiction. The discussion of the original decision suggests how the issue might arise in the future. Section 1983 reads:

> Every person who, under color of any statute, ordinance, regulation, custom, or usage, of any State or Territory or the District of Columbia, subjects, or causes to be subjected, any citizen of the United States or other person within the jurisdiction thereof to the deprivation of any rights, privileges, or immunities secured by the Constitution and laws, shall be liable to the party injured in an action at law, suit in equity, or other proper proceeding for redress . . .

AT&T Wireless had been refused a special use permit for PCS construction. The denial was not in writing; nor, said the panel, was the refusal supported by substantial evidence in a written record. In vacating the

District Court on the Section 1983 issue, the panel placed great weight on the "no implied effect" statement in Section 601(c) of the 1996 Act, which reads: "This Act and the amendments made by this Act shall not be construed to modify, impair, or supersede Federal, state, or local law unless expressly so provided in such Act or amendments."

In a special concurrence on the matter of the carrier's entitlement to attorney's fees, Judge Carnes said: "AT&T is no civil rights victim."

Some Lessons from the Above

- DON'T allow Section 704 of the 1996 Act to be turned on its head. It is mainly an affirmation of local zoning authority, not a federal preemption.

- DON'T play such a clever game of "gotcha" with your zoning ordinance that it looks like an "effective prohibition."

- DO err on the side of a written set of findings and conclusions, with references to a writtten record, when you decide to deny an application.

- DO keep faith in the power and acceptability of alternatives to carrier proposals.

- DON'T confuse zoning authority under Section 704 with the FCC's plenary authority to control operational interference to other radio services and to RF-vulnerable equipment.

Other Pertinent Telecom Cases and Limited Commentary: Case Law Decisions Under the Telecommunications Act of 1996 Local Zoning Provisions (Sec. 704) http://www.als.edu/glc/wireless_cases.html[2]

Anyone wishing to research telecom cases should look into the ones listed below.

Alexandra Cellular Corp. v. Town of Rochester, slip op. (Sup. Ct. Ulster Co. 1997).

---

[2] List gathered from the Albany Law School at this website.

American PCS v. Fairfax County ZBA, 40 Va. Cir. 211 (Cir. Ct. Va. 1996).

AT&T Wireless Services of Fla. v. Orange County, slip op. (M.D. Fl. 1997).

AWACS v. Hearing Board of Newtown Township, 702 A.2d 604 (Pa. Commw. 1997).

Bell Atlantic Nynex Mobile v. Lonergan, slip op. (Sup. Ct. West. Co.1997).

Bellsouth Mobility v. Gwinnett County, 944 F. Supp. 923 (N.D. Ga. 1996).

> The Federal District Court for the Northern District of Georgia was called upon in this case to apply the Telecommunications Act of 1996 provisions requiring denials of applications to build wireless facilities to be supported by substantial evidence. Noting that this does not allow a court to substitute its judgment for that of the decision maker, it reversed the City's decision denying the tall permit structure applied for by Bellsouth. Bellsouth had submitted numerous documents to support its application, including evidence from experts that on other occasions, monopole construction had not hurt property values. The only opposition was presented by residents, who did not have expert opinions or other evidence to back them up. The court concluded that such non-expert opinions were insufficient to create the substantial evidence required to uphold the denial of a permit application. Of particular note here is that, instead of remanding the case to the board for further proceedings, [the court] ordered the permit granted.

Campanelli v. AT&T Wireless Services, slip op. (Ohio Ct. Appl. 1997).

Century Cellunet of So. Mich. v. City of Ferrysburg, slip op. (W.D. Mi. 1997).

Crown Communications v. Zoning Hearing Board of the Borough of Glenfield, 679 A.2d 271 (Pa. Commw. 1996).

Genesee Telephone Co. Szmigel, slip op., 1997 W.L. 800699 (Sup. Ct. Monroe Co. 1997).

Illinois RSA No. 3 v. County of Peoria, 963 F. Supp. 732 (C.D. Ill. 1997).

Two related requirements of the Telecommunications Act of 1996 caused the Federal District Court for the District of Illinois to overturn the County of Peoria's decision denying plaintiff's request to build a cellular tower. While the Court found that the decision made by the County was made within a "reasonable time" under the Act — here the decision was made in six months — the written decision was not sufficient to meet the Act's "written decision" requirement. The denial simply stated, "On July 11, 1996, the Peoria County Board DENIED your request for a Special Use for a utility communication tower in the R1 zoning district." According to the Court, the decision must state reasons for the denial, not just that a denial has been issued. While the court states that this would have been enough to reverse the denial under the Act, it also noted that the only reasons for denial that could be found in the record were based on the local opposition to the project. "But under substantial evidence review, the mere existence of opposition is insufficient to suppport an agency decision against a request." A final constitutional claim against the County was denied because there was no evidence that the County acted in an arbitrary and unreasonable fashion. The court, however, did not remand the case for further decision making at the local level, but instead directed that the permit be issued.

In re Graeme, 975 F. Supp. 570 (D. Vt. 1997).

Kapton v. Bell Atlantic Nynex Mobile, 700 A.2d 581 (Pa. Commw. 1997).

New Brunswick Cellular Telephone Co. v. Borough of South Plainfield Board of Adjustment, 701 A.2d 1281 (N.J. Super. 1997).

OPM - USA - Inc. v. Board of County Commissioners of Brevard County (FL), slip op. (M.D. Fl. 1997).

Paging, Inc. v. Board of Zoning Appeal, 957 F. Supp. 805 (W.D. Va. 1997).

This case involved the application for a radio common carrier relay tower, which was denied based on a finding that

Paging Inc., the plaintiff, was not a public utility under appropriate local regulations. If it was a public utility, Paging would not have to apply for the otherwise required special use permit. Plaintiff argued, and the court accepted, that the county had found other wireless carriers to be public utilities, and that failure to treat them as the same violated the Telecommunications Act of 1996's prohibition against treating "functionally equivalent service providers" differently. The County had asked the Federal Court to abstain from becoming involved in the case on the basis that it involved purely local, and thus nonfederal, issues. As the court found that the potential for inconsistent treatment of functionally equivalent services existed in violation of the Telecommunications Act, it refused to abstain from hearing the case.

Smart SMR of New York Inc. v. Borough of Fair Lawn Board of Adjustment, slip op. (N.J. 1998).

Sprint Spectrum LP v. Zoning Hearing Board of East Nottingham Township, slip op. (E.D. Pa. 1997).

Sprint Spectrum LP v. Town of Easton, slip op. (D. Ma. 1997).

Sprint Spectrum LP v. Town of Farmington, slip op. (D. Ct. 1997).

This case involves the application for permits to build two towers by Sprint Spectrum. Sprint had originally applied for permission, and for some reason the applications were not addressed. A subsequent moratorium was imposed, during which time Sprint was advised it should seek a rezoning and a special use permit. After the moratorium expired, no action was taken on the new applications. The court (a trial level court), held that under New York law, Sprint was a public utility [see, Cellular Telephone Co. vs Rosenberg, 82 N.Y.2d 364, 604 N.Y.S.2d 895, 24 N.E.2d 990 (1983)] and entitled to a variance on a showing of "public necessity" including a gap in service. In addition, that the town had failed to act within a reasonable time; that the town must [support denial of] any applications [with a] writing supported by substantial evidence, and that the town had effectively denied service in violation of the Telecommunications Act. The Court did not order the permits granted, but instead required that the applications be dealt with at the next Town Board meeting.

Sprint Spectrum v. Medina, 924 F. Supp. 1036 (W.D. Wash. 1996).

Federal district court upheld the imposition of a six-month moratorium by the City, which had justified the moratorium as necessary to study the issues surrounding tower siting. During the pendency of the moratorium, the City had made measurable, demonstrable progress on the development of an ordinance to address wireless facilities. The court held that the "reasonable time" requirements of the Telecommunications Act of 1996 were to be interpreted to be the time normally required for processing of similar applications. The court noted that in Washington, the imposition of a moratorium was figured into the reasonable time for processing of applications, and as such was not a violation of the Act's requirements.

Sprint Spectrum LP v. Jefferson County, 968 F. Supp. 1457 (N.D. Al. 1997).

Sprint v. Town of West Seneca, slip op. (Sup. Ct. Erie Co. 1997).

Sprint Spectrum LP v. Willoth (Town of Ontario), slip op. (W.D. N.Y. February 19, 1998).

Sprint Spectrum LP v. Zoning Board of Appeals of Guilderland, slip op. (Sup. Ct. Alb. Co. 1997).

TCG Detroit v. City of Dearborn, 977 F. Supp. 836 (E.D. Mi. 1997).

Westel-Milwaukee Co. v. Walworth County, 205 Wisc. 2d 242, 556 N.W.2d 107 (Ct. Appl. Wisc.1996).

The Court of Appeals found that the Telecommunications Act of 1996, which was enacted after the denial by the Commission of a permit to build a cellular facility, required that the case be remanded for a new fact-finding hearing concerning the effect of the new law on the pending application.

Western PCS II Corp. v. Extraterritorial Zoning Authority, 957 F. Supp. 1230 (D.N.M. 1997).

Westinghouse Electric Corp. v. Council of Town of Hampton, 686 A.2d 905 (Pa. Commw. 1996).

> The Township had determined that a cellular phone company was not a public utility under its ordinance; that its radio-frequency radiation might pose possible health hazards; and that the tower would not be aesthetically appropriate for the area. The Court (a mid-level appeals court) first held that a cellular telephone company was a public utility under the ordinance, which required that public utilities be "a service distributing water, gas, electricity, etc. by means of a network of overhead or underground lines." The court concluded that evidence before the Township indicated wires were used in the distribution of cellular service, and that the definition was therefore met. As to the health claim, the court noted that § 704 of the Telecommunications Act preempts regulation based on perceived health concerns. Finally, as to the aesthetic basis for denial, the court stated, "Aesthetics alone has never served as an adequate reason to deny a property owner the legal use of . . . property."

James R. Hobson, Esq.
Miller & Van Eaton, PLLC
1155 Connecticut Ave.
Suite 1000
Washington, D.C. 20036-4306
Email: jhobson@millervaneaton.com

Chapter 10

Preserving Scenic and Historic Sites: The Dilemma of Siting Cell Towers and Antennas in Sensitive Areas

By: Jeffrey Anzevino, Regional Planner
Scenic Hudson, Inc.

Scenic Hudson

Scenic Hudson is a 37-year old nonprofit environmental organization and a separately incorporated land trust. Scenic Hudson is dedicated to protecting and enhancing the scenic, natural, historic, agricultural, and recreational treasures of the Hudson River and its valley. To date Scenic Hudson has protected more than 17,200 acres in nine counties, and created or enhanced 28 parks and preserves for public enjoyment.

Poets' Walk Romantic Landscape Park, on the banks of the Hudson River in Red Hook, N.Y., is one of our most popular parks. To the west, the peaks of the Catskill Mountains are visible from the park. Scenic Hudson's Riverfront Communities Program (RCP) works to ensure that development along the Hudson River protects views and provides public access to the shore, and complements and strengthens existing town centers. We promote development based on sound planning principles through a meaningful public process among stakeholders. One of our objectives is to convert underutilized and abandoned sites along the Hudson into vibrant parkland, recreation areas, or mixed-use development.

Telecommunications Towers

Why does Scenic Hudson care about telecommunications facilities? It's apparent by our name. Scenic Hudson was formed in 1963 to fight the visual and environmental impact of a power plant on Storm King Mountain. After a seventeen-year court battle, we prevailed. The land is now a State Park. That fight formed the basis for our modern environmental movement, including the formation of the National Environmental Policy Act (NEPA), the New York State Environmental

Quality Review Act (SEQRA), and citizens standing in favor of environmental issues.

The Telecommunications Act of 1996

Communities are frustrated by the mixed messages sent by the Federal Telecommunications Act of 1996. On one hand the Act affirms a community's responsibility for — and jurisdiction over — land use matters. On the other hand, telecommunications providers assert that if a proposed tower cannot be sited at their preferred location, at the desired height, or designed as they see fit, the facility will not be practicable. Therefore, the providers often claim that a municipality asserting its rights is in violation of the Federal Telecommunications Act because the municipality is, in effect, prohibiting service or discriminating between providers. Batteries of lawyers representing well-funded telecommunications providers can easily intimidate small towns and villages, which are often staffed with volunteers or part-time elected officials. But nothing in the Act says that these facilities must be constructed in the manner first proposed by providers, or in the cheapest possible manner for the applicant.

SEQRA implications

Scenic Hudson filed an amicus brief in an important court case in 1992 — *WEOK Broadcasting Company v. the Planning Board of the Town of Lloyd*. In that landmark case, the New York State Court of Appeals ruled that "the potential negative impact of a proposed project is a valid reason under SEQRA for denying a permit needed to approve a project." The court said, in effect, that if the town was able to substantiate its argument that the radio towers would be detrimentally visible from the FDR Roosevelt home — the "Franklin D. Roosevelt National Historic Site," a site designated on the National Register of Historic Places — the planning board would be justified in denying the permit for the tower. This is an important ruling in light of so many telecommunications towers being proposed for sensitive areas.

Scenic Hudson's Telecom Towers Initiatives

Recognizing that the Telecommunications Act was unleashing a rash of tower applications, Scenic Hudson's Riverfront Communities Program (RCP) advanced a Strategic Cell Tower Initiative in February of 1998. Three press conferences were held in Albany, New Paltz, and Greenburgh, to inform the press and interested municipalities throughout the region. The press conferences announced the release of a telecom towers report published by Scenic Hudson. It also announced a 1998 Cell Tower Summit to be held in conjunction with The Catskill Center for Conservation, along with twenty-two co-sponsors. Interest in the subject was overwhelming. The co-sponsors included: six county planning departments, two chapters of the American Planning Association, the Association of Towns of New York, the New York Conference of Mayors, four municipalities, and others. The conference was well attended.

The RCP continues to provide technical assistance to municipalities developing local laws to regulate wireless telecommunications facilities, and citizens fighting towers in their communities.

Other Initiatives

- Scenic Hudson published "Protecting Our Region's Sense of Place in the Age of Wireless Telecommunications."
- 1998 and 1999 Scenic Hudson helped thwart industry-sponsored legislation that would have imposed a statewide siting process on every community in New York State, except New York City. If

successful, these bills would have undermined the efforts of over 250 municipalities, which have invested the time and resources to develop and adopt local laws regulating these facilities. Under the provisions of these bills towers would have been classified as "Type II Actions," and thus not subject to New York's SEQRA law, thereby avoiding the opportunity for coordinated environmental reviews and environmental impact statements. Towers up to 300-feet high would have been allowed in small towns. Towers would have needed to comply only with setback requirements in underlying zoning districts. One can imagine how a tower in excess of 100 feet in height would loom over adjacent property 25 feet away. The bills would have provided only the most marginal consideration of towers within 500 feet of a historic park.

What's At Stake In The Hudson Valley?

Our scenic vistas attract tourists from all over the world. Tourism is our number two industry — just behind agriculture — in the state, and a leading source of tax revenue. In fact, tourism is the number one or two industry in every county. In the Hudson Valley, tourism employs 90,000 people, creating a $1.3 billion annual payroll, and $2.5 billion annual revenue.

Community character in the Hudson Valley attracts new residents and business, in addition to tourists, and the quality of life is also key to attracting new businesses.

Several important gains in protecting the unique, historic Hudson River corridor have been made over the past few years. The Hudson was declared an American Heritage River through President Clinton's initiative, and was designated a National Heritage Area by Congress in 1998. (There are only thirteen such designated sites in the country.) A comprehensive management plan is being developed.

Scenic areas are of significance throughout the state, but there is an inherent problem with telecommunications towers. Telecom providers seek out the highest ground for maximum signal range. But scenic ridgelines are, of course, the most visible and sensitive areas. Towers automatically intrude upon viewsheds. Here are some case examples:

While the New York State Thruway carries no designation as a scenic byway, it nonetheless has many stretches that possess outstanding scenic qualities. An Environmental Impact Statement (EIS) prepared without much fanfare, or public notice, now proposes 150 towers positioned along a 461-mile stretch of highway. That's one tower every 3.2 miles along a beautiful rural highway. Since the thruway is operated by a state authority, local zoning does not apply.

An example of poor tower siting is this tower, north of Saugerties. It is positioned too close to the road. Positioning like this raises safety issues — such as tower failure/collapse, and falling ice — along with aesthetic concerns. It is also directly in line with northbound motorists' field of vision for a considerable length of time.

An example of better tower siting is in New Paltz. The Town of New Paltz developed a local law that encouraged co-location on this tower sited at the town landfill. Their local law was designed to encourage co-location on an existing tower at the town landfill.

This tower is visible southbound, pictured above, but barely visible northbound.

Another negative example is this Omnipoint tower. Town officials were livid to find that a tower was built without their knowledge at the Thruway exit.

And in Kingston this monster looms over the information kiosk greeting visitors to Kingston as they exit the Thruway.

This tower greets people at the gateway to the Catskills.

An example of how tower siting negatively affects individuals is that of Jimmy & Micheala Bulich, a young couple who bought a 135-acre organic farm in the foothills of Catskills.

The Buliches were approached by SBA Inc. — an independent tower company that builds towers on speculation — and asked to locate a 199-foot high spec tower on their land. (Keep in mind that 150 towers are already planned along the thruway, which runs right by this area.) When the Buliches declined, SBA signed a lease with their neighbors to site the tower on property next door to the Buliches with only a 50-foot setback from their property. Below is what it might look like:

As of this printing, the applicant has withdrawn the proposed site and has applied to site the tower on another portion of the Bulich property that is not within their view of the Catskills. Unfortunately, if approved as now proposed, the tower would be visible from Trumpbour's Corner Farm and Museum, a National Register site dating back to 1732.

This is another example of something that could have been better planned. This tower near West Point was not the subject of an Environmental Impact Statement required under SEQRA. This tower is visible from the Hudson River, and the photo was taken from a scenic overlook on a state-designated Scenic Byway — Route 9W. It could have been designed as a flagpole and saved this kind of visual blight.

In Red Hook, at a 1999 public informational meeting, the applicant said this tower would barely be visible except in the winter months when the trees were without leaves. But look what happened... Both the town and the applicant refused to consider camouflage techniques. There was a perfect co-location opportunity on a 109-foot high water tower nearby. But the town water department was afraid of corrosion on the tank and therefore was not interested.

Scenic Hudson received phone calls complaining about the Red Hook tower before it was even completed. Now, the tower looms over a rural road. It is considered by many to be a blight on the landscape — visible from at least five or six locations throughout the town.

The town supervisor promises this will be the only tower in Red Hook, but that remains to be seen. The goal of the town was to site the tower on municipal property so that taxpayers would benefit from leasing revenues. But ironically, the town only receives $1200 per month in licensing revenue for this eyesore. And unfortunately the lease was drawn up to permit expansion to 160 feet in the future. This was never mentioned at the public meeting.

There is currently a very insensitive plan by Crown Castle that endangers the Taconic State Parkway. Crown Castle plans 39 towers along this state-designated Scenic Byway, which is eligible for the National Register of Historic Places. They plan one tower every couple of miles. The Taconic is a beautiful rural thoroughfare reminiscent of a bygone time. Scenic Hudson is fighting to preserve its integrity through the Corridor Management Plan. We developed guidelines that steer towers out of the right-of-way and off of the ridgelines, as well as calling for camouflaging facilities if they must be visible from Parkway.

The stakes are high with this proposal. Crown Communications plans 120-foot high towers, each less than three miles apart. That's 39 towers along a 105-mile length — or a tower every 2.6 miles. Crown Communications claims that since each tower will handle five co-locations, this minimizes the impacts.

When their "Master Plan" was presented to the Corridor Management Plan Committee, Scenic Hudson and a coalition of concerned others urged the Department of Transportation (DOT) to require an Environmental Impact Statement. The DOT agreed and sent Crown Castle back to the drawing board. But this is not the last we will see of this multi-tower project. Like SBA, Crown Castle is also an independent tower builder — not a telecommunications service provider.

In Putnam Valley this tower is 650 feet from the Parkway. Putnam Valley's cell tower law prohibited facilities within 1000 feet of an historic site or district. They apparently did not realize that Taconic State Parkway was eligible for listing on the National Register of Historic Places. The town amended their regulations to exclude towers on historic roads, even though the applicant might have asked for a variance. The town could also have required mitigation to reduce visual impacts. But the applicant testified at the public hearing that the tower would barely be visible. Today it is seen by thousands of vehicles per day traveling southbound. The town was unfortunately not interested in requiring camouflage techniques.

What Needs to Be Done?

- Every municipality needs a strong local law regulating telecommunications facilities. The time to act is before applications arrive.

- Ensure that Section 106 of the National Historic Preservation law is complied with. Applications for wireless telecommunications must comply with Section 106 of the National Historic Preservation Act. Federal agencies must consider the effect of actions on cultural and historic resources. (Regulations implementing Section 106 are found in 36 Code of Federal Regulations Part 800.) The Advisory Council on Historic Preservation is an independent federal agency responsible for promulgating the regulations and providing oversight in implementation. The FCC is also responsible, but often delegates this responsibility to the applicants or the designees. Towns must be wary of this.

- Inter-municipal and regional planning is particularly important when regional resources are at stake, such as the Hudson River, the Taconic State Parkway, and other like resources.

- It is important to amend the Telecommunications Act. We need to strengthen the role of local government in tower siting, and protect our First Amendment Rights of free speech at public forums. People raising important issues are often shut down.

- As a society, we need to encourage telecommunications systems that are not dependent on ground-based facilities — satellite systems, for example.

- We need more frequent and effective use of camouflage and stealth facilities. Until satellite systems can be more effectively deployed, we must encourage and require camouflage and stealth facilities such as barn silos, imitation trees, flagpole designs and antennas mounted flush on other structures.

- Conservation should also be considered. Just like the energy conservation and recycling efforts of the past that have now become part of our consumer consciousness, people should be aware that cell phone use can be voluntarily curtailed. If people used their cell phones less, there would be less need for towers. People should think of the public airwaves as the natural resource that they are, worthy of conservation.

Conclusion

Much is at stake in the Hudson Valley and elsewhere. We are being called upon to protect our communities as never before. Tourism, our quality of life, our scenic vistas, and our property values are all at risk from a burgeoning wireless technology.

photo by Jeffrey Anzevino

This lasting image of Storm King serves as an inspiration to remind us that in 1963 a concerned group of citizens banded together to oppose a Con Edison power plant on this mountain. The adage says, "You can't fight City Hall." But not only was the power plant stopped, an entire environmental movement was born that gave citizens legal standing to intervene in environmental issues. In the wake of that struggle, a new wave of environmental regulations was passed.

We must galvanize around the issue of wireless telecommunications facilities to ensure that this technology serves us in a manner that doesn't jeopardize our environment.

By: Jeffrey Anzevino, Regional Planner
Scenic Hudson, Inc.
9 Vassar St.
Poughkeepsie, NY, 12601
Email: JAnzevino@scenichudson.org

Chapter 11

Brief Overview of the Effects of Electromagnetic Fields on the Environment

By: Raymond S. Kasevich, BSEE, MSE, PE

Introduction

The generation, radiation, and propagation of electromagnetic waves are generally well understood from both the engineering and scientific viewpoints. What is less well understood is the effect of the interaction of electromagnetic fields or waves with material and biological systems — such as humans, animals, plants, trees, and insects.

In clinical medicine, however, there has been considerable success involving the application of microwaves, or radiofrequency energy, especially with thermal (tissue heating) models such as thermal treatment to relieve benign prostatic hyperplasia (BPH), and electrical therapy used to treat cardiac arrhythmia. In fact, radiofrequency ablation of certain types of arrhythmia is now the treatment of choice.

Some tumors are also being treated with microwaves. A very precise temperature range from 41.5 to 44.5 degrees Celsius is required to kill tumors by hyperthermia. Such applications require precise management and control of the electromagnetic energy for proper thermal dosimetry and thermal pattern positioning. Other applications can be found in the attached reference below.[1]

It is vital to remember that, however positive and successful the use of microwave applications are in medicine, they are based on the destructive powers of radiofrequency energy. Precise management and control of this energy is fundamental in any therapeutic application. But once released into the natural environment, it is very difficult to predict radiation patterns with any precision.

The physics of electromagnetic waves, and their interactions with material and biological systems, is based on the concept that the electromagnetic wave is a force field which exerts a mechanical torque, pressure, or force on electrically charged molecules, groups of charged

---

[1]Kasevich, R.S., *Understand the Potential of Radiofrequency Energy*, Chemical Engineering Progress, January 1998, American Institute of Chemical Engineers, New York, N.Y., pp. 75 – 81.

molecules, positive or negative ions, free electrical charges, or bound electrical charges that may be in motion, or which may be stationary. A simple example of a charged molecule is ordinary water. The special arrangement of two hydrogen atoms with one atom of oxygen produces what is called an 'electric dipole moment,' which is a positive charge separated from a negative charge at a very small distance of separation (measured in angstroms). All living things contain these electric dipoles. In many cases, the thermal effects produced by absorption of electromagnetic energy is the direct result of water molecules acted upon by the oscillating electric field, thereby rubbing against each other to produce heat. Sometimes, non-thermal effects are produced, but they are much more difficult to understand and separate from electromagnetically induced thermal effects.

Trees, plants, soil, grass, shrubs, etc. have the ability to absorb electromagnetic wave energy over a very broad range of wavelengths. Water molecules, ions, and molecularly charged groups within the cellular structure of these items will interact, and generate volumetric heating, as well as other bioeffects. Electromagnetic bioeffects in humans and animals have been intensively studied.[2] Research work is continuing to understand low-level bioeffects at intensities lower than about 10 milliwatts per square centimeter ($10mW/cm^2$), for example, at microwave frequencies.

Electromagnetic radiation in the microwave or radiofrequency bands from cell-tower antennas will interact to some extent with all surrounding vegetation and wildlife. Even though the main beam within half-power points of a microwave antenna is generally directed above treetop level, sidelobe energy and backlobe energy is present — albeit at considerably lower power levels. These levels depend on where a microwave antenna is pointing, the aperture size, the power gain, the frequency and the height above ground level at which an antenna is mounted.

At lower radiofrequencies, when dipoles or monopoles are employed for radiation, the radiation pattern is not beam-like but rather is shaped like a giant doughnut in an omnidirectional pattern. In this case the wave propagation is over 360 degrees of azimuth and follows a cosine pattern in the far field and in the vertical plane of the antenna pattern for any radial cut through the pattern. Energy will easily propagate toward the ground and upward with this type of antenna, which is a normal free space mode of propagation.

---

[2] *Biological Effects and Exposure Criteria for Radiofrequency Electromagnetic Fields*, NCRP Report No. 86, 1986, 1995, National Council on Radiation Protection and Measurements, Bethesda, MD.

Jungle treetops were used by U.S. troops in the Vietnam War to provide radio communications over long distances by what is known as the lateral wave mode. The energy actually clings to the trees as it propagates. A similar mode of propagation was used by the U.S. Army in Operation Desert Storm. The desert floor guided the wave energy as a lateral mode for combat communications. A horizontal wire along the ground acted as either the transmitting or receiving antenna.

In a forested area, a cell tower may couple energy into this so-called lateral mode of electromagnetic wave propagation. This may result in the shedding of some part of the radiation field energy of the tower antenna directly into trees or along the ground, with the affect of enhanced propagation away from the antenna. The wave energy will attenuate by giving up its energy to the tree branches and trunk, or to ground shrubs, as well as by normal geometric spreading.

It should also be noted that electromagnetic waves that reflect from the ground can theoretically quadruple in power density because of the phase relationships inherent over different propagation pathways. This is known as Fresnel reflection, and the region over ground that produces this effect is defined by Fresnel zones.[3]

The following examples of electromagnetic effects should provide some background and insights on possible electromagnetic effects on vegetation and birds. A short discussion on insect mortality from electromagnetic effects is also included.

Trees

Experiments with pine trees growing within high-tension powerline rights-of-way have shown visible branch damage from induced corona. The needle tips dry out and die back in a kind of self-pruning, as if to escape the electric field. Such studies have been largely confined to the 60-Hertz (Hz) range, but with the advent of extensive radio and microwaves in the environment, any material capable of absorbing electromagnetic energy will tend to heat thin dielectric objects such as pine needles.[4] The thinness factor actually amplifies the local radiofrequency or microwave electric field intensity because the electric field induced polarization charge in the pine needle is large compared to a hypothetical round dielectrically equivalent object. Polarization charges exist in all dielectric materials and produce

[3] Beckmann, P., Spizzichino, A., *The Scattering of Electromagnetic Waves from Rough Surfaces*, Pergamon Press Ltd., Oxford, England, 1963.
[4] Levitt, B. B., *Electromagnetic Fields: A Consumer's Guide to the Issues and How to Protect Ourselves*, Harcourt Brace & Company, New York, NY, 1995, p. 498.

electromagnetic effects similar to what one normally associates with free electrons in metal conductors — such as currents when a voltage or electric field is applied.

There is also this important fact: *any tree may act as a receiving dielectric rod or monopole antenna* with the ability to both absorb energy from the wave passing by and to scatter the wave in many directions. If the polarization of the transmitting tower antenna matches the particular tree or trees (i.e., vertical orientation of the antenna which is usually the case for collinear dipole arrays on towers), maximum coupling or absorption of the wave energy by the tree will occur. Polarization and conduction currents will generally flow to the root system.

Dr. Wolfgang Volkrodt, a retired Siemens engineer and physicist in Germany, led an environmental dialogue related to electromagnetic damage to trees over large areas of deforestation in the German and Swiss Alps.[5] *He believed that electromagnetic energy — not acid rain — is the underlying cause of the deforestation.* This is not hard to understand, or believe, in view of the basic physics discussed above and particularly if the frequencies employed cause a resonant interaction between the tree structure and incident wave.

The resonance concept is well known in electromagnetic science and engineering. It encompasses a range of frequencies — from the light technologies all the way to low frequency electromagnetic waves — in the non-ionizing bands of the electromagnetic spectrum. A human being, who is standing, will interact resonantly at the frequency of an incident electromagnetic wave (vertically polarized electric field, which is ½ wavelength of odd or even multiples thereof). In other words, we are capable of acting as receiving antennas for some frequencies. The absorbed energy is maximized under a resonant condition.

The reason the sky appears blue is based on the same principle. But in that situation, it is the scattered light energy that is maximized in the blue light frequency range by a resonant interaction with the atmosphere.

Birds

Electromagnetic fields absorbed by living tissue may produce heat (hyperthermia) and other not-so-well known athermal effects. This absorbed energy is characterized by a number called the Specific Absorption Rate (SAR) which is measured in watts per kilogram of tissue. As an example, it has been shown — both theoretically and with phantom models — that a cell phone held next to the human head will produce a SAR value capable of

---

[5] Ibid , Chapter 4.

heating brain tissue. The bioeffects of this unintentional heating are not well understood at this time but there is on-going research to evaluate the effects on humans.

The affect of heat on birds' eggs has shown some effects on growth and differentiation of the vascular zone. Other studies have shown clear morphologic effects, e.g., retarded development of the whole or parts of the body in 65% of chicks irradiated at 200 mW/cm², for 8 minutes, on day two of embryonic growth. Note that 200 mW/cm², for 8 minutes, is 96 joules of energy and is therefore equivalent on an energy basis to about one day at a power density of 1mW/cm². *This level is comparable to some near fields of cellular towers!* Also, subsequent studies on the same chicks indicated a reduced growth rate, *in vivo*, when exposed to about 550 microwatts per square centimeter (μW/cm²), at 880 MHz.[6]

Insects

A considerable amount of data exists on the ability of radiofrequency energy to selectively kill insects in stored grains at electric fields on the order of one kilovolt per centimeter (kv/cm). This knowledge was acquired by the U.S. Department of Agriculture in the early 1960s. Injuries and delayed effects of radiofrequency exposure were also studied and reported.[7] Mortality curves are presented over a wide range of temperatures and exposure times — up to about one week.

Bernd Heinrich, Professor of Biology at the University of Vermont, has published extensively on insect endothermy (internal heat production) and thermoregulation for a wide variety of insects.[8] Careful reading of his book, *The Thermal Warriors*, clearly will demonstrate to the reader how critical insect heat balance is to insect survival. Without a doubt, radiofrequency or microwave energy absorbed by the insect may alter insect survival mechanisms in dramatic ways. Insects are dielectrics with water content from the perspective of electromagnetic absorption. Even though SAR values for insects may be small, a small temperature change will have a significant effect on insect behavior based on Heinrich's scientific work. Much greater temperatures induced by radiofrequency energy — as shown in the research work published by the USDA — will definitely kill grain-related insects over a one week period at levels of one kv/cm as noted above. Longer exposure

---

[6] Thuery, J. *Microwaves: Industrial, Scientific, and Medical Applications*, ed. Grant, E. H., Artech House, New York, NY, 1995.

[7] Effects of High-Frequency Electric Fields on Certain Species of Stored-Grain Insects, U.S. Department of Agriculture, Marketing Research Report No. 455, 1986.

[8] Heinrich, B., *The Thermal Warriors*, Harvard University Press, Cambridge, MA, 1996, 1999.

times, and lower power densities of radio frequency electric field intensities may prove to be as lethal.

Summary

This short overview on environmental electromagnetic effects with an emphasis on the interaction of radiofrequency and microwave energy with vegetation, birds, plants, and insects is based on the writer's extensive experience with the science and engineering of electromagnetic waves — both for military and commercial applications. I am presently involved with microwave and radiofrequency energy in medical applications, enhanced oil recovery, and soil environmental remediation projects. A review of some of these applications is in the footnoted paper published in the January 1998 issue of *Chemical Engineering Progress.*

The study of low-level effects, thermal and athermal, of electromagnetic radiation on humans, animals, vegetation, insects, etc. is in its infancy. Clearly, the scientific principles and engineering of wave propagation in air and in dielectric materials in most materials — as well as in the many biological effects related to humans — have been studied extensively. However, how the overall biological system responds or behaves to absorbed or scattered electromagnetic energy of any wavelength or intensity, is still largely unknown. Far more needs to be understood concerning how whole-systems react to environmental energy exposures.

Great caution is therefore urged in the propagation and spreading of electromagnetic wave energy into our natural environment because of the inherent difficulty in managing and controlling the energy once it is launched by an antenna system. The antenna system itself may be well engineered, but the vegetation and terrain features will generally play a key role in guiding and directing the flow of energy as dictated by the laws of electromagnetic theory as contained in Maxwell's equations.

The interaction of electromagnetic energy flow with vegetation, wildlife, insects, and birds is still mostly uncharted scientific territory. But indications in the literature are that there may well be negative bioeffects at very low power density levels (much less than $1 \, mW/cm^2$) on myriad species.

Raymond S. Kasevich, BSEE, MSE, PE
Registered Professional Electrical Engineer
94 West Street, Great Barrington, MA, 01230
Email: raykase@taconic.net

Chapter 12

Prediction and Measurement of Exposure to Radiofrequency Electromagnetic Fields

By: Mark Hutchins

Determining radiofrequency (RF) exposure at wireless facilities often has two conflicting goals. The more common objective is to determine compliance with the relevant exposure guidelines, generally as a percentage of Maximum Permissible Exposure (MPE). This may not require measurements, particularly where worst-case predictions for all emitters show cumulative exposure significantly below MPE. At a co-location site with many emitters, however, it may be easier to measure the RF levels. This will be more accurate, absent the worst-case margins, and measured levels will always be lower than such predictions. Although there are exceptions, the typical cellular/PCS co-location site (with a half-dozen providers) will result in general population exposure of less than 10% MPE.

On the other hand, there is increasing interest in obtaining accurate measurements expressed as an unequivocal value instead of a percentage of MPE. One rationale is for easier comparison with guidelines adopted in other countries; another is for comparison with laboratory investigation of similar exposures. The latter may be hampered by the inability to easily correlate specific absorption rates (used in the laboratory) with field measurements of equivalent plane-wave power density.

Unlike a laboratory, the off-site world will impact results. Particularly at levels below 1 microwatt per square centimeter ($\mu W/cm^2$), ambient signals will produce significant measurement variability. The presence of a nearby high-power emitter, such as a 50,000-watt AM radio station, can greatly increase measured power density, but minimally increase the percentage of MPE. For these reasons, relating broadband field measurements to laboratory studies will usually be problematic.

Nonetheless, the case can be made for more detailed and accurate measurements. The incremental cost is not significant and guideline compliance can easily be determined. Local officials and residents are more likely to trust measurements than predictions. Plus, the resulting data compilation could also help guide studies of human effects at the levels being measured.

Case Study

I will outline a recent process to evaluate exposure at a new Cellular One facility in Moreau, New York. As you can see in Figure 1, it occupies the lowest level on a 180-foot tower with radiation center at 155 feet. I am the consultant for the town of Moreau in a situation involving discussion between attorneys for the town and Cellular One over RF radiation compliance. Cellular One said, "We'll be in compliance with FCC emissions requirements." But as noted in Dr. Cleveland's presentation in Chapter 7, there is a difference between emissions and exposure. What the town said was, "We want to know if you're going to be in compliance with 'microwave exposure' requirements." The attorney for Cellular One said they weren't going to utilize "any microwaves."

Figure 1

Verizon Mobile

NEXTEL

CellularOne

There was considerable back and forth until I was put in touch with the Cellular One engineering department, who acknowledged that — if they were in the 800 MHz band — they would technically be utilizing microwaves. The confusion there — and perhaps for many others in general — was considering microwave "dishes" that operate at considerably higher frequency, to be "microwaves." But the town's exposure concern was the entire RF exposure. At this Crown Castle site we already had two carriers, and Cellular One didn't want to pay for measurements for Nextel and Verizon. I explained that when I measure, I look at the exposure from everyone, and it doesn't cost any extra to do so.

It doesn't hurt to ask applicants to underwrite site surveys. Moreau was one case where the town said, "We want measurements." Originally they wanted what is known as the Cobbs Protocol,[1] but Cellular One objected to its use as "overly burdensome." What they agreed to was something in conformity with FCC methods to determine compliance with the exposure guidelines. Dr. Cleveland made this point in his presentation: at any location where you have human access at a site like that in Moreau in the 800 MHz range — specifically at Cellular One frequencies — you would need to limit exposure to the general public to around 580 μW/cm^2. Another of Dr. Cleveland's points was that typically we would find 1 μW/cm^2 or less at this type of cell site.

Figure 2

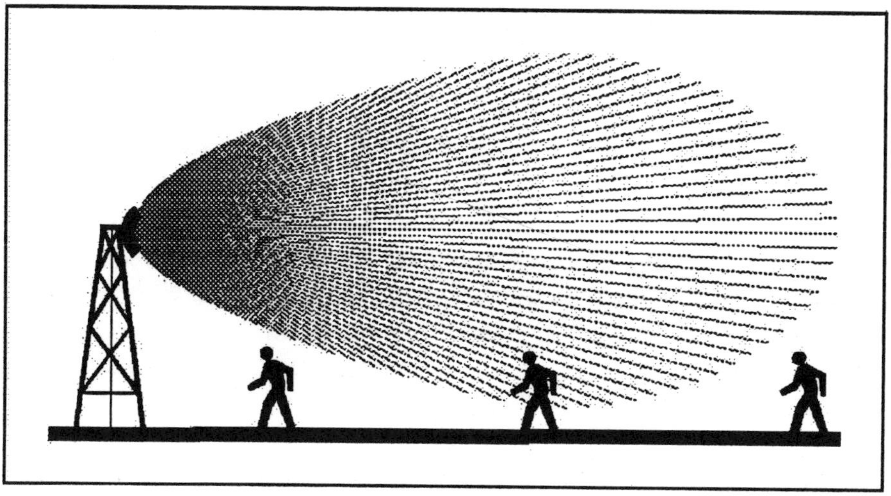

Courtesy Narda Microwave

---

[1] See Appendix D for the Cobbs Protocol.

The previous iiiustration shows an over-simplified view of exposure from a particular antenna. A frequently asked question is whether the person in the middle receives more exposure, and we often find that to be the case. The cell-site exposures are generally very low but, in comparison, someone farther away may have more exposure than someone directly under the antennas. The person on the right, because the signal level drops so quickly with distance, will probably also receive lower exposure than the person in the middle.

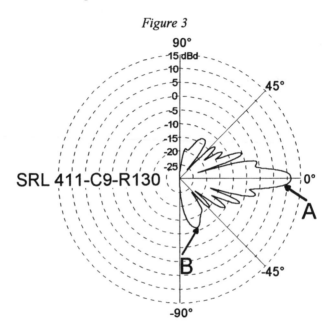

Figure 3

Moving to the more realistic view of Figure 3, what I used in my prediction program was the actual antenna type being used by Cellular One. Applicants often talk about how they are "beaming the signal" at the horizon, and they really are. If we look at the majority of the power — in this case 100 watts effective radiated power for each channel — it's aimed at the horizon. The letter "A" marks the 3dB point, where the power of the beam is effectively half; so the 100 watts aimed at the horizon is 50 watts aimed in that downward direction.

In calculating where that will hit the ground, I consider the variation of terrain, and the 50 watts is aimed at a point on the ground about 2,800 feet away from this antenna. If one was aiming the beam at a person standing at that point (which the antenna does), even though it aims most power at the horizon, everything below gets some signal. This is what is shown in Figure 3. We often see a lobe of energy (the "B" point) — something that causes concern among lay people since it looks like there is quite a bit of power beaming down. However, these charts are in decibels, a comparative unit in which 3 decibels (dB) lower power is half the power. In Figure 3, point B means a reduction to an effective radiated power level more like half a watt. At that angle, the signal is aimed at a point on the ground about 60 feet from the base of this tower. Even at sixty feet, we have started to accumulate the distance from the antenna that so rapidly helps attenuate the signal. The prediction program shows that where the "A" point meets the ground, there will be a power density of 0.008 μW/cm² and at the "B" point there will be 0.02 μW/cm² (from every channel). Cellular One uses more than one channel, and before performing measurements, we must also consider activity by the other carriers to make sure we have the correct probes for the survey.

Figure 4

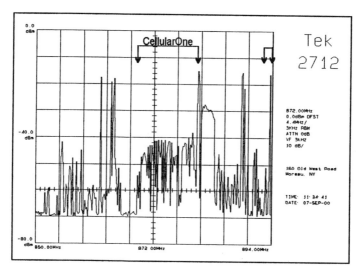

We can now compare spectrum analysis plots before (Figure 4) and after (Figure 5) site activation. Both show the 800 MHz spectrum occupied by all three carriers for transmitting at this site. Cellular One operates primarily in the marked portion, with some channel utilization indicated at the upper end of the display. Note the higher levels (Figure 5) following activation of the site. This is exactly what the provider seeks, and might lead you to believe there has been quite a power increase.

Figure 5

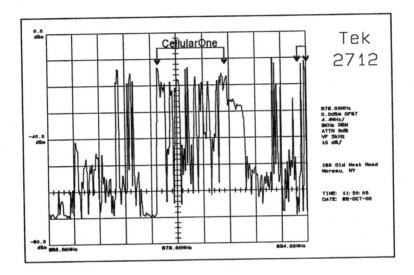

The spectrum analyzer shows the signal that will be detected by a cell-phone antenna. The voltage, or the excitation of the wire that is the antenna, is quite different than the power deposited over the surface of a human being. This more-than-adequate signal at the antenna can still be extremely low in terms of power density. But clearly there is more going on here after activation of the base station.

Figure 6

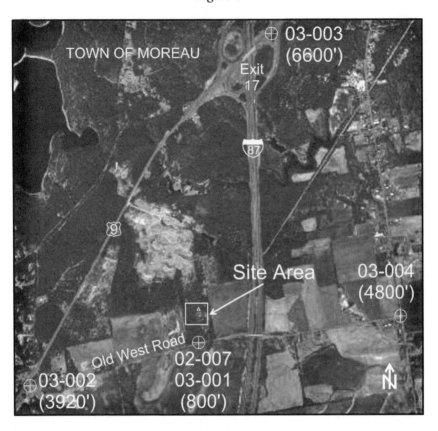

Figure 6 shows measurement points in addition to those normally made close to a facility. We ordinarily examine levels within a few hundred feet, but in this case we went considerably beyond the site. I measured at the beginning of the access road — 800 feet south of the site. To the west, about 3,900 feet away, was the second point. A third point was located north, at Exit 17 of Interstate 84, about 6,600 feet away. A final point was about 4,800 feet to the east. These distant measurements were fairly unusual, but the town was interested to see what was going on farther from the site. It was also unusual in that we had a provider willing to pay not only for before-and-after testing, but also for these additional test points.

Figure 7

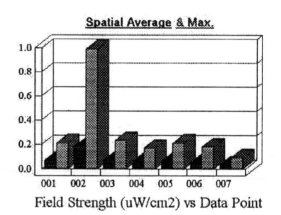

METER: 8718B	S/N: 1534	Cal. Date: 10/19/00	Due: 10/19/01
PROBE: 8760D	S/N: 02020	Cal. Date: 12/15/99	Due: 12/15/00
PROBE CORRECTION:	Frequency: N/A		Corrrection Factor 1.00
Run Ref. Number: 02	Record #2 of 3	Date: 10/26/00	Start Time: 11:37

Data Point #	Average uW/cm2	Max uW/cm2
001	0.07	0.21
002	0.18	0.99
003	0.07	0.23
004	0.06	0.17
005	0.06	0.21
006	0.05	0.18
007	0.03	0.09

Spatial Average & Max.

Field Strength (uW/cm2) vs Data Point

Figure 7 shows measurement results using a very sensitive probe — accurate as low as 0.05 μW/cm^2 — close to the tower. Keeping in mind that the guideline maximum at the 800 MHz frequencies is between 500 and 600 μW/cm^2, clearly we have quite low values in the area near the tower. The bar graph shows two values for each data point: spatial average (bar to the left) and maximum at the point (bar to the right). The former is due to the requirement that we average the exposure over the space that a body would occupy; the latter lets us know the highest reading we encountered over that same space. With the exception of the second point, these averages were less than 0.1 μW/cm^2. This probe measures exposure over the RF spectrum as high as 3 GHz, and measures exposure from all emitters simultaneously. On the spectrum analyzer I also looked at the general activity, particularly in the VHF spectrum (between 30 and 300 MHz) where the guidelines are the most stringent. In this case there was a lot of activity from FM, TV, and other stations — most at some distance — but all contributing to power density at the test location.

Figure 8

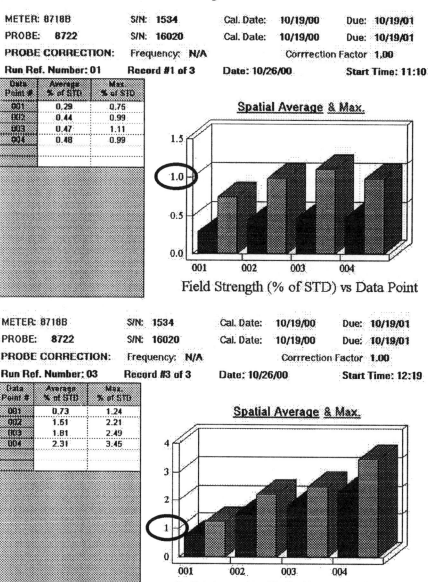

METER: 8718B   S/N: 1534   Cal. Date: 10/19/00   Due: 10/19/01
PROBE: 8722   S/N: 16020   Cal. Date: 10/19/00   Due: 10/19/01
PROBE CORRECTION: Frequency: N/A   Corrrection Factor 1.00
Run Ref. Number: 01   Record #1 of 3   Date: 10/26/00   Start Time: 11:10

Data Point #	Average % of STD	Max % of STD
001	0.29	0.75
002	0.44	0.99
003	0.47	1.11
004	0.48	0.99

Spatial Average & Max.

Field Strength (% of STD) vs Data Point

METER: 8718B   S/N: 1534   Cal. Date: 10/19/00   Due: 10/19/01
PROBE: 8722   S/N: 16020   Cal. Date: 10/19/00   Due: 10/19/01
PROBE CORRECTION: Frequency: N/A   Corrrection Factor 1.00
Run Ref. Number: 03   Record #3 of 3   Date: 10/26/00   Start Time: 12:19

Data Point #	Average % of STD	Max % of STD
001	0.73	1.24
002	1.51	2.21
003	1.81	2.49
004	2.31	3.45

Spatial Average & Max.

Field Strength (% of STD) vs Data Point

Figure 8 shows results from a probe that yields results as percentage of the MPE for the controlled, or occupational, environment. We can roughly translate these to uncontrolled/general-public environment percentage exposure by multiplying readings by 5. I used this second probe because I didn't know, when I moved some distance from the site, what other types of exposures I would encounter from RF spectrum outside the 800 MHz range. This probe allows a greater range of power and frequency—from 300 kHz to 40 GHz—so these results indicate exposure across the entire RF spectrum. The upper chart shows results near the tower site, and even the peak values were below 1% occupational or (approximately) less than 5% of the limit for the general public. Because this graphing program changes the vertical scale, I have circled the 1% point on each chart. The lower chart has values from the 4 locations noted earlier that are some distance (between 800 and 6,600 feet) from the tower. The 800 foot point was more in line with what I found at the site: a little less than 1%. But the other locations — at some distance from the site — were actually higher.

There is a possible explanation for this. Since the site (as can be seen through close examination of the Figure 6 photograph) is very protected by terrain and heavy woods, the ground-level survey points are much better shielded from the numerous signals. Also, at such low levels — and given the extremely numerous emitters — there can be much more going on and much greater signal variability. We often see a lot of 'up' and 'down' with measurements, but it is interesting that measurements away from the site were consistently higher.

Mark Hutchins, Radiofrequency Engineer
P.O. Box 6418
Brattelboro, VT 05302-6418
www.MarkHutchins.com

Chapter 13

Planning and Zoning Regulations: Some Local Solutions

By: Tony Blair

Let's assume, for the moment, that you live in a town with no cellular towers and you want to help the town create zoning regulations that will allow for maximum control and oversight, consistent with federal law. Or, maybe your town has already been approached by wireless service providers. You have applications for cell towers pending and you have discovered that your current regulations do not adequately protect the community. How do you get effective regulations in place, or tighten the ones you have? What are the rights and responsibilities of the average citizen to effect change at the local level? What is reasonable to ask of municipal agents? Where do you start?

What Citizens Can Do

Perhaps a cell tower or wireless installation has been proposed in your neighborhood. You've hit the panic button and don't know where to start. The first tasks at hand are to educate yourself about the existing regulations in town, persuade the proper officials to recognize the need for a solid planning approach, and to bring effective, persistent political pressure on decision makers until they do what is necessary and consistent with their mandate to protect the health, safety, and welfare of the community.

Organizing at the local level takes hard work. The very first step is to educate yourself about the local process and find out which board or office is responsible for drafting land-use regulations or zoning codes. A copy of such regulations can usually be gotten from the town or city clerk, the building inspector, or the zoning enforcement officer.

Find out which board or office is responsible for permitting special uses such as cellular towers. Is it the zoning board? The zoning board of appeals? The city council? The planning board? Every state is different in how land-use powers are vested. Land-use regulation often differs from town to town.

You will need to know which board is responsible for writing such regulations. It may not be the same board as is given the siting powers, or later — enforcement powers. For instance, in Massachusetts, the planning board may write the regulations, but a Special Permit Granting Authority (SPGA) may be the board of selectmen or the zoning board of appeals (ZBA).

Once you've determined the specifics of your situation, find out when and where the decision-making board meets. Attend some meetings to get a flavor for the personalities of the board members and a sense of the way they approach their work.

It helps to contact other municipalities for information, or local newspapers that have run articles about other tower-siting scenarios. Network. You will find that people who have been active in this field love to share their stories, expertise, and resources. Consider placing an ad in the local newspaper to attract other citizens who are concerned. An ad as simple as: "Interested in the issue of cellular towers in our neighborhoods? Call me at . . ." will cost only a few dollars and may help you begin a citizens group that can share the workload.

It's fair to say one person cannot do this alone. Few people have the spare time, energy, or tenacity to move such issues onto center stage and pressure public officials to act constructively. Plus, there is power in numbers. No city council, or planning board can afford to ignore a room full of people who have a clear agenda. But they have little problem ignoring one citizen (or even a small group) whom they can dismiss as NIMBY's.

By organizing your neighbors and others throughout the community, you will develop a larger voice that will attract the local media. When you attend municipal meetings to speak about the issues, you will be heard in a very different way than before.

Our local group in Great Barrington, Massachusetts — Folks for Appropriate Cellular Tower Sites, or FACTS — became a force to be reckoned with when it could consistently, and on very short notice, get fifty or so people to any meeting where the tower issues were up for discussion. It did not matter than only about three or four of those people were really working diligently on the issue. The group took on a force far greater than the individual efforts of the members.

An Overview of Zoning:
What It Can – And Cannot Do – According To Federal Law

The parameters of zoning for "personal wireless service facilities" are set out in federal law, in the Telecommunications Act of 1996, Section 704.[1]

Cutting through the legalese of the Telecom Act, a community can still regulate many aspects of tower siting. Where a tower is located, how tall it can be, what can go on the tower, and how such installations are monitored for radiofrequency (RF) emissions to make sure they are in compliance with the FCC standards — among many other things, still fall under local jurisdiction. But, there are better and certainly worse ways of going about the exercise of that control.

The Telecom Act also stipulates that communities must be careful in denying permits. Denials should be for substantial reasons created in a written record of the proceedings. The better the zoning regulations are, the better will be the template for denials when siting requests are inappropriate. Good regulations are the blueprint for successful legal actions, should that come to pass.

What a community cannot do is to completely ban personal wireless service from that community. Does that mean it must allow a tower or base station within the community? Not necessarily. If the company could provide service from another adjacent community, and is already located on a tower in that nearby town, where — by adding antennas they could also cover your town — then you might be able to keep that company from building a new tower in your town.[2] The basic legal argument is that your town is not preventing the company from providing service to the community but rather disallowing a new base station to be erected within town boundaries. The reason for doing so is that the company can already provide service from an existing tower to which the company already has legal access.

Under the Telecom Act, communities cannot "unreasonably" discriminate among providers. This means the town cannot block one cellular company from providing service in the community if other

---

[1] See B. Blake Levitt, Chapter 1, for the exact language of the Telecommunications Act.
[2] Recent case law supports this. See James Hobson's presentation, Cellular Telephone Co. v. Zoning Board of Adjustment.

providers have already established service.[3] But towns can — and usually do — require the new company to co-locate on an existing tower. That is reasonable discrimination — allowing them both to cover the same area from the same location. You might hear carriers arguing that they want a better location, or to provide better service — but your town is not required to provide the carriers the absolute best possible location — just a reasonable location. If another carrier is already providing service from an existing location, then it is probably good enough.

In addition, your community must act within a reasonable period of time in dealing with applications. Towns cannot put service providers off indefinitely. State statutes establish precise timelines on land-use applications. In some states or municipalities, a permit is automatically granted if a decision-making board does not act within a specified time frame. It's a decision by default.

One of the most vexing clauses in the Telecom Act — for citizens in particular who are worried about health effects — concerns the restriction on considering the environmental effects of RF. Municipalities cannot use the environmental effects of radio frequency radiation — which is widely interpreted by many, though not all, to include health effects in humans — as a basis for making a siting decision "to the extent that such facilities comply with the Commission's regulations concerning such emissions."

Although towns cannot regulate for RF, it is important to know there are other concerns that parallel environmental and health concerns that can be used as a basis for zoning. Examples include the use of large setbacks and vegetative screening. This will prevent facilities from being sited too close to dwellings, reduce visual impacts, and help protect property values. Large setbacks will also reduce the potential damage if a tower collapses or has ice fall from it. Another important avenue is the fact that towers can create an "attractive nuisance" — especially to students who may dare each other to climb them. Attractive nuisance is a legal term that could come in handy when denying applications near schools.

All such provisions can result in the tower being located at a reasonable distance from residential areas and schools, thereby reducing RF exposures, but without directly depending on that rationale to do so.

---

[3] There is recent case law on this point that appears to be in direct conflict with the Telecom Act. See James Hobson, Chapter 9, presentation, APT Pittsburgh v. Penn Township.

In addition, towns can require monitoring to make sure that all facilities meet the maximum FCC emissions guidelines — no matter how many providers are co-located at a particular site. Very few people at the local level understand that the responsibility for compliance monitoring has shifted to municipalities.

Hiring Experts

Telecommunications regulation and application-review is one of the most complex forms of land-use law today. Done correctly, it is unlike anything that most planners and zoners have been called upon to do. Many shy away from it because of the complexity. But what individual board members are unfamiliar with can — and should — be provided by hiring outside expertise.

One of the first things you will need to know is what telecommunications coverage already exists in your area. It is not enough to speculate that a company "ought" to be able to provide coverage from somewhere else. Wireless coverage is a function of tower height, signal strength, frequency, antenna direction, topography and several other factors. You need to know with precision if another location can work. And to know, you need expert assistance from an independent RF engineer who is working for the municipality — not the telecommunications industry. Such an RF engineer will be familiar with the systems and technology of radiofrequency communication and will help the town determine if the information on an application is accurate, or if other solutions would be better for the town's interests.

A telecommunications engineer can be helpful whether an application is pending or not. One proactive approach used by communities is to hire an engineer to help create a telecommunications master plan or overlay district, where facilities can be placed to provide adequate service — while still protecting the town's vital interests. By having an expert do a few radial or tile plots — diagrams that model RF coverage patterns — of likely sites, it can help town officials, as well as interested citizens, understand how topography and demography work as a whole. If a town can anticipate what the carriers want and do their own prior assessment, rather than passively wait for the industry to define its own goals in town, a win-win situation may result.

The town will have to front money for an RF engineer but the expense is worth it. A master plan will help with better siting decisions and fewer lawsuits by the industry (if applications are denied), or by irate citizens (if siting decisions are poor ones.)

A note of caution, however, is warranted. Do not invite the industry in on early planning efforts in the name of listening to all "stakeholders." Be wary when they "want to help the town." They are skilled at co-opting the local process and you may find yourself pulled more toward accommodating their needs than your own. Such co-optation can be subtle. It often seems friendly. They want to help you "avoid law suits" — which can be a veiled threat. Inviting them to the planning table will also provide an early window into town dynamics and give them an edge later on.

Another note of caution: most telecommunications engineering firms work for the industry and so would have a conflict of interest in working for a community. But there *are* competent independent engineers who can provide what the town needs. This is where networking with other towns is especially helpful. You may be able to find out the names of one or more engineers from other town boards. If not, try local universities with engineering departments. The EMR Network also recommends independent engineers to municipalities.[4] Ask for references from other towns the individual has worked for. When you contact those references, you will have found a gold mine of information — not just about the engineer you are thinking about hiring, but also about the process the other town went through, the lessons they learned, and the pitfalls they encountered.

The other important expert you will need is a lawyer who is familiar with the recent telecommunications case law. In 1996 when the Telecom Act was passed, very little such case law existed regarding where this technology intersects with the rights of local governance. Today, that case law is accumulating. Many important decisions in federal courts back local decision-making powers. The town's municipal attorney may not be familiar with the implications of these decisions. Often, the municipal attorney defines his or her mandate as avoiding lawsuits for the town and may advise the path of least resistance. But, this not the best course of action with this particular issue. Towns need not roll over for the telecom industry.

---

[4] See Appendices E & F for websites.

Moratoriums

If the town needs time to study the issue, going into a moratorium period is the wisest thing to do. During the pre-determined time-period, no applications can be accepted, therefore no legal obligation exists to act on them. A moratorium is especially helpful before applications come in. It will give the town breathing room to do a proactive job of creating good zoning regulations. If a town is not in a legal moratorium, any applications for telecom sites will apply to whatever regulations are in place at the time. Telecom providers have been known to flood some towns with applications just before the start of a moratorium in order to avoid stricter regulations.

The FCC has set out voluntary moratorium guidelines for communities.[5] In general, moratoriums cannot be used as smokescreens for obstruction. They cannot be indefinite.[6] They must be good-faith efforts to get one's regulatory house in order. Many communities begin with a three-month time frame and extend it to six months, if necessary. Those are considered reasonable periods.

Any applications that are pending before the moratorium must be heard in a timely manner. The moratorium will not apply to them.

A moratorium is a legal entity. It must be enacted by the appropriate authority in your town. Moratorium language should be precise and include a statement that the purpose of the moratorium is to develop appropriate regulations to control the placement, construction, and modification of personal wireless service facilities, in accordance with the Telecommunications Act of 1996, and applicable state and local laws. The time-period must be specified. Extensions should be voted on again.

Once a moratorium is in place, the community must work quickly on the bylaws you will be drafting.

How Do You Start?

It helps to define your goals up front:

❑   What are we trying to accomplish?
❑   Is our goal to place facilities in specific locations?

---

[5] See Chapter 7, Robert Cleveland's presentation for the FCC's website.
[6] A federal court up held one community's right to two, back-to-back, six-month moratoriums. See Sprint Spectrum v. Medina in Chapter 9, James Hobson's presentation.

- ❑ For how many carriers do we anticipate needing to provide service?
- ❑ What is the infrastructure already in place — here and in neighboring communities?
- ❑ Are there areas you really want to avoid — scenic ridgelines, other vulnerable areas?
- ❑ Are there appropriate and acceptable town-owned sites where the town could gain some revenue?
- ❑ How are you going to handle the NIMBY phenomenon? Are *we* the NIMBY phenomenon?
- ❑ How have neighboring communities fared in their dealings with the carriers?
- ❑ Do we need a whole new bylaw, or a revamp of the existing bylaws?
- ❑ Is there a process for input from citizens and from experts into the end product? Who has control over that process? Is that Board or person on your side?
- ❑ What sides are likely to be drawn up during this process? Who is likely to be opposing whom?
- ❑ Do you have a consensus about these and other questions as you start? Or are you going to have to work out these issues as you go forward?
- ❑ Is an application already pending?
- ❑ Are the necessary experts in place? Are you going to be using the town attorney for legal advice as you proceed? What is that person's orientation on this subject? Are they up to speed on wireless telecommunications issues and case law? If not can they consult with another firm that is?

The basic attitude you take into the process will often determine what you get out of it. The more professional you are, the better. Understand that, according to the Telecom Act, you may have to allow these facilities somewhere. You are trying to balance the best interests of your community with those of the telecommunications providers.

The best way to accomplish that balance is to create a stringent, thorough, and fair bylaw to locate wireless facilities that will be adequate for the carriers, and have the least detrimental impact possible.

Good Telecom Regulations

As mentioned before, this is a different kind of land-use regulation than most planners or zoners are familiar with. It requires a lot of engineering detail for wireless energy — something invisible that exists in space. This is not the average three-bedroom colonial house proposed for a residential plot, or a sub-division request.

Great Barrington, Massachusetts, was one of the first communities in the country to incorporate the requirement for such RF engineering detail, as well as thorough monitoring, and proof of liability coverage for the town, into zoning regulations. (Numerous communities across the country have subsequently used this model, with various adaptations.) It set the bar for telecom siting regulation at a new high for a local municipality.[7]

Great Barrington is located in the southern Berkshire Mountains of Massachusetts. The area is scenic and laden with historic assets to protect. Its economy is heavily dependent on tourism dollars. Inappropriately placed telecom towers are seen as a direct threat to the local economy and the underlying aesthetic sensibilities of the community.

The following bylaw was written while the town and some private citizens were involved in a court case, appealing a special permit for a cellular tower on a private school campus near a residential neighborhood. (After six years, the case was won by the town.)

The following Great Barrington bylaw, with italicized comments, is fourteen pages long. Some towns have expanded it to 30-40 pages.[8] The point is to be thorough and adapt it to your town's needs. Note that it is written to conform with both Great Barrington existing bylaws (so the numbering is specific to Great Barrington) and with Massachusetts law. Any adaptations must be consistent with your own state.

---

[7] The Great Barrington regulations effect many of the same provisions used by the Connecticut Siting Council – a state agency with vastly greater resources – in reviewing telecom proposals.

[8] See Appendix D, for the regulations of Cabot, VT.

Great Barrington Personal Wireless Service Facilities and Towers By-Law

I § 171- 120. Purposes:

The purposes of this Personal Wireless Service Facilities and Towers Article are to:

A. Preserve the character and appearance of the Town while simultaneously allowing Adequate Personal Wireless Services to be developed.

B. Protect the scenic, historic, environmental, and natural or man-made resources of the community.

C. Provide standards and requirements for regulation, placement, construction, monitoring, design, modification and removal of Personal Wireless Service Facilities.

D. Provide a procedural basis for action within a reasonable period of time for requests for authorization to place, construct, operate or modify Personal Wireless Service Facilities.

E. Preserve property values.

F. Minimize the total number and height of Towers throughout the community.

G. Locate Towers so that they do not have negative impacts, such as, but not limited to, attractive nuisance, noise and falling objects, on the general safety, welfare and quality of life of the community.

H. Require owners of Towers and Personal Wireless Service Facilities to configure them so as to minimize and mitigate the adverse visual impact of the Towers and Facilities.

I. Require Tower sharing and the clustering of Personal Wireless Service Facilities where possible.

A listing of purposes is useful because it tells your Special Permit Granting Authority (SPGA) what it is trying to accomplish, and gives it the reasons it needs if it is going to deny the permit. It also addresses one of the Telecomm Act issues — timely consideration.

II § 171- 121. Consistency with Federal Law:

These regulations are intended to be consistent with The Telecommunications Act of 1996 in that: a) they do not prohibit or have the effect of prohibiting the provision of Personal Wireless

Services; b) they are not intended to be used to unreasonably discriminate among providers of functionally equivalent Services; c) they do not regulate Personal Wireless Services on the basis of the environmental effects of radio frequency emissions to the extent that the regulated Services and Facilities comply with the FCC's regulations concerning such emissions.

This language allows the SPGA to demonstrate that they were cognizant of the federal law and are striving to comply with it.

III § 171-122. Definitions and word usage:

As used in this Personal Wireless Service Facilities Article, the following terms shall have the meanings indicated. The word "shall" or "will" indicate mandatory requirements; "may" is advisory and indicates recommendations which are not mandatory.

ACT - The Telecommunications Act of 1996.

ADEQUATE COVERAGE - Coverage is considered to be "adequate" within that area surrounding a Base Station where the predicted or measured median field strength of the transmitted signal is greater than -95 dBm. It is acceptable for there to be holes within the area of Adequate Coverage where the signal is less than -95 dBm, as long as the signal regains its strength to greater than -95 dBm further away from the Base Station. For the limited purpose of determining whether the use of a Repeater is necessary or desirable, there shall be deemed not to be Adequate Coverage within said holes. The outer boundary of the area of Adequate Coverage, however, is that location past which the signal does not regain a strength of greater than -95 dBm.

The telelcommunications industry was upset that the town defined its own signal strength. Such a right has subsequently been reserved to the towns and upheld in federal case law in Sprint Spectrum v. Willoth. It is VERY important that YOU define the level of signal strength that is adequate. This is an engineering detail. DO NOT LET THE CARRIERS DEFINE EITHER ADEQUATE COVERAGE OR ADEQUATE CAPACITY! You have the right to set these parameters, as long as they are reasonable and do not have the effect of prohibiting the carriers from providing service. NOTE: The definition needs to be updated to the signal strength levels that are appropriate for today's equipment and for technologies that have evolved since this was written.

ADEQUATE CAPACITY - Capacity is considered to be "adequate" if the Grade of Service is p.05 or better for at least 50% of the days in a preceding month, prior to the date of Application, as measured using direct traffic measurement of the Personal Wireless Service Facility in question, where the call blocking is due to frequency contention at the antenna(s).

ANTENNA - A device which is attached to a Tower, or other structure for transmitting and receiving electromagnetic waves.

AVAILABLE SPACE - The space on a Tower or structure to which Antennas of a Personal Wireless Service Provider are both Structurally Able and Electromagnetically Able to be attached.

BASE STATION - The primary sending and receiving site in a wireless telecommunications network. More than one Base Station and/or more than one variety of Personal Wireless Service Provider can be located on a single Tower or structure.

CHANNEL - The segment of the radiation spectrum from an Antenna which carries one signal. An Antenna may radiate on many Channels simultaneously.

COMMUNICATION EQUIPMENT SHELTER - A structure located at a Base Station designed principally to enclose equipment used in connection with Personal Wireless Service transmissions.

dBm - Unit of measure of the power level of an electromagnetic signal expressed in decibels referenced to 1 milliwatt.

ELECTROMAGNETICALLY ABLE - The determination that the new signal from and to the proposed new Antennas will not significantly interfere with the existing signals from and to other Facilities located on the same Tower or structure as determined by a qualified professional telecommunications engineer. The use of available technologies to alleviate such interference shall be considered when making this determination.

EMF - Electromagnetic Frequency Radiation

FACILITY SITE - A property, or any part thereof, which is owned or leased by one or more Personal Wireless Service Providers and upon which one or more Personal Wireless Service Facility(s) and required landscaping are located.

FCC - Federal Communications Commission. The Government agency responsible for regulating telecommunications in the United States.

FCC 96-326 - A Report and Order which sets new national standards for emissions of Radio-Frequency emissions from FCC-regulated transmitters.

GHZ - Gigahertz: One billion hertz.

GRADE OF SERVICE - A measure of the percentage of calls which are able to connect to the Base Station, during the busiest hour of the day. Grade of Service is expressed as a number, such as p.05 - which means that 95% of callers will connect on their first try. A lower number (p.04) indicates a better Grade of Service.

HERTZ - One hertz is the frequency of an electric or magnetic field which reverses polarity once each second, or one cycle per second.

MAJOR MODIFICATION OF AN EXISTING FACILITY - Any change, or proposed change in power input or output, number of Antennas, change in Antenna type or model, repositioning of Antenna(s), change in number of Channels per Antenna above the maximum number approved under an existing Special Permit.

MAJOR MODIFICATION OF AN EXISTING TOWER - Any increase, or proposed increase in dimensions of an existing and permitted Tower or other structure designed to support Personal Wireless Service transmission, receiving and/or relaying antennas and/or equipment.

MHZ - Megahertz: One million hertz.

MONITORING - The measurement, by the use of instruments in the field, of the radiation from a Site as a whole, or from individual Personal Wireless Service Facilities, Towers, Antennas or Repeaters.

MONITORING PROTOCOL - The testing protocol, initially the Cobbs Protocol, which is to be used to monitor the emissions from existing and new Personal Wireless Service Facilities upon adoption of this Article. The SPGA may, as the technology changes, require, by written regulation, the use of other testing protocols. A copy of the Monitoring Protocol shall be on file with the Board of Selectmen and the Town Clerk.

MONOPOLE - A single self-supporting vertical pole with no guy wire anchors, usually consisting of a galvanized or other unpainted metal, or a wooden pole with below grade foundations.

PERSONAL WIRELESS SERVICES - Commercial Mobile Services, unlicensed wireless services, and common carrier wireless exchange access services. These services include: cellular services, personal communications services (PCS), Specialized Mobile Radio Services, and Paging Services.

PERSONAL WIRELESS SERVICE FACILITY - All equipment (including any Repeaters) with which a Personal Wireless Service Provider broadcasts and receives the radio-frequency waves which carry their services and all locations of said equipment or any part thereof. This Facility may be sited on one or more Towers or structure(s) owned and permitted by another owner or entity.

PERSONAL WIRELESS SERVICE PROVIDER - An entity, licensed by the FCC to provide Personal Wireless Services to individuals or institutions.

RADIATION PROPAGATION STUDIES OR RADIAL PLOTS - Computer generated estimates of the radiation emanating from Antennas or Repeaters sited on a specific Tower or structure. The height above ground, power input and output, frequency output, type of antenna, antenna gain, topography of the site and its surroundings are all taken into account to create these simulations. They are the primary tool for determining whether a site will provide Adequate Coverage for the Personal Wireless Service Facility proposed for that Site.

REPEATER - A small receiver/relay transmitter of not more than 20 watts output designed to provide service to areas which are not able to receive Adequate Coverage directly from a Base Station.

SPECIAL PERMIT GRANTING AUTHORITY (SPGA) - The Board of Selectmen shall be the SPGA for this Article.

STRUCTURALLY ABLE - The determination that a Tower or structure is capable of carrying the load imposed by the proposed new Antennas under all reasonably predictable conditions as determined by professional structural engineering analysis.

TELEPORT - A facility utilizing satellite dishes of greater than 2.0 meters in diameter designed to uplink to communications satellites for transmitting in the C-Band (4 - 6 GHz) spectrum.

TOWER - A lattice structure or framework, or Monopole, that is designed to support Personal Wireless Service transmission, receiving and/or relaying antennas and/or equipment.

IV § 171 - 123. Exempted Wireless Telecommunications Uses:

This Article specifically exempts the following wireless telecommunications facilities: police, fire, ambulance and other emergency dispatch; amateur (ham) radio; citizens band radio; any existing commercial radio tower; radio dispatch services for local businesses. No Personal Wireless Service Facility shall be considered exempt from this Article for any reason whether or not said Facility is proposed to share a Tower or other structure with such exempt uses.

> *You don't want to interfere with your local emergency services or antagonize HAM radio operators. But you also don't want Ham operators to lease their towers to other carriers. Radio dispatch for local businesses is a judgment call. The Telecom Act only preempts local authority for cellular telecommunications services. Broadcast facilities for TV and radio can still be banned outright in communities.*

V § 171 - 124. Provision of Independent Consultants:

A. Upon submission of an Application for a Special Permit under this Article, the SPGA shall hire independent consultants whose services shall be paid for by the Applicant(s) under the terms of Selectmen's Policies and Procedures in accordance with Chapter 593 of the Acts of 1989. These Consultants shall each be qualified professionals with a record of service to municipalities in one of the following fields: a) telecommunications engineering, b) structural engineering, c) monitoring of electromagnetic fields, and, if determined necessary by the SPGA, d) other consultants.

B. The SPGA shall select the Independent Consultant(s) after consultation with the Planning Board, the Board of Health, and the Conservation Commission, which may propose a list of qualified candidates.

Because applications for these facilities (when they include everything they should) are voluminous and technical, you need to be able to hire independent consultant(s). The Applicant should pay for consultants, not the Town. This language allows that to happen. Again, note the reference to Massachusetts law and change as necessary.

VI § 171 - 125. Prohibition of Teleports:
There shall be no Teleport(s) within the Town of Great Barrington.

Teleports create a lot of radiation, are not protected in the Telecommunications Act, and you don't want them anywhere near residential areas.

VII § 171 - 126. Application Requirements:
A. No Tower or Personal Wireless Service Facility shall be erected, constructed, or installed without first obtaining a Special Permit from the SPGA. One or both of two kinds of Special Permits are required; a) for new Tower construction (or Major Modification Of An Existing Tower); b) for Personal Wireless Service Facilities (or Major Modification Of An Existing Facility) to be mounted on an existing, or newly permitted, Tower or structure. If Applicant is applying for both Permits, they shall be submitted and examined concurrently. Applications shall be submitted using the Long Form Application (SP-2), in accordance with the requirements of Article X of the Bylaw. The following additional information must also be submitted:

Details of the application process are specific to Great Barrington, and would need to be adapted to fit your local and state requirements. We require two different types of permits because the first carrier, who may build a tower will need to get both a Tower permit and a Facility permit, but subsequent carriers, co-locating on that Tower, need only get a Facility permit. However, note that Major Modifications also require new permits.

B. **Adequate Coverage, Adequate Capacity, and Justification of Need:**

1.   Applicant shall provide written documentation of any Facility Sites in Great Barrington, in abutting towns and in Mount Washington, MA, in which it has a legal or equitable interest, whether by ownership, leasehold or otherwise. From each such Facility Site, it shall demonstrate with written documentation that these Facility Sites are not already providing, or do not have the potential by adjusting the Site, to provide Adequate Coverage and/or Adequate Capacity to the Town of Great Barrington. The documentation shall include, for each Facility Site listed, the exact location (in longitude and latitude, to degrees, minutes and seconds), ground elevation, height of Tower or structure, type of Antennas, Antenna gain, height of Antennas on Tower or structure, output frequency, number of channels, power input and maximum power output per channel. Potential adjustments to these existing Facility Sites, including changes in Antenna type, orientation, gain, height or power output shall be specified. Radial Plots from each of these Facility Sites, as they exist, and with adjustments as above, shall be provided as part of the Application.

2.   Applicant shall demonstrate with written documentation that they have examined all Facility Sites located in Great Barrington, in abutting towns and in Mount Washington, MA, in which Applicant has no legal or equitable interest, whether by ownership, leasehold or otherwise to determine whether those existing Facility Sites can be used to provide Adequate Coverage and/or Adequate

Capacity to the Town of Great Barrington. The documentation shall include, for each Facility Site examined, the exact location (in longitude and latitude, to degrees, minutes and seconds), ground elevation, height of Tower or structure, type of Antennas proposed, proposed Antenna gain, height of proposed Antennas on Tower or structure, proposed output frequency, proposed number of channels, proposed power input and proposed maximum power output per channel. Radial Plots from each of these Facility Sites, as proposed, shall be provided as part of the Application.

3. Applicant shall demonstrate with written documentation that they have analyzed the feasibility of Repeaters in conjunction with all Facility Sites listed in compliance with VII,B,1&2 (above) to provide Adequate Coverage and/or Adequate Capacity to the Town of Great Barrington. Radial Plots of all Repeaters considered for use in conjunction with these Facility Sites shall be provided as part of the Application.

4. Notwithstanding anything else in this §171-126.B (entitled "Adequate Coverage, Adequate Capacity, and Justification of Need"), Applicant may request that the requirement to provide written documentation as to any existing Facility Site (as specified in §171-126.B.1 and §171-126.B.2) be waived or modified as to any such existing Facility Site outside the Town of Great Barrington which is located more than four miles from any boundary of the Town of Great Barrington. Such a request shall be submitted by the Applicant in writing and shall be supported by a statement of reasons and supporting material. The SPGA may waive or modify said requirement only if it finds that consideration of the documentation regarding any such existing Facility Site as to which the Applicant seeks a waiver is not necessary because the intended technology is clearly not technically feasible for use at said site. The SPGA's finding as to the waiver request shall be based on all the evidence, which may include but is not limited to: then-current industry standards, government regulatory standards or materials, and input from the SPGA's Independent Consultant.

The purpose of this section is to require the carriers to show what they can already provide and to demonstrate conclusively that they <u>need</u> the new facility they are applying for. It may be that they <u>want</u> the new facility (because it may produce income for them as they rent out space on the new tower to other competitors), but they may be able to provide completely adequate coverage from an existing tower (on which they would be paying rent). In this circumstance, the town is not <u>required</u> to allow a new tower, but could insist that the carrier co-locate on the existing tower.

C. **Required Documentation:**

1. Copies of all submittals and showings pertaining to: FCC licensing; Environmental Impact Statements; FAA Notice of Construction or Alteration; Aeronautical Studies; and, all data, assumptions and calculations relating to service coverage and power levels regardless of whether categorical exemption from Routine Environmental Evaluation under the FCC rules is claimed.

   It is very important to obtain all the data you need from the carrier! The following sections spell this out in detail.

2. Copies of all information submitted in compliance with requirements of Massachusetts Department of Public Health, 105 CMR 122 Fixed Facilities Which Generate ELECTROMAGNETIC FIELDS IN THE FREQUENCY RANGE OF 300 KHz TO 100 GHz AND MICROWAVE OVENS, or any revisions thereof as the Department of Public Health may, by written notice, create.

   This is a Massachusetts regulation, but there may be something similar in your state. Check with your State's Health Department to see.

3. The exact legal name, address or principal place of

business and phone number of the Applicant. If any Applicant is not a natural person, it shall also give the state under which it was created or organized.

4. The name, title, address and phone number of the person to whom correspondence or communications in regard to the application are to be sent. Notice, orders and other papers may be served upon the person so named, and such service shall be deemed to be service upon the Applicant.

5. Name, address, phone number, and written consent to apply for this permit, of the owner of the property on which the proposed Tower shall be located, or of the owner(s) of the Tower or structure on which the proposed Facility shall be located.

6. Details of proposed method of financial surety as required in §171-131.

7. Required Plans and engineering plans, prepared, stamped and signed by a Professional Engineer licensed to practice in Massachusetts. (Note: survey plans should also be stamped and signed by a Professional Land Surveyor registered in Massachusetts.) Plans shall be on 24" x 36" sheets, on as many sheets as necessary, and at scales which are no smaller (i.e. no less precise) than listed below, and which show the following information:

   a. Each plan sheet shall have a title block indicating the project title, sheet title, sheet number, date, revision dates, scale(s), and original seal and signature of the P.E. and other professionals who prepared the plan.

D. **For new Tower construction, or Major Modification Of An Existing Tower, a Tower Construction Special Permit is required.**

1. Applicant shall provide a written, irrevocable commitment valid for the duration of the existence of the Tower, to rent or lease Available Space for co-location on the Tower at fair-market prices and terms, without discrimination to other Personal Wireless Service Providers.

You will want this language if you are encouraging co-location. Some bylaws in towns where the visual impact is a high priority use the Overlay District approach [see the end of this bylaw] and require towers to be camouflaged and as low in height as possible. They do not include this language, since co-location generally increases the necessary height of a tower.

2.   If Applicant is not simultaneously applying for a Personal Wireless Service Facilities Special Permit, it shall provide a copy of its existing lease/contract with a Personal Wireless Service Provider. A Tower Construction Special Permit shall not be granted for a Tower to be built on speculation.

It is important not to allow towers to be built in the hopes that a service provider will come. Only allow a tower if the applicant is a service provider. The Telecomm Act preempts local zoning for service providers — not tower builders! Some towns require that the tower owner, service provider, and land owner — all of whom may be different entities — be signatories to, and responsible for an application, otherwise the application is incomplete and can be turned down. All share liability. This is one way to stop towers built on speculation.

3.   The following plans and maps:
   a. **Location Map:** Copy of a portion of the most recent U.S.G.S. Quadrangle map, at a scale of 1:25,000, and showing the area within at least two miles from the proposed tower site. Indicate the Tower location and the exact Latitude and Longitude (degrees, minutes and seconds).
   b. **Vicinity Map** at a scale of 1" = 200' (1:2400) with contour intervals no greater than 10 feet (3 meter) showing the entire vicinity within a 2000' radius of the Tower site, and including the topography, public and private roads and driveways, buildings and

structures, bodies of water, wetlands, landscape features, historic sites, habitats for endangered species. Indicate the property lines of the proposed Tower Site Parcel and of all abutters within 300' of the Tower Site Parcel, (from assessors maps or available surveys). Include the names of all abutters within 300' of the Tower Site Parcel. Indicate any access easement or right of way needed for access from a public way to the Tower, and the names of all abutters or property owners along the access easement or who have deeded rights to the easement.

c. **Existing Conditions Plan:** A recent survey of the Tower Site at a scale no smaller than 1" = 40' (1:480 or metric equivalent 1:500) with topography drawn with a minimum of 2' (0.6 meter) contour intervals, showing existing utilities, property lines, existing buildings or structures, stone walls or fence lines, wooded areas, individual trees with diameters greater than 12" within a 200' radius from the base of the proposed Tower (labelled with their current heights). Show the boundary of any wetlands or floodplains or watercourses, and of any bodies of water included in the Watershed Protection District within 200' from the Tower or any related facilities or access ways or appurtenances. The survey plan must have been completed on the ground, by a Professional Land Surveyor, within two years prior to the application date.

d. **Proposed Site Plans:** Proposed Facility Site layout, grading and utilities at the same scale or larger than the Existing Conditions Plan.

    i.   Proposed Tower location and any appurtenances, including supports and guy wires, if any, and any accessory building (Communication Equipment Shelter or other). Indicate property boundaries and setback distances to the base(s) of the Tower and to the nearest corners of each of the appurtenant structures to those boundaries, and dimensions of all proposed improvements.

ii.   Indicate proposed spot elevations at the base of the proposed Tower and at the base of any guy wires, and the corners of all appurtenant structures.

iii. Proposed utilities, including distance from source of power, sizes of service available and required, locations of any proposed utility or communication lines, and whether underground or above ground.

iv.   Limits of areas where vegetation is to be cleared or altered, and justification for any such clearing or alteration.

v.   Any direct or indirect wetlands alteration proposed.

vi.   Detailed plans for drainage of surface and/or sub-surface water; plans to control erosion and sedimentation both during construction and as a permanent measure.

vii. Plans indicating locations and specifics of proposed screening, landscaping, ground cover, fencing, etc; any exterior lighting or signs.

viii. Plans of proposed access driveway or roadway and parking area at the Tower Site. Include grading, drainage, travelled width. Include a cross section of the access drive indicating the width, depth of gravel, paving or surface materials.

e. **Proposed Tower and Appurtenances**:

i.   Plans, elevations, sections and details at appropriate scales but no smaller than 1" = 10'.

ii.   Two cross sections through proposed Tower drawn at right angles to each other, and showing the ground profile to at least 100 feet beyond the limit of clearing, and showing any guy wires or supports. Dimension the proposed height of tower above average grade at Tower Base. Show all proposed antennas, including their location on the Tower.

iii.   Details of proposed Tower foundation, including cross sections and details. Show all ground attachments, specifications for anchor bolts and other anchoring hardware.

iv.   Detail proposed exterior finish of the Tower.

v.   Indicate relative height of the Tower to the tops of surrounding trees as they presently exist, and the height to which they are expected to grow in ten years.

vi.   Illustration of the modular structure of the proposed Tower indicating the heights of sections which could be removed or added in the future to adapt to changing communications conditions or demands.

vii.   A Structural Professional Engineer's written description of the proposed Tower structure and its capacity to support additional Antennas or other communications facilities at different heights and the ability of the Tower to be shortened if future communications facilities no longer require the original height.

viii.   A description of Available Space on the tower, providing illustrations and examples of the type and number of Personal Wireless Service Facilities which could be mounted on the structure.

f. **Proposed Communications Equipment Shelter:**

i. Floor Plans, elevations and cross sections at a scale of no smaller that 1/4" = 1' (1:48) of any proposed appurtenant structure.

ii.   Representative elevation views, indicating the roof, facades, doors and other exterior appearance and materials.

g. **Sight Lines**:

i. A minimum of eight (8) view lines in a zero (0) to two (2) mile radius from the site, shown beginning at True North and continuing clockwise at forty-five degree intervals.

ii. A plan map of a circle of two (2) miles radius of the Facility Site on which any visibility of the proposed Tower from a public way shall be indicated.

iii. Applicant shall utilize the U.S.G.S. Quadrangle map, at a scale of 1:25,000, and submit profile drawings on a horizontal scale of 1"= 400', with a vertical scale of 1"= 40'. Trees shall be shown at existing heights and at projected heights in ten years.

h. **Balloon Test:**

Within 35 days of submitting an Application, Applicant shall arrange to fly, or raise upon a temporary mast, a three-foot diameter brightly colored balloon at the maximum height and at the location of the proposed Tower. The dates, (including a second date, in case of poor visibility on the initial date), times, and location of this balloon test shall be advertised, by the Applicant, at 7 and 14 days in advance of the first test date in a newspaper with a general circulation in the Town of Great Barrington. The Applicant shall inform the SPGA and the Planning Board, in writing, of the dates and times of the test, at least 14 days in advance. The balloon shall be flown for at least four consecutive hours sometime between 9:00 am and 5:00 pm of the dates chosen.

Balloon Tests are an effective way to visualize the Tower's height and impact. But the test must be run when people are aware of it and when the balloons can be seen!

E. **For new Personal Wireless Service Facility, or Major Modification of An Existing Facility, a Personal Wireless Service Facility Special Permit is required.**

1. The following plans and maps:

a. **Location Map:** Copy of a portion of the most

recent U.S.G.S Quadrangle map, at a scale of 1:25,000, and showing the area within at least two miles from the proposed Facility Site. Indicate the location of the proposed Personal Wireless Service Facility, or of the Facility undergoing Major Modification, and the exact Latitude and Longitude (degrees, minutes and seconds).

b. **Proposed Facility Plan:** A recent survey of the Facility Site at a scale no smaller than 1" = 40' (1:480 or metric equivalent 1:500) showing:

   i. Horizontal and radial distances of Antenna(s) to nearest point on property line.

   ii. Horizontal and radial distances of Antenna(s) to nearest dwelling unit.

   iii: Proposed utilities, including distance from source of power, sizes of service available and required, locations of any proposed utility or communication lines, and whether underground or above ground.

   iv. Any changes to be made to the existing Facility's landscaping, screening, fencing, lighting, drainage, wetlands, grading, driveways or roadways, parking, or other infrastructure as a result of this proposed Modification of the Facility.

c. **Proposed Communications Equipment Shelter:**

   i. Floor Plans, elevations and cross sections at a scale of no smaller that 1/4" = 1' (1:48) of any proposed appurtenant structure.

   ii. Representative elevation views, indicating the roof, facades, doors and other exterior appearance and materials.

d. **Proposed Equipment Plan:**

   i. Plans, elevations, sections and details at appropriate scales but no smaller than 1" = 10'.

   ii. Number of Antennas and Repeaters, as well as the exact locations, of Antenna(s) and of all Repeaters (if any) located on a map as well as by degrees, minutes, and seconds of Latitude and Longitude.

iii. Mounting locations on Tower or structure, including height above ground.

iv. Antenna type(s), manufacturer(s), model number(s).

v. For each Antenna, the Antenna gain and Antenna radiation pattern.

vi. Number of channels per Antenna, projected and maximum.

vii. Power input to the Antenna(s).

viii. Power output, in normal use and at maximum output for each Antenna and all Antennas as an aggregate.

ix. Output frequency of the Transmitter(s).

This information is critical as it gives your independent consultant the information needed to assess the coverage and to generate a Radial Plot to determine whether the information being provided by the carrier is accurate and complete. Do not be tempted to jettison the engineering detail just because it is technical, or because you do not understand the meaning of the terms. It is not necessary for laypeople to understand such detail. If this detail is not required in the application, the industry does not have to provide it. Your engineer will then be working with incomplete information.

VIII § 171 - 127. General Requirements:

A. New Towers shall be set back at least one (1) time the height of the Tower, plus 50', from all boundaries of the Site on which the Tower is located.

B. If the Facility or Tower Site is in a wooded area, a vegetated buffer strip of undisturbed trees shall be retained for at least 50 feet in width around the entire perimeter except where the access drive is located. Applicant shall obtain a financial surety to cover the cost of the remediation of any damage to the landscape which occurs during the clearing of the Site.

C. Fencing and Signs: The area around the Tower and Communication Equipment Shelter(s) shall be completely fenced for security to a height of six feet and gated. Use of razor wire is not permitted. A sign no greater than two (2) square feet indicating the name of the facility owner(s) and a 24-hour emergency telephone number shall be posted adjacent to the entry gate. In addition, No Trespassing or other warning signs may be posted on the fence.

D. Communication Equipment Shelters and Accessory Buildings shall be designed to be architecturally similar and compatible with each other, and shall be no more than 12 feet high. The buildings shall be used only for the housing of equipment related to this particular site. Whenever possible, the buildings shall be joined or clustered so as to appear as one building.

E. New Towers shall not exceed the minimum height necessary to provide Adequate Coverage for the Personal Wireless Service Facilities proposed for use on the Tower. Applicant may submit a request for additional height to accommodate future sharing, and shall provide design information to justify such additional height.

Some towns place a maximum tower height number in this area, based on the RF Engineer's analysis and the vegetation in the area where the tower is proposed. The tower may be allowed to be fifteen or so feet above surrounding growth, for instance. Also, because towers fail in various ways — meaning, they don't just break at the base and fall neatly over — many towns require larger fall zones, sometimes up to four-times the height of the tower, depending on tower-failure modeling.

F. Tower Finish: New Tower(s) shall have a galvanized finish unless otherwise required. The SPGA may require the Tower(s) to be painted or otherwise camouflaged to minimize the adverse visual impact.

G. Tower(s) must be of a type which will maximize potential sharing. Lattice type structures are preferred, but where a Monopole is requested, Applicant must demonstrate the future utility of such structure for expansion of service for Applicant and other future Applicants.

When this regulation was written, Great Barrington is hoping for just <u>one</u> (ugly) tower, but other towns (especially where they have used the overlay district approach) want multiple, smaller and less conspicuous towers. Unfortunately with the advent of the digital PCS systems, which are higher frequency and therefore lower power, many more installations may be required. PCS claims to need antennas every 1-5 miles apart.

H. The use of Repeaters to assure Adequate Coverage, or to fill holes within areas of otherwise Adequate Coverage, while minimizing the number of required Towers is permitted and encouraged. An Applicant who has received a Personal Wireless Service Facility Special Permit under this Article, may, with at least 30 days written notice to the SPGA, the Planning Board, Board of Health, Conservation Commission, Building Inspector and Town Clerk, install one or more additional Repeaters by right. Site Plan Review before the Planning Board shall be required. The Planning Board shall publish written notice of the public meeting date at least 14 days in advance. Applicants shall detail the number, location, power output, and coverage of any proposed Repeaters in their systems and provide engineering data to justify their use.

Repeaters may be a useful tool to allow a carrier to use an existing tower since they can help fill holes in the coverage area. Great Barrington decided to allow them by right — no Special Permit is required, as a "carrot" to encourage their use. Other towns require full permitting. Because repeaters are still RF generating sources, towns vary in how high they allow them to be, and how close they will allow them to dwellings.

I. If primary coverage (greater than 50%) from proposed Personal Wireless Service Facility is outside Great Barrington, then permit may be denied unless the Applicant can show that they are unable to locate within the Town which is primarily receiving service from the proposed Facility.

If your town is being used to provide service to another town, get the carrier to go to the other town! Regional approaches, where there is a regional master plan for wireless telecommunications would be ideal, but they are rare. Most towns keep their fingers crossed that towers "won't happen to them." Few towns cooperate with each other for a regional approach. Until then, your obligation is to your own town.

J. Commercial advertising shall not be allowed on any Antenna, Tower, or Accessory Building or Communication Equipment Shelter.

K. Unless required by the Federal Aviation Administration, no night lighting of Towers, or the Personal Wireless Service Facility, is permitted, except for manually operated emergency lights for use only when operating personnel are on site.

L. No Tower or Personal Wireless Service Facility that would be classified as a hazard to air navigation, as defined by the Federal Aviation regulations (Title 14 CFR) is permitted.

M. No Tower or Personal Wireless Service Facility with the exception of Repeaters shall be located:

    1. a. Closer than 1500', on a horizontal plane, to any structure, existing at the time of Application, which is, or is able to be, occupied or habitable, on the property of any school (both public and private).

       b. Closer than 750', on a horizontal plane, to an existing Dwelling Unit, or, day-care center, hospital, nursing home, church, synagogue or other place of worship.

These setbacks are the teeth of this bylaw — telling where a tower or facility may go in relation to other uses. We checked by doing radial plots and found that there were still areas in town where a carrier could locate and have adequate coverage, before we set out these distances. Otherwise we might have "had the effect of prohibiting" the provision of *services. These distances are justifiable by reference to the opening 'Purposes' (especially I: E, G, H). The greater distance to schools is based primarily on attractive nuisance. But <u>NOTE</u> in N1d (below) that we are also mentioning that we are taking radiation into account <u>in case emissions exceed FCC guidelines</u>.*

2. No Repeater shall be located closer than 50' to an existing Dwelling Unit, nor less than 25' above ground.
3. Within any of the following prohibited areas:
   a. Massachusetts or federally regulated wetland;
   b. A Massachusetts Certified Vernal Pool;
   c. The habitat of any State-listed Rare or Endangered Wildlife or Rare Plant Species;
   d. Within 100' horizontally from any Massachusetts regulated wetland;
   e. Within the 200' horizontally of the Outer Riparian Zone measured horizontally from any river or perennial stream;
   f. Within 500' horizontally from any Historic District or property listed or eligible to be listed on the state or federal Register of Historic Places;
   g. Within 500' horizontally from any known archaeological site.
N. Parameters of appropriate siting:
   1. Towers and Personal Wireless Service Facilities shall be located so as to minimize the following potential impacts:
      a. Visual/Aesthetic: Towers shall, when possible, be sited off ridgelines, and where their visual impact is least detrimental to highly rated scenic areas.[9]
      b. Diminution of residential property values: Siting shall be in as low population density areas as possible.
      c. Safety: In cases of structural failure and attractive nuisance.

---

[9] See Massachusetts Landscape Inventory, MGL §131, Sec. 39A: conducted by Massachusetts Dept. Of Environmental Management, 1982.

      d. Safety from excessive electromagnetic radiation: In case the Tower or Personal Wireless Service Facility is found to exceed the FCC guidelines.

2. The following locations are ranked in order of preference:
   a. Shared use of existing Personal Wireless Service Facilities shall be encouraged.
   b. Clustering of Towers: Applications for Towers adjacent to Existing Towers shall be encouraged.
   c. The use of municipal lands which comply with other requirements of this Article, and where visual impact can be minimized and mitigated, shall be encouraged.
   d. The use of Repeaters to provide Adequate Coverage without requiring new Tower(s) shall be encouraged.
   e. The use of land, distant from higher density residential properties, and where visual impact can be minimized shall be encouraged.

3. Towers and Personal Wireless Service Facilities shall be located so as to provide Adequate Coverage and Adequate Capacity with the least number of Towers and Antennas which is technically and economically feasible.

4. The SPGA shall request input from the Chiefs (or their designees) of Fire, Police and other Emergency services regarding the adequacy for emergency access of the planned drive or roadway to the site.

IX § 171 - 128. Evaluation by Independent Consultants.

    A. Upon submission of a complete Application for a Special Permit under this Article, the SPGA shall provide its Independent Consultant(s) with the full Application for their analysis and review.

    B. Applicants for any Special Permit under this Article shall obtain permission from the Owner(s) of the proposed property(s) or Facilities Site(s) for the Town's Independent Consultant(s), to conduct any necessary site visit(s).

X § 171 - 129. Approval Criteria:

    A. In acting on the Special Permit Application, the SPGA shall proceed in accordance with the procedures and timelines established for Special Permits in Article X of the Bylaw.

B. In addition to the findings required by the Bylaw in Section 171-45, the SPGA shall, in consultation with the Independent Consultant(s), make all of the applicable findings before granting the Special Permit, as follows:

1. That Applicant is not already providing Adequate Coverage and/or Adequate Capacity to the Town of Great Barrington; and

2. That Applicant is not able to use Existing Towers/Facility Sites either with or without the use of Repeaters to provide Adequate Coverage and/or Adequate Capacity to the Town of Great Barrington; and

3. That the Applicant has agreed to rent or lease Available Space on the Tower, under the terms of a fair-market lease, without discrimination to other Personal Wireless Service Providers; and

4. That proposed Personal Wireless Service Facility or Tower will not have an undue adverse impact on historic resources, scenic views, residential property values, natural or man-made resources; and

5. That the Applicant has agreed to implement all reasonable measures to mitigate the potential adverse impacts of the facilities; and

6. That the proposal shall comply with FCC Reg 96-326 regarding emissions of electromagnetic radiation and that the required Monitoring program is in place and shall be paid for by the Applicant; and

These findings create the basis for approval or denial. If the application does not comply with the requirements of the bylaw, and the SPGA can include that determination in a written record, it has a good chance of prevailing in a denial of the Application.

C. Any decision by the SPGA to deny an Application for a Special Permit under this Article shall be in conformance with SEC. 332 [47 U.S.C. 332] (7)(B)(iii) of the Act, in that it shall be in writing and supported by substantial evidence contained in a written record.

XI § 171 - 130. Monitoring and Evaluation of Compliance:

A. **Pre-testing:** After the granting of a Special Permit and before Applicant's Personal Wireless Service Facilities begin transmission, the applicant shall pay for an Independent Consultant, hired by the Town, to Monitor the background levels of EMF radiation, around the proposed Facility Site and/or any Repeater locations to be utilized for Applicant's Personal Wireless Service Facilities. The Independent Consultant shall use the Monitoring Protocol. A report of the Monitoring results shall be prepared by the Independent Consultant and submitted to the Board of Selectmen, the Planning Board, the Board of Health, the Town Engineer, the Building Inspector and the Town Clerk.

B. **Post-testing:** After transmission begins, the owner(s) of any Personal Wireless Service Facility(s) located on any Facility Site shall pay for an Independent Consultant, hired by the Town, to conduct testing and Monitoring of EMF radiation emitted from said Site, and to report results of said Monitoring, as follows:

   1. There shall be routine annual Monitoring of emissions by the Independent Consultant using actual field measurement of radiation, utilizing the Monitoring Protocol. This Monitoring shall measure levels of EMF radiation from the Facility Site's primary Antennas as well as from Repeaters (if any). A report of the Monitoring results shall be prepared by the Independent Consultant and submitted to the Board of Selectmen, the Planning Board, the Board of Health, the Town Engineer, the Building Inspector, and the Town Clerk.

   2. Any Major Modification of Existing Facility, or the activation of any additional permitted channels, shall require new Monitoring.

C. **Excessive Emissions:** Should the Monitoring of a Facility Site reveal that the Site exceeds the FCC 96-326 standard, then the owner(s) of all Facilities utilizing that Site shall be so notified. The owner(s)shall submit to the SPGA and the Building Inspector a plan for the reduction of emissions to a level that complies with the FCC 96-326 standard within 10 business days of notification of noncompliance. That plan shall reduce emissions to the standard within 15 days of initial notification of non-compliance. Failure to accomplish this reduction of emission within 15 business days of initial notification of non-compliance shall be a violation of the Special Permit and subject to penalties and fines as specified in Article XII, §171-65 of the Bylaw. Such fines shall be payable by the owner(s) of the Facilities with Antennas on the Facility Site, until compliance is achieved.

D. **Structural Inspection:** Tower owner(s) shall pay for an Independent Consultant (a licensed professional structural engineer), hired by the Town, to conduct inspections of the Tower's structural integrity and safety. Guyed towers shall be inspected every three years. Monopoles and non-guyed lattice towers shall be inspected every five years. A report of the inspection results shall be prepared by the Independent Consultant and submitted to the Board of Selectmen, the Planning Board, the Board of Health, the Town Engineer, the Building Inspector, and the Town Clerk. Any Major Modification of Existing Facility which includes changes to Tower dimensions or antenna numbers or type shall require new structural inspection.

E. **Unsafe Structure:** Should the inspection of any Tower reveal any structural defect(s) which, in the opinion of the Independent Consultant render(s) that Tower unsafe, the following actions must be taken. Within 10 business days of notification of unsafe structure, the owner(s) of the Tower shall submit a plan to remediate the structural defect(s). This plan shall be initiated within 10 days of the submission of the remediation plan, and completed as soon as reasonably possible. Failure to accomplish this remediation of structural defect(s) within 10 business days of initial notification shall be a violation of the Special Permit and subject to penalties and fines as specified in Article XII, §171-65 of the Bylaw. Such fines shall be payable by the owner(s) of the Tower, until compliance is achieved.

XII § 171 - 131. Removal Requirements:

Any Personal Wireless Service Facility which ceases to operate for a period of one year shall be removed. Cease to operate is defined as not performing the normal functions associated with the Personal Wireless Service Facility and its equipment on a continuous and ongoing basis for a period of one year. At the time of removal, the Facility Site shall be remediated such that all Personal Wireless Service Facility improvements which have ceased to operate are removed. If all Facilities on a Tower have ceased to operate, the Tower shall also be removed, and the Site shall be revegetated. Existing trees shall only be removed if necessary to complete the required removal. Applicant shall, as a condition of the Special Permit, provide a financial surety or other form of financial guarantee, payable to the Town of Great Barrington and acceptable to the SPGA, to cover the cost of removal of the Personal Wireless Service Facility and the remediation of the landscape, should the Facility cease to operate.

XIII § 171 - 132. Fees and Insurance:

A. Towers and Personal Wireless Service Facilities shall be insured by the owner(s) against damage to persons or property. The owner(s) shall provide a Certificate of Insurance to the Selectmen's Office on an annual basis in which the Town of Great Barrington shall be an additional named insured.

B. A schedule of fees for Towers and Personal Wireless Service Facilities permitting and renewal, any Monitoring of emissions and inspection of structures, and any other fees shall be established by the SPGA as provided for in Article X, §171-40.B. of the Zoning Bylaw. This schedule may be amended from time to time.

XIV §171- 133. Severability Clause:

The invalidity of any section or provision of this Article shall not invalidate any other section or provision hereof.

****

That is the end of the Great Barrington by-law.

Overlay Districts

The advantage of an "overlay district" is that the municipality can map out where the facilities can go, and restrict them to those areas. Thus, the town controls the sites where the carriers can place the facilities. The disadvantage is that it may be politically difficult to come up with sites that don't raise concerns of abutters.

Overlay districts are a proactive approach. They work less well when a carrier is already considering a site in your community. Under such reactive circumstances, overlay districts are often seen as a NIMBY effort by the proponents, and are less likely to be politically acceptable. But with careful consideration of possible sites, determined with the help of an RF engineer, towns should be able to place the overlay districts where the adverse impacts are as minimal as possible.

If you want to create an overlay district, it needs to be done before you write the bylaw. If your zoning bylaw already defines certain districts — and most do, then the definition of the telecommunications overlay district goes in that section. It has been adequate in the Berkshires to define the overlay district by reference to the assessor's maps and parcel numbers, which, although not a surveyed definition, is close enough for the purposes your town will need.

It is important to include in the zoning language that the telecommunications overlay district is mapped over other districts. It modifies — and where there is inconsistency, supersedes — the regulations of other districts. Except as so modified or superseded, the regulations of the underlying districts remain in effect. This clarifies that the overlay district does not result in an overall rezoning of the area affected.

Final Thoughts

There are many challenges your town will face as it prepares to use zoning to regulate the location of wireless telecommunications facilities. But with careful and thorough work, your community can exercise a great deal of control.

Be aware that the telecommunications industry continues to try, by a variety of means, to reduce the degree of local control available to communities across the country. So it is critical to remain vigilant with regard to both federal and state regulations and laws. Massachusetts nearly enacted a statewide law last year that would have allowed a new telecommunications facility on existing structures with a simple building permit. This industry-written law was promoted as community friendly! This law went down to defeat, but only after intensive lobbying by the many folks who have been active in local efforts to retain local control.

Tony Blair
Former Member of the Planning Board and the Board of Selectmen
17 Round Hill Rd.
Great Barrington, MA 01230
Email: TonyBlair@worldnet.att.net

Biographical Notes
(In the order of presentations in the book.)

B. Blake Levitt:

B. Blake Levitt is an award-winning journalist who has specialized in medical and science writing for nearly two decades. She has researched the biological effects of non-ionizing radiation since the late 1970s. A former *New York Times* writer, she has written widely on medical issues for both the lay and professional audience. Her work has appeared in numerous national publications.

She is the author of *Electromagnetic Fields, A Consumer's Guide to the Issues and How to Protect Ourselves* (Harcourt Brace, 1995), for which she won an Award of Excellence from the American Medical Writers Association. Ms. Levitt is also the author of *50 Essential Things To Do When The Doctor Says It's Infertility* (Penguin, 1995), and the co-author of *Before You Conceive, The Complete Prepregnancy Guide* (Bantam, 1989), for which she also won an Award of Excellence from the American Medical Writers Association.

Ms. Levitt earned two Bachelor of Arts degrees magna cum laude from Quinnipiac University with subsequent post-graduate work in journalism and essay writing at Yale University. She is a member of the American Medical Writers Association, the National Association of Science Writers, the New York Academy of Sciences, and the Bioelectromagnetics Society, as well as the Author's Guild. She is listed in *Who's Who of American Women, Who's Who in the World, Who's Who in Science and Engineering, and Who's Who of International Writers and Authors.*

Ms. Levitt's work is referenced in numerous government publications and other resources on EMF. She has helped several congressional offices write legislation for energy research appropriations and land-use issues pertaining to tower siting. She lectures widely on the subject of environmental energy and consults for municipalities considering telecommunications regulations.

Carl F. Blackman, Ph.D. (Keynote)

Dr. Carl F. Blackman is a biologist in the Biochemistry and Pathobiology Branch of the Environmental Carcinogenesis Division of the National Health and Environmental Effects Research Laboratory at the U.S. Environmental Protection Agency (EPA), Research Triangle Park, NC. He received his master's degree and Ph.D. in biophysics from Pennsylvania State University, and postdoctoral training at Brookhaven National Labortory. In 1970, Dr. Blackman joined the Public Health Service's Bureau of Radiological Health. His position was transferred to the EPA at that agency's inception. He has been with the EPA since that time.

For many years, Dr. Blackman studied the complexities of electric and magnetic field interactions with biological systems. His work resulted in several discoveries, including the demonstration that the earth's magnetic field is involved with some biological responses and that it may be a scientific variable in research models. His research is often referred to as "the window effects" work — based on his observation that living systems are sensitive to some frequencies and intensities, but not to others. Dr. Blackman's more recent work has focused on possible mechanisms underlying cancer promotion processes. He and colleagues discovered that the hormone, melatonin, which has oncostatic properties, can mediate communication between the cells and partially block the action of tumor promoting agents.

Dr. Blackman has received numerous awards and is a member of 11 scientific societies. He has sat on committees for the Office of Naval Research, the National Council on Radiation Protection and Measurements, the American National Standards Committee on Non-Ionizing Radiation, the National Institutes of Health, and the Oak Ridge National Laboratory, among many others. He has been an invited speaker at the National Academy of Sciences and at numerous workshops sponsored by the Department of Energy. He has been on numerous international committees including the World Health Organization subcommittee and the International Agency for Research on Cancer on non-ionizing radiation. He is one of the founders of the Bioelectromagnetics Society. Dr. Blackman has published 77 professional papers; given 47 invited presentations; and 121 meeting reports.

Henry C. Lai, Ph.D.

Dr. Henry C. Lai is a research professor at the Department of Bioengineering at the University of Washington, Seattle. He holds a Bachelor of Science degree with honors in physiology from McGill University, and a Ph.D. in psychology from the University of Washington, Seattle. He received postdoctoral training in the Department of Pharmacology at the University of Washington where he subsequently became a faculty member for several years. He has been a research professor in the Department of Bioengineering since 1997.

Dr. Lai's recent work includes the discovery that radiofrequency radiation (RFR), similar to that emitted by cell phones, causes double and single strand DNA breakage. He also discovered spatial-learning deficits in test animals exposed to the radiation, and that certain RFR increases free radical activity in cells.

Dr. Lai has conducted research for the National Institute of Environmental Health Sciences at the National Institutes of Health, the Office of Naval Research, the National Institute of Aging, the Fetzer Institute, Wireless Technology Research, the Breast Cancer Fund, and many others.

Dr. Lai has consulted for numerous governmental agencies, and testified at government hearings in the U.S. and Great Britain. He is a former member of the USA-USSR Exchange Program on the Study of Biological Effects of Physical Factors in the Environment, and the Special Emphasis Panel of the Radiation Study Section at the National Institutes of Health. Dr. Lai is also a member of the United States National Committee for the International Union of Radio Science.

Among many other service appointments, Dr. Lai also reviews grants for the U.S. Air Force Office of Scientific Research. He is a past member of the Board of Directors of the Bioelectromagnetics Society. He has published more than 100 papers in peer-reviewed and professional journals, and given numerous invited presentations worldwide.

Albert M. Manville, II, Ph.D.

Dr. Albert M. Manville is a Wildlife Biologist with the Division of Migratory Bird Management, U.S. Fish and Wildlife Service, Arlington, VA. Dr. Manville received a Bachelor of Science degree in zoology and ecology from Allegheny College with a research focus on black bears. He received a master's degree in natural resources and wildlife management at the University of Wisconsin, studying the parasites and diseases of black bears. He earned a Ph.D. at Michigan State University in wildlife ecology and management, studying black bears in the wild using radio tracking devices to assess their movements, dispersion, den site selection, and survival, as well as the impact of humans on bear populations. Dr. Manville was also a Mandarin Chinese interpreter for the National Security Agency while in the U.S. Navy.

Among many varied career positions, Dr. Manville has served as Director of Science Policy for Defenders of Wildlife, and was a member of the U.S. Scientific Delegation on High Seas Driftnetting, which led to significant victories at the United Nations in stopping large-scale driftnet fishing. He helped write and pass seven environmental laws dealing with marine plastic debris, oil spills, and military plastic dumping. He chaired a coalition of more than 50 environmental groups that helped win $16.2 million in federal research appropriations to investigate marine entanglement issues. He founded the Nongame Coalition, and co-founded the Ad Hoc Advisory Committee on Plastics/Keystone Dialogue on Plastics, which helped convince the Navy to stop all dumping of plastics worldwide.

Dr. Manville was also the Executive Director of the Adirondack Mountain Club in Upstate New York. He has served on the Steering Committee of the Endangered Species Coalition in Washington, D.C. In 1977, he became branch chief with the Office of Migratory Bird Management with the U.S. Fish & Wildlife Service where he now works as a wildlife biologist in charge of bird strikes, policy, and international migratory bird issues for his division. In 1999, Dr. Manville received the Conservation Service Award from the Secretary of the Interior for bird conservation efforts with the electric utility industry.

Dr. Manville currently chairs the Communications Tower Working Group which works with the communications industry, academicians, federal and state agencies, conservationists, and others. He also co-chairs the Inter-Agency Seabird Working Group with members of the National Marine Fisheries Service and the Department of State.

Dr. Manville has testified over 35 times in Congress and at other governmental bodies, and conducted numerous research efforts globally. He has published over 90 professional and popular papers, and given 90 invited presentations. He has served on the Editorial Advisory Board of the Nature Conservancy Magazine. He also served as the wildlife consultant in the Walt Disney production of the movie *White Fang*.

Dr. Manville held faculty positions at Michigan State University, George Mason University, and the USDA Graduate School Evening Programs. He is currently an adjunct professor at Johns Hopkins University.

Andrew A. Marino, Ph.D., J.D.

Dr. Andrew A. Marino holds professorships in the Department of Orthopaedic Surgery at Louisiana State University Medical Center; the Department of Cellular Biology and Anatomy at Louisiana State University; and the Department of Bioengineering at Louisiana Tech University. He received a Bachelor of Science degree in physics from St. Joseph's University and a master's degree and Ph.D. in biophysics from Syracuse University. He also earned a Doctor of Jurisprudence at Syracuse University. He is admitted to the bar in the states of New York and Louisiana.

Dr. Marino was one of the early proponents of understanding EMFs as a potential public health issue and for using caution when siting high-tension lines near residences. He worked with a pioneering research team in the 1970s that demonstrated low-level electrical current can stimulate new growth in intractable bone breaks.

He is the author of *Electromagnetism and Life*, with Robert O. Becker (Albany: State University of New York Press, 1982); *Electric Wilderness*, with Joel Ray (San Francisco Press, 1986); and the editor of the seminal work *Foundations of Modern Bioelectricity* (Marcel Decker, 1988).

Dr. Marino is the former chairman of the Louisiana State University Institutional Review Board for Human Research; the Committee on Promotions Guidelines; and the Medical Communications Committee. He is the former president of the Faculty of the Medical School, and the International Society for Bioelectricity. He is the former editor of the *Journal of Bioelectricity*, and an associate editor of the *Journal of Electro- and Magnetobiology*, as well as an editorial consultant in biophysics and medical physics for the *Encyclopedia of Applied Physics*. He is on the advisory and editorial boards at the Center for Frontier Sciences at Temple University.

Dr. Marino is a member of the American Association for the Advancement of Science, the International Society for Bioelectricity, the New York Academy of Sciences, the Bioelectromagnetics Society, the American Statistical Society, the Bioelectrochemistry Society, and the Society for Epidemiological Research.

Dr. Marino is the author of 123 papers in professional journals, as well as 50 abstracts and editorials.

Bill P. Curry, Ph.D.

Dr. Bill P. Curry is the founder and consulting physicist of EMSciTek — an electromagnetics/technology consulting firm. He has 40 years of experience in applied physics. Dr. Curry received a Bachelor of Science degree in physics from Vanderbilt University, a master's degree in physics from the University of Tennessee Sace Institute, and a Ph.D. in electrical engineering from Kennedy-Western University.

Dr. Curry's professional focus has been on visible light scattering from particles, among other things. He is a former staff member at Lawrence Livermore Laboratory where he worked on the Nuclear Readiness Program. He was also a staff member in the Engineering Physics Division at Argonne National Laboratory where he worked on charged particle beam aberrations and large ion source stimulation. He also modeled laser induced ablation of unusual composite materials there. Dr. Curry was also a Senior Physicist at Sverdrup/Aro, Inc. where he worked on simulation models for nuclear X-ray EMP satellite electronics tests. He has been a consultant for MTI Analytical Instruments, Rayex Corp., Dunlee, Inc., and the Pittway Corporation. As a staff member at the Physics International Corp., he co-authored a U.S. Army report on nuclear weapons. He has also reviewed research proposals for the National Institutes of Health and has developed expertise in the non-ionizing bands of the electromagnetic spectrum. EMSiTek also consults for municipalities concerned with radiofrequency issues.

Dr. Curry has published more than 80 papers, including 9 in peer-reviewed journals. He is listed in *American Men and Women of Science, Who's Who in Science and Engineering*, and *Who's Who in the Midwest*.

Robert F. Cleveland, Jr. Ph.D.

Dr. Robert F. Cleveland is a senior scientist in the Office of Engineering and Technology at the Federal Communications Commission (FCC) in Washington, D.C. Dr. Cleveland earned a Bachelor of Science degree in physics from Virginia Polytechnic Institute, and a master's degree and Ph.D. in biophysics at Pennsylvania State University.

Dr. Cleveland's background includes research and teaching in the fields of radiation biology, biophysics, biochemistry, physics and engineering. After graduating from Penn State, Dr. Cleveland worked as a research associate at Temple University Medical School before accepting a position with a Washington, D.C. consulting firm dealing with issues of environmental safety and health. He has worked at the Federal Communications Commission (FCC) since 1980.

At the FCC, Dr. Cleveland is responsible for coordinating agency policy and activities related to environmental safety and health, particularly those aspects pertaining to potential health risks associated with human exposure to radiofrequency emissions. He has conducted numerous exposure assessment studies, and is the author or co-author of many scientific publications, papers, and government reports. He was instrumental in the recent updating of FCC Bulletin 56, *Questions and Answers about Biological Effects and Potential Hazards of Radiofrequency Electromagnetic Fields*.

Joel M. Rinebold

Joel M. Rinebold is the Executive Director of the State of Connecticut Siting Council where he has directed activities for the site regulation of energy, telecommunications and waste management facilities since 1985. Prior to serving with the Siting Council, Mr. Rinebold was a land-use consultant and worked as the District Manager for the U.S. Department of Agriculture, Litchfield County Conservation District.

Mr. Rinebold has a bachelor's degree in urban planning and geology from Central Connecticut State University, and a master's degree in community planning and area development from the University of Rhode Island.

Mr. Rinebold is also an adjunct faculty member at Central Connecticut State University, teaching senior and graduate level environmental planning classes. He is considered an expert in energy and telecommunications issues and has lectured throughout the United States.

James R. Hobson, Esq.

James Hobson has 28 years of experience in cable television and communications as an FCC official, corporation lawyer and private legal practitioner. He is currently in private practice and maintains offices at Miller and Van Eaton in Washington, D.C., where he specializes in telecommunications law.

Mr. Hobson earned a Bachelor of Arts degree in English from Cornell University; a master's degree in government/international relations from Georgetown University; and a law degree from the University of San Francisco. He is admitted to the bar in California and in the District of Columbia.

Mr. Hobson served as Special Assistant to the Chairman at the FCC, as well as Chief of the Cable Television Bureau there. In private practice, he was the Washington Counsel for GTE for 12 years, working on the early stages of wireless (cellular) telephony and telephone company provision of video services. He is a skilled mediator and arbitrator and has worked on statutory panels that effected changes in the fee structures paid for the satellite carrier delivery of superstation and network TV signals to backyard dish receivers. He has served on the American Arbitration Association's National Panel.

Among Mr. Hobson's many cases, he argued for the Ad Hoc Association of Parties Concerned About the Federal Communications Commission's Radio Frequency Health and Safety Rules, in the case known as *Cellular Phone Taskforce v. FCC*, at the Second Circuit U.S. Court of Appeals.

Mr. Hobson is the co-author of *Preemption of Local Regulation of Radio Antennas* (46 Federal Communications Law Journal, No.3, 1994), and the co-editor of *The Communications Act: A Legislative History of the Major Amendments, 1934-1996*, (Pike & Fischer, 1999.)

Jeffrey Anzevino

Jeffrey Anzevino is a regional planner with Scenic Hudson, Inc. — a 37-year old nonprofit organization protecting the Hudson Valley. He has been a member of Scenic Hudson's Riverfront Communities Program since 1991, providing technical assistance to communities on planning, land-use, and transportation issues.

Mr. Anzevino graduated cum laude from the University of Maryland, Baltimore County, with a Bachelor of Arts degree in geography. He was a planner for the City of Cape Coral, Florida, where he wrote the city's historic preservation ordinance; served on the Lee County Historic Preservation Board; and chaired the Metropolitan Planning Organization's Technical Advisory Committee.

Mr. Anzevino returned to his native Hudson Valley in 1991 to advance the goals of Scenic Hudson. In 1998, the Riverfront Communities Program created a cell towers initiative to minimize the number and visibility of telecommunications facilities, helping local officials and citizens better understand the issues. Mr. Anzevino helped organize three conferences on the subject. Through Mr. Anzevino's work at Scenic Hudson, industry-friendly bills were defeated in the New York State Legislature.

Mr. Anzevino has represented Scenic Hudson at the New York Planning Federation Annual Conference, and at the New York State Association of Town's 75th Anniversary Fall Conference. He serves as Scenic Hudson's representative on the Board of Trustees of the Tri-State Transportation Campaign.

Scenic Hudson publications, *Protecting Our Region's Sense of Place in the Age of Wireless Telecommunications* and *Understanding Traffic: A Primer,* were written by Mr. Anzevino.

Mr. Anzevino founded the Hudson Valley Bluegrass Association, a nonprofit arts and educational organization promoting the appreciation of bluegrass music. He served as president of the board from 1994-1999. He recently founded the Hudson Valley Sunfish Fleet and established the annual Great Scenic Hudson River Sunfish Race, which benefits Big Brothers/Big Sisters of Orange County, N.Y.

Raymond S. Kasevich

Raymond S. Kasevich is the founder, Chairman of the Board, and Chief Scientist of KAI Technologies, Inc. — a company using electromagnetic energy in various medical applications, including the treatment of cancerous tumors and cardiovascular disease with microwaves. He is the president and chief scientist of CS Medical Technologies, and vice-president and CEO of Kase Energy. He received a Bachelor of Science degree in electrical engineering at the University of Hartford, a master's degree in electrical engineering from Yale Unversity, and worked toward a Ph.D. at the University of Michigan and the Massachusetts Institute of Technology.

Mr. Kasevich has thirty years of corporate research and development experience in electromagnetic science and engineering applications, covering a wide range of uses — from radiofrequency oil recovery and environmental remediation systems, to medical cathether systems for microwave hyperthermia. Before founding KAI, Mr. Kasevich worked at Raytheon for 14 years as the principal scientist in the Advanced Development Laboratory, and was the technical director of programs that covered a broad range of electromagnetic applications. Prior to that, he was employed with Westinghouse as senior engineer overseeing the development of microwave components used in radar systems.

Mr. Kasevich has been on the adjunct faculty in electrical engineering at the University of Massachusetts at Lowell, Northeastern University, and the University of Hartford. He is a member of the Institute of Electrical and Electronics Engineers, the Society of Petroleum Engineers, and the USNC URSI Commission F of the National Research Council Academy of Sciences and Engineering. He is the recipient of a Ford Foundation Grant; a Regents Award for Academic Excellence; and a twice-recipient of a NATO Research Grant in Optical Oceanography from Max Planck Institute for Meteorology and the University of Hamburg, among other awards.

He holds 30 patents, and has published 39 papers.

Mark F. Hutchins

Mark Hutchins is a radiofrequency engineer, consultant, and a former broadcast station owner and communications site landlord. He holds a lifetime first-class (General) FCC license, and is a Senior Member of the Society of Broadcast Engineers. He has been SBE-certified as a Senior Broadcast Engineer for 24 years. He is a member of the Institute of Electrical and Electronic Engineers (IEEE) Antennas and Propagation Society; the IEEE Communications Society; the IEEE Microwave Theory and Techniques Society; and the IEEE Standards Association. He is also a member of the Vermont Planners Association. Mr. Hutchins is the Vermont FCC/SBE Frequency Coordinator for broadcast frequencies below 2 Gigahertz.

Mr. Hutchins consults for municipalities across the country. He is experienced with facility co-location engineering; radiofrequency (RF) propagation modeling; RF analysis and design; and terrain analysis — as well as spectrum compliance; coverage testing; and system design and integration.

Mr. Hutchins' corporate clients have included Cellular One, Cox Broadcasting, Hearst-Argyle Television, Hubbard Communications and U.S. Cellular. He has also done work for Vermont Public Radio, the Atlanta Board of Education, and many other FCC licensees.

Mr. Hutchins chaired the engineering panel at the University of Vermont Environmental Law Center forum on telecommunications facilities in 1996. He assisted in a multi-emitter RF radiation study of Mount Mansfield, Vermont, — the results were submitted to the FCC in two rule-making proceedings. He has reviewed facility applications for the New Hampshire Office of State Planning, and assisted in numerous application reviews for municipalities nationwide. He helped draft model ordinances for the Vermont League of Cities and Towns in 1998.

Mr. Hutchins is a court-recognized expert witness in several states and has testified before district environmental commissions and the Vermont Environmental Court, among others. He was invited by U.S. Senators Patrick Leahy and James Jeffords to participate in a staffers briefing on telecommunications issues in 1999.

Tony Blair

Tony Blair is a former Selectman (and former member of the Planning Board) from Great Barrington, Massachusetts, and is a student at Boston College Law School where he expects to graduate in 2002. He will clerk for one of the Justices on the Massachusetts Supreme Judicial Court after graduation.

Mr. Blair has a bachelor's degree in behavioral science from Lesley College, and a master's degree in social work from Boston College.

Mr. Blair has been involved with a number of land-use issues with a particular interest in telecommunications siting. He was one of several citizens who drafted the Great Barrington Wireless Facilities bylaw, which has been adopted by municipalities across the country. He is a founding member and co-chair of Folks for Appropriate Cell Tower Sites (FACTS) and has assisted many other towns in drafting telecommunications regulations. He is also active in monitoring and lobbying both national and state legislators in support of local control of the siting of wireless telecommunications facilities.

Appendices

Appendix A

No.

In the
Supreme Court of the United States
————◆❶◆————

CITIZENS FOR THE APPROPRIATE PLACEMENT
OF TELECOMMUNICATIONS FACILITIES *et al.*,

Petitioners,

vs.

FEDERAL COMMUNICATIONS COMMISSION
and THE UNITED STATES OF AMERICA,

Respondents.

PETITION FOR WRIT OF CERTIORARI TO
THE UNITED STATES COURT OF APPEALS
FOR THE SECOND CIRCUIT

PETITION FOR WRIT OF CERTIORARI

WHITNEY NORTH SEYMOUR, JR.*
PETER JAMES CLINES
LANDY & SEYMOUR
Attorneys for Petitioners
363 Seventh Avenue, Room 1300
New York, New York 10001
(212) 629-0590

* *Counsel of Record*

QUESTIONS PRESENTED

1. Whether Congress, by requiring local zoning boards to approve the construction of cellular phone towers[1] without regard to the health impact of high frequency radiation, has commandeered legislative processes of the states to administer a federal program, in violation of the Tenth Amendment as interpreted by this Court in *New York v. United States*, 505 U.S. 144 (1992) and *Printz v. United States*, 521 U.S. 898 (1997).

2. Where Congress has failed to fund continuing Federal research into potential adverse health effects of radiation emission from cellular phone towers, does Congress have the power to prohibit State and local governments from protecting the health of their citizens by taking into account available research and official standards from other countries in regulating the placement of cellular phone towers?

---

[1] For convenience, the phrase "cellular phone towers" is used as shorthand in this petition to cover all personal wireless services facilities (PWSF).

iv

TABLE OF CONTENTS

vi

TABLE OF AUTHORITIES

Page(s)

Cases:

vii

viii

Other Authorities:

ix

OPINIONS BELOW

The original opinion of the Court of Appeals is reported as *Cellular Phone Taskforce v. FCC*, 205 F.3d 82 (2d Cir. 2000) and reproduced herein in the Appendix ("A") at A-1. The opinion of the United States Court of Appeals for the Second Circuit denying the petition for rehearing by the Cellular Phone Taskforce is reproduced at A-23. The opinion of the Second Circuit denying the petition for rehearing by Communications Workers of America is electronically reported at 2000 WL 862305 and reproduced herein at A-26. The Orders of the FCC are reported at 11 F.C.C. Rcd. 15123 (1996) and 12 F.C.C. Rcd. 13494 (1997) and have been lodged with the Clerk of this Court, due to their voluminous nature.

JURISDICTION

On February 18, 2000, the Court of Appeals affirmed the Orders of the FCC, thereby upholding the validity of the statutory and regulatory provisions in question. (A-22) On June 15, 2000, the Court of Appeals denied the timely petition for rehearing by the Communications Workers of America. Pursuant to Supreme Court Rule 13, this petition is filed within 90 days of that decision. The jurisdiction of this Court is invoked under 28 U.S.C. Sec. 1254(1). Jurisdiction in the Court of Appeals was based on 28 U.S.C. § 2342(1).

CONSTITUTIONAL PROVISIONS

The constitutional provisions involved in this case are as follows:

Article I, Clause 8 of the United States Constitution, which provides that "Congress shall have power to regulate commerce . . . among the several states. . . ."

Additional constitutional and statutory authorities are reproduced in the Appendix at A-28 through A-39.

2

STATEMENT OF THE CASE

This case challenges the Constitutionality of the Telecommunications Act of 1996 and FCC implementing regulations. Petitioners seek review of a Second Circuit decision upholding the constitutionality of the Act, to determine whether it conflicts with a line of Tenth Amendment/Commerce Clause decisions rendered by this Court in *New York v. United States*, 505 U.S. 144 (1992), *Printz v. United States*, 521 U.S. 898 (1997), *Alden v. Maine*, 527 U.S. 706 (1999) and *United States v. Morrison*, 529 U.S. __, 120 S. Ct. 1740 (2000). Review is also sought to resolve the direct conflict between the Second Circuit decision and a recent concurring opinion by Fourth Circuit Judge Niemeyer in *Petersburg Cellular Partnership v. Board of Supervisors*, 205 F.3d 688 (4th Cir. 2000).

In *New York*, this Court determined that under the Tenth Amendment, Congress could not compel states to pass legislation addressing a critical problem of public policy, *i.e.*, the shortage of disposal sites for hazardous radioactive waste. (505 U.S. at 175-177) This holding was expressly reconfirmed in *Printz*. 521 U.S. at 933. This case is the mirror-image of *New York*, inasmuch as it presents the issue of whether Congress may compel state or local governments to pass zoning legislation which *fails* to adequately address a crucial policy issue: *i.e.*, the health risks associated with radio frequency radiation from cellular phone tower sites. Petitioners contend that such an Act of Congress violates the holdings of both *Printz* and *New York*, as well as that of the very recent decision in *Alden*, which prohibits the Federal Government from infringing upon the "residuary and inviolable sovereignty" retained by the states (527 U.S. at 715, *quoting The Federalist No. 39*, at 245), and *Morrison*, which reconfirms that states possess a plenary police power which cannot be overridden by Congress. (120 S.Ct. at 1754) In *Petersburg, supra*, Circuit Judge Niemeyer concluded in his concurring opinion that provisions of the Act imposing

3

conditions on state and local regulation of the siting of cellular phone facilities were inconsistent with the principles of Federalism enunciated by this Court in these decisions.

Proceedings Below

Petitioners are "Citizens for the Appropriate Placement of Telecommunications Facilities" of Charlotte, Vermont, together with numerous other community citizens organizations and individual citizens from other parts of the country. Petitioners participated in administrative and judicial challenges to FCC regulations concerning the environmental and health effects of radio frequency emissions from cellular telephone facilities. The challengers appealed to the Second Circuit Court of Appeals from two final opinions and orders of the FCC. These orders set standards for human exposure to radio frequency radiation emitted from transmitters and facilities regulated by the FCC, including "personal wireless service facilities," commonly known as cellular phone towers. They also, *inter alia*, announced rules implementing section 704 (c)(7)(B)(iv) of the Telecommunications Act of 1996, which precluded state or local governments from regulating the siting of wireless service facilities on the basis of environmental effects, including health effects, provided the facilities comply with the aforementioned FCC emissions standards. *See Guidelines for Evaluating the Scientific Effects of Radiofrequency Radiation*, 11 F.C.C. Rcd. 15123 (1996) ("First Report and Order"); *Procedures for Reviewing Requests for Relief from State and Local Regulations Pursuant to Section 332(c)(7)(B)(v) of the Communications Act of 1934*, 12 F.C.C. Rcd. 13494 (1997) ("Second Memorandum Opinion and Order").[2] Petitioners challenged the substantive guidelines on a number of statutory grounds and asserted that the regulatory prohibition, as well as the statutory provision on which it is

---

[2] Due to their voluminous nature, copies of these agency opinions have been lodged with the Clerk's office.

4

based (*codified* at 47 U.S.C. Sec. 332(c)(7)(B)(iv)), is unconstitutional facially and as applied.

The Second Circuit rejected all of petitioners' claims and
upheld both of the FCC Orders. With respect to the Constitutional claims, the panel found that the prohibition on state
regulation of the siting of wireless facilities was within the
scope of Congress' legislative power under the Commerce
clause and that the "statute does not commandeer local authorities to administer a federal program in violation of the
federalism principles embodied in the Tenth Amendment and
set forth" in *New York* and *Printz*. (205 F.3d at 96.) (A-21)
By decisions dated June 6, 2000 and June 15, 2000, respectively, the Second Circuit denied rehearing of its decision.
(A-23) (A-26)

The Telecommunications Act of 1996:
The Clash Between Federal Policy and State Regulation

A primary purpose of the Telecommunications Act of 1996
was to "encourage the rapid deployment of new telecommunications technologies" such as wireless or cellular telephone
service. (Pub. L. No. 104-104.) The Act instituted a major
overhaul of wireless telecommunications regulation, in order
to encourage the construction of a broad national network of
communications towers for use by providers of cellular telephone and other wireless services. *See Petersburg*, 205 F.3d
at 697. As Congress recognized, there were obvious tensions
between the federal policy to encourage proliferation of cellular telephone facilities and state and local governments' desire
to maintain control over local land use regulation. A clash between the two was inevitable. Indeed, as the legislative history
reflects, a primary purpose of the Act was to override local
zoning regulators, who were believed to standing in the way
of industry plans for expansion. (*See id. quoting* H.R. Rep.
No. 104-204 at 94 (1995) noting the legislators' view that "a
conflicting patchwork" of state and local zoning requirements

5

was "inhibiting deployment" of wireless services.) Local concerns over the environmental effects of radio frequency emissions were a particular bone of contention, and local zoning
decisions based on such concerns were singled out for preemption, allegedly because they were "at times not supported
by scientific and medical evidence." (*See id quoting* H.R.
Rep. No. 104-204 at 95.)

State and Local Input In Siting Decisions:
The Compromise Enacted Into Law

Despite Congress's wish to prevent local governments from
frustrating the federal policy of expansion, it also recognized
that "there are legitimate State and local concerns involved in
regulating the siting" of cellular telephone towers (*see* H.R.
No 104-204 at 94-95), and that these authorities could not
be completely excluded from the siting process. Congress
therefore considered ways to provide for limited state and
local input, while denying localities authority to base siting
decisions on their independent assessment of health effects
of radio frequency radiation in their communities. Under the
House version of the Act, the FCC was given "authority . . .
to regulate directly the siting of towers" (*Petersburg* at 205
F.3d at 698), while input from State and local governments
was to come through their participation in a "negotiated
rulemaking committee," along with industry representatives
and public safety agencies. H.R. Conf. Rep. No. 104-458 at
207 (1996). The committee's purpose was to recommend a
national siting policy for the FCC to implement which ensured that "the siting of facilities cannot be denied on the basis
of Radio Frequency (RF) emission levels which are in compliance with Commission (RF) emission levels." (H.R. 104-
204 at 94.)

6

In contrast to the House bill, the Senate version of the Act permitted local governing bodies to continue to regulate the siting of cellular towers. *See Petersburg*, 205 F.3d at 698.

To resolve the conflict between the House and Senate versions of the bill, the Conference Committee created a new section 704 which was eventually enacted into law. This section preserved state and local authority over zoning and land use, *provided* that these governing bodies regulate in accordance with federally imposed standards enumerated in that section. (*See infra.*) The statute thereby delegates *responsibility* for siting decisions to local government, while retaining significant federal control over the *outcome* of such local regulation. In considering the constitutionality of such a siting arrangement, it is important to bear in mind the observation of this Court in *New York*, in connection with the choice of radioactive waste sites:

> If a federal official is faced with the alternative of choosing a location, or directing the states to do it, the official may well prefer the latter as a means of shifting responsibility for the ultimate decision.

(505 U.S. at 183)

Section 704

Specifically, Section 704 imposes substantive, procedural and evidentiary standards on state and local siting regulation, which in practical terms can effectively dictate the outcome of local zoning board deliberations. The procedural/evidentiary standards include requirements that zoning decisions regarding the placement, construction or modification of towers be issued "in writing," "in a reasonable period of time" and be "supported by substantial evidence contained in a written record." (47 U.S.C. Sec. 332 (c)(7)(B)(ii) and (iii).)

7

Substantively, the section prohibits state and local regulators from "unreasonably discriminating among providers"; mandates that local regulations "not prohibit or have the effect of prohibiting the provision of personal wireless services" (47 U.S.C. Sec. 332(c)(7)(B)(i)) and, most significantly for this petition, provides that:

> No state or local government or instrumentality thereof may regulate the placement, construction or modification of personal wireless service facilities on the basis of the environmental effects of radio frequency emissions to the extent that such facilities comply with the Commission's regulations concerning such facilities.

47 U.S.C. Sec. 332 (c)(7)(B)(iv).

The section also provides an enforcement mechanism, which makes the decisions of local authorities reviewable in state or federal Court "on an expedited basis." (47 U.S.C. Sec. 332(c)(7)(B)(v).)

The FCC Standards

The FCC adopted radio frequency emission standards in 1996 based on "thermal effects" from radiation (that is, the heating of human tissue — as in microwave ovens). The standards do not require any minimum distance between transmitters and human habitations. Although these standards are revised every ten years, to date no emission standards have been established by the FCC based on non-thermal "biological effects" from emissions at below-heating levels (that is, alterations of human cells, various cancers and other diseases).[3]

---

[3] As applied, the FCC standards do not take into account numerous research reports finding non-thermal effects. *See* B. Blake Levitt, *Electromagnetic Fields: A Consumer's Guide to the Issues and How to Protect Ourselves.* (Harcourt Brace, 1995).

8

Recent research in Europe, Australia and elsewhere has shown that cell phone frequencies may cause biological harm. In England, the U.K. Independent Expert Group on Mobile Phones, commissioned by the British government, issued a report in May, 2000, recommending that children under age 16 be discouraged from using cell phones. The report further recommends avoiding the siting of cell phone antenna installations near residences, schools, and hospitals. (One can examine the report at: http://www.iegmp.org.uk) The British minister of education has already sent notices to all British schools about the potential health risks for children from mobile phones.

Practical Consequences of Supreme Court
Reversal of Opinion Below

In the event the Court should decide to set aside the pre-emption provisions of the Telecommunications Act of 1996 and the obsolescent FCC RF emissions regulations, the result will not be an anarchy of obstinate small town resistance to communications progress in the nation. Every local community has its share of residents and institutions who *want* access to reliable wireless communications technology, including:

Fire departments
Local and state police
Emergency ambulance services
Small businesses
Parents of teenagers
Repair services, etc.

These citizens, taxpayers, and public servants already do, and will continue to, urge elected zoning boards to approve construction of telecommunications towers.

The major change will be that local tower siting decisions will be made by *local* elected officials familiar with local

9

conditions who will be sensitive to the placement of towers close to schools, playgrounds, recreation areas, nursing homes, hospitals, residential areas and the like, and will exercise judgment based on these local conditions in light of current research into potential health effects of RF emissions. Concerned local citizens and public health officers are now able to keep elected local government officials informed about research developments *around the world* thanks to universal access to the Internet.[4]

The objective of this case is not to hobble technological progress, but to empower local officials to make intelligent decisions based on reliable information and direct knowledge of the communities they serve.

There is a wealth of information available about how other nations are handling human health concerns. The following schedule shows present maximum emission standards set by other countries around the world — *all* of them lower than the 1996 FCC permitted levels. These standards are sugges-

---

[4] Some of the leading websites are:

www.bioelectromagnetics.org
(Research organization of scientists)

www.iegmp.org.uk/IEGMPtxt.htm
(The Stewart report from England)

www.nrpb.org.uk.NIR-is.htm
(National Radiological Protection Board in England)

www.rsc.ca
(Royal Society of Canada)

www.microwavenews.com
(Newsletter edited by former NRDC staffer)

www.land-sbg.gv.at/
celltower/english/salzburg_resoluton_e.pdf
(Salzburg Resolution)

10

tive of what might be applied by individual local communities to tower siting decisions.

	Measurement in Public Exposure Limits: Microwatts Per Centimeter Squared[5]
United States	200.0
Italy	10.0
Poland	10.0
China	6.6
Switzerland	4.2
Russia	2.4
Moscow	2.0
Austria	0.1

The real answer, of course, is for Congress to appropriate funds for a comprehensive and continuing EPA-supervised study of non-thermal biological effects at different emission levels — that is why the outcome of this case is so important.

---

[5] The FCC limits vary depending on frequency. VHS limits are shown in the table. At cellular and personal communication services telephone frequencies, the FCC limits begin at about 500 microwatts and run as high as 1,000. *See FCC OET Bulletin 65*, (ed. 97-01) at pp. 67-68. Data for the other countries comes from: *Microwave News*, January/February 2000 "Switzerland Adopts Strict Limits for Cell Towers and Power Lines." pp. 1-6; *Microwave News*, January/February 2000, "Italian Wireless Radiation Limits Enter Second Year,"p.7; *Microwave News*, July/August 2000, "Efforts to Harmonize RF/MW Exposure Standards in Disarray," pp. 1-8; *Microwave News*, September/October 1999, "U.K. Parliamentary Panel Seeks Stricter RF Limits, More Research," pp. 1-10; *Microwave News*, September/October 1999 "Chinese RF/MW Exposure Standard Is the Strictest," pp. 9-10.

11

Currently there is no U.S. Government-funded research program into the non-thermal biological effects of RF emissions. EPA, which formerly conducted such research, lost all of its research funding in 1996, and has done nothing since. So long as telecommunications companies only have to comply with "thermal effects" standards and can otherwise put up towers pretty much wherever they want, the industry will obviously do all it can to *prevent* more research into biological effects. Right now, the federal government's approach is: let's permit the cell phone companies to put up the towers, and we'll worry about human health problems later.

REASONS FOR GRANTING CERTIORARI

Much as *New York v. United States*, this case "implicate[s] one of our Nation's newest problems of public policy and perhaps our oldest question of constitutional law." 505 U.S. at 149. The public policy problem here concerns the health effects of radio frequency emissions from cellular phone facilities. The constitutional question concerns the proper relationship between "the Federal government and the states" *id.* — or, more precisely, state-created local zoning boards. Specifically, the issue is who will be accountable to the electorate for the Federal radio frequency emissions standards: The Federal government itself, which is responsible for setting the standards, or the local zoning boards, which, as demonstrated below, have had the standards thrust upon them. Petitioners submit that while Congress has substantial power to preempt State legislation under the commerce clause, the Tenth Amendment precludes Congress from treating state and local legislative bodies as puppets on a Federal string.

Both the public policy question and the constitutional question are of overriding national importance necessitating review by this Court. Indeed, the gravity of the policy question underscores the great significance of the constitutional question. Since the mid-1990s, there has been a veritable

12

explosion in the number of telecommunication facilities for wireless phone systems, which customarily consist of a tower, antennas and an equipment box with radios. *See* Foster, Heverty and Pugh, "An Analysis of Facility Siting Issues Under Section 704 of the Telecommunications Act of 1996," 30 *The Urban Lawyer*, 729 (1998).[6]

As a result of such cell tower proliferation, federal standards which govern tower emissions have a critical impact on virtually every community across the country, and the effects of those regulations, for good or ill, reach as far as the radio-emissions themselves that penetrate the very homes of millions of Americans. As noted above, under the Telecommunications Act of 1996, these federal standards are *exclusive* and preempt local health regulation. As the authors of a recent article put it:

> In one fell swoop, Congress removed from control of the local governments one of the biggest issues confronting them in the tower siting arena: local opposition based on fear of cancer or other ill effects from the radio emissions of wireless facilities.

Foster, *et al.*, 30 *Urban Lawyer* at 740, *citing Genessee Tel. Co. v. Szmigel*, 174 Misc.2d 567, 570, n. 3 (Sup. Ct. Monroe Cty, 1997).

It is imperative that such a sweeping exercise of federal power with such far reaching consequences in such a crucial area of public health and safety (1) be made in accordance with constitutional principles, and (2) be subject to the effective scrutiny of the people through the electoral process.

---

[6] As one commentor has noted, "the wireless communication industry in America has consistently grown at a rate that has outpaced the wildest predictions of economists and industry leaders." Note, "Wireless Facilities Are A Towering Problem," 40 *Wm. & Mary L. Rev.*, 975, 979 (1999).

13

Regrettably, neither is the case here, as further demonstrated below. Rather, this is a case where Congress has violated the Tenth Amendment by compelling state-created entities to "enact and enforce a federal regulatory program," (*New York, supra*, 505 U.S. at 151,[7] quoting *Hodel v. Virginia Surface Mining & Reclamation Ass'n., Inc.*, 452 U.S. 264, 288 (1981)), thereby evading Congressional accountability to the public (*New York*, 504 U.S. at 168-69) and "restrict[ing] those political processes which can obviously be expected to bring about the repeal of undesirable legislation. . . ." *United States v. Carolene Products*, 304 U.S. 144, 152-53 n.10 (1938).

Petitioners do not ask the Court to act as an ultimate arbiter of whether the federal standards are desirable or undesirable, but only to grant review to determine whether the *manner* in which they have been imposed upon localities is in conformity with the democratic structures of the constitution established by the Framers. *Cf.* Calabresi, "Textualism and the Counter-majoritarian Difficulty," 66 *Geo.Wash.L.Rev.* 1373, 1391 (1998) (Supreme Court enforcement of jurisdictional lines of federalism and separation of power is "democracy enhancing" and "has the potential to make our system of Madisonian democracy function better.")

This Court has recently granted certiorari in Tenth Amendment cases where, arguably, the significance of the underlying issues pales in comparison to that presented here. For example, in *Printz*, the federal regulation in question consisted of relatively innocuous, temporary requirements that local chief law enforcement officers perform background checks on would-be purchasers of firearms. 521 U.S. at 903-04. Similarly, in *Reno v. Condon*, the Court granted certiorari to review the Tenth Amendment ramifications of the Driver's

---

[7] The holding in *New York* is fully applicable to *local* subdivisions of states, as this Court made clear in *Printz*, which invalidated legislation impressing local chief law enforcement officers into federal service.

14

Privacy Protection Act, 528 U.S. ___, 120 S. Ct. 666, 671 (2000). While *Printz* and *Reno* undoubtedly involved important issues, of still greater importance are those presented in the case at bar.

THE 10ᵗʰ AMENDMENT PRESERVES THE SYSTEM OF DUAL SOVEREIGNTY ESTABLISHED BY THE FRAMERS

A recent line of decisions handed down by this Court has breathed new life into the Tenth Amendment. Chief among these are the decisions in *New York v. United States* and *Printz v. United States*. In *New York* and *Printz*, this Court forcefully reconfirmed the long-standing principle that "Congress may not simply 'commandeer the legislative processes of the States by directly compelling them to enact and enforce a federal regulatory program.'" 505 U.S. at 161 *quoting Hodel, supra*, 452 U.S. at 288. *See also New York, supra*: "the Constitution has never been understood to confer upon Congress the ability to require states to govern according to Congress' instructions." *citing Coyle v. Smith*, 221 U.S. 559, 565 (1911); *Printz*, 521 U.S. at 925: ". . . the Federal Government may not compel the states to implement, by legislation or executive action, federal regulatory programs."[8]

The historical record conclusively establishes that the Framers "designed a system in which the state and federal governments would exercise concurrent authority over the people — who were, in Hamilton's words, 'the only proper objects of government.'" *Printz*, 521 U.S. at 919-20, *quoting The Federalist No. 15; Accord, Alden, supra*, 527 U.S. at 714.

---

[8] Commandeering the legislative power of the states to serve federal ends is antithetical to the "system of dual sovereignty" established by "the Framers, who explicitly chose a Constitution that confers upon Congress the power to regulate individuals, not states." *Printz*, 521 U.S. at 918, 920, *quoting Gregory v. Ashcroft*, 501 U.S. 452, 457 (1991); *New York, supra*, 505 U.S. at 166.

15

Moreover, any act which threatens to "compromise the structural framework of dual sovereignty" is "categorically" unconstitutional and "no comparative assessments of the various interests [involved] can overcome that fundamental defect." *Printz*, 521 U.S. at 932-33.

RESPECTING THE SPIRIT OF DUAL SOVEREIGNTY PRESERVES DEMOCRACY

While the categorical rule may appear doctrinaire and inflexible, it serves vital constitutional purposes, *inter alia*, by preserving the accountability of elected officials to the electorate — the very basis of democratic government. As explained in *New York*:

> . . . where the Federal Government directs the States to regulate, it may be *state officials who will bear the brunt of public disapproval*, while the federal officials who devised the regulatory program may remain insulated from the electoral ramifications of their decision. (505 U.S. at 169) (Emphasis added.)

Accord Petersburg, 205 F.3d at 701. *See also Printz*, observing that where state governments are forced to implement a Federal program, state officials are "put in a position of taking the blame for its burdensomeness and its defects." (521 U.S. at 930, *quoting* Merrit, *Three Faces of Federalism: Finding a Formula for the Future*, 47 Vand. L. Rev. 1563, 1580, n. 65 (1994)).[9]

---

[9]   *See also Alden*, 527 U.S. at 715: "When the Federal Government asserts authority over a State's most fundamental political process, it strikes at the heart of the political accountability so essential to our liberty and republican form of government."

16

ARGUMENT

POINT I

CERTIORARI IS WARRANTED TO RESOLVE THE CONFLICT BETWEEN THE FOURTH CIRCUIT AND THE SECOND CIRCUIT ON THE CONSTITUTIONALITY OF SECTION 704 OF TELECOMMUNICATIONS ACT OF 1996

The Fourth Circuit Decision

In *Petersburg, supra*, a divided panel of the Fourth Circuit reversed the District Court and upheld a decision of the Board Supervisors of Nottaway County, Virginia denying an application to erect a cellular telephone tower. Applying the federalism principles elucidated above, Fourth Circuit Judge Niemeyer wrote a concurring opinion declaring that Section 704 of the Telecommunications Act "'commandeers' the County's legislative process and is therefore unconstitutional under the Tenth Amendment." 205 F.3d at 705 *quoting New York*, 505 U.S. at 175.

Judge Niemeyer recognized that the functions of the local zoning board were legislative in nature. 205 F.3d at 699. The Telecommunications Act therefore effectively imposes federal standards on this legislative process.

As Judge Niemeyer recognized:

through a compromise involving a partial preemption approach, [Congress] enacted § 704(a) of the Telecommunications Act, imposing federal standards on state and local legislative processes, thus leaving state and local legislative boards responsible and accountable for any fall-out in making siting decisions. Through this blend of assigned power, Congress apparently believed it could effect a federal policy promoting the erection of

17

telecommunications towers, while preserving local interests in the process. But this particular blend erases the
constitutional lines dividing power between the federal
and state sovereigns and therefore becomes a categorical violation of the Tenth Amendment.

(205 F.3d at 705-06)[10]

The Second Circuit Decision

Despite the serious federalism issues raised by the Telecommunications Act, the Second Circuit in this case brushed
aside petitioners' constitutional arguments in a single paragraph. *Cellular Phone Task Force, supra,* 205 F.3d at 96.
(A-21) According to the Circuit Court, Congress did not
commandeer local authorities in violation of *Printz* and *New
York,* because "[s]tate and local governments are [purport-
edly] not required to approve or prohibit anything" under the
statute. (*Id.*) (A-21) This conclusion is directly contrary to
the Second Circuit's own jurisprudence, which demonstrates
that local authorities are routinely required to approve tower
construction under the Act.

For example, in *Cellular Telephone Co. v. Town of Oyster
Bay,* 166 F.3d 490 (2d Cir. 1999), the Second Circuit reviewed a decision by a local town board on Long Island to
deny permits to construct two wireless communication "cell
sites." At public hearings on the applications before the board,
the "vast majority" of speakers "expressed concern that the
rfes [radio frequency emissions] emitted by the cell sites might

---

[10] By its express terms, Judge Niemeyer's opinion does not deal with
subsection (iv) of Section 332(c)(7)(B), which is at issue here. Nonetheless, his reasoning is fully applicable to the case at bar. No less than
subsection (iii), subsection (iv) imposes federal standards on local zoning
boards and therefore contravenes the Tenth Amendment under the holding espoused by Judge Niemeyer — a holding which is in direct conflict
with the decision of the Second Circuit in this case.

18

cause cancer." (*Id.* at 492.) Finding that the health concerns expressed by residents could not constitute substantial evidence under the Telecommunications Act and that the remaining evidence was insufficient to support the board's decision, the Second Circuit expressly held "that an injunction ordering the Town to issue the permits was an appropriate remedy." (166 F. 3d at 497.) Thus, despite the town board's obvious misgivings about the health effects of the cell sites, it was *compelled* by the Telecommunications Act to exercise its legislative authority in accordance with the mandate of the Federal government, rather than its own policy preferences, and to approve construction. This is precisely the unconstitutional result which the Second Circuit panel in *this* case said would *not* come about under the Act. Clearly, the Second Circuit was wrong and ignored its own prior case law in this field.

Nor is *Oyster Bay* an aberration. The Court explicitly noted that "the majority of district courts which have heard these cases have held that the appropriate remedy is injunctive relief, in the form of an order to issue the relevant permits." (*Id.* citing *Iowa Wireless Servs., v. City of Moline* 1998 WL 879518 (C.D. Ill.) at *9 (ordering defendant to grant plaintiff a special use permit "with all deliberate speed"); *OmniPoint Corp. v. Zoning Hearing Bd. of Pine Grove, TP*, 20 F. Supp. 2d 875, 881-92 (E.D. Pa. 1998) (ordering zoning board to issue requested special exception permit and declining to remand because to do so would "frustrate the TCA's intent to provide aggrieved parties full relief on an expedited basis"), *aff'd*, 181 F.3d 403 (3rd Cir. 1999); *Illinois RSA No. 3 v. County of Peoria*, 963 F. Supp. 732, 747 (C.D. Ill. 1997) (concluding that injunction directing defendant to issue permit is appropriate relief under TCA); *BellSouth Mobility Inc. v. Gwinnett County Georgia*, 944 F. Supp. 923, 929 (N.D. Ga. 1996) (granting plaintiffs' request for writ of mandamus and ordering defendant to grant plaintiffs' requested permit).

19

These cases also conclusively refute the Second Circuit's
suggestion that Congress was merely exercising its "authority
to offer states the choice of regulating the activity according
to federal standards or having state-law pre-empted by federal regulation." (205 F.3d at 96, *quoting New York*, 505 U.S.
at 167.) (A-21) As *Oyster Bay* and the cases cited therein
demonstrate, *there is no choice at all*. If the local authorities
fail to follow the federal standards on their own, the federal
courts will compel them to do so. *Accord Petersburg*, 205
F.3d at 702.

This conclusion is borne out by the legislative history of
Section 704 cited above, which demonstrates that Congress
did not leave local governments with a choice, but con-
sciously chose to require them to continue to consider cell
tower zoning issues in conformity with *federal* standards.

In addition, Judge Niemeyer recognized that any choice offered to local authorities under the Act is at best a Hobson's
choice:

The choice suggested — that Nottoway County comply
with § 704(a) of the Telecommunications Act or end its
role as a land-use regulator — is no less coercive than
the choice offered the states in *New York*. Indeed, it is
not a choice at all. The Telecommunications Act does
not suggest it, and it cannot be implied except in an
ontological sense: one has a "choice" to avoid obeying
a governmental body by ending his own existence. To
suggest that a local body withdraw from land-use regulation and leave the construction of structures in the
community to the whims of the market is nothing short

20

of suggesting that it end its existence in one of its most vital aspects. *Petersburg*, 205 F.3d at 703. (*Id.*) [11]

The concurrence went on to note that "land use decisions are a core function of local government," and described the chaos that would follow should local authorities "abandon their land use power." (*Id.*) Requiring local zoning boards to forego this fundamental power violates the residuary inviolable sovereignty retained by the states. *Alden*, 527 U.S. at 715.

Petitioners respectfully submit that Judge Niemeyer's interpretation is clearly the more persuasive, and that the Second Circuit's reading of the statute disregards its obvious effect. Plainly, to prohibit local authorities from disapproving cell tower construction based on health concerns has exactly the same effect as expressly requiring them to approve such construction.

Finally, the Second Circuit declared that it had "no doubt" that Congress possessed the legislative authority under the Interstate Commerce Clause "to preempt state and local governments from regulating the operation and construction of a national telecommunications infrastructure. . . ." (205 F.3d at 96.) Evidently, the Court considered this to be the decisive factor establishing the constitutionality of the Act. However, the conclusion that Congress has legislative jurisdiction under the commerce clause to regulate telecommunications simply does not resolve the constitutionality of the act under the Tenth Amendment. As this Court recently observed:

> In *New York* and *Printz*, we held federal statutes to be unconstitutional not because Congress lacked legislative

---

[11] In *New York*, states were given the coercive "choice" of "either accepting ownership of [radioactive] waste, or regulating according to the instructions of Congress." (505 U.S. at 175.)

21

authority over the subject matter, but *because those statutes violated the principles of federalism contained in the Tenth Amendment.*

Reno v. Condon, 120 S. Ct. at 671. (Emphasis added.)

POINT II

THE SECOND CIRCUIT DECISION CONFLICTS WITH RECENT DECISIONS OF THIS COURT PRESERVING THE INVIOLABLE SOVEREIGNTY RETAINED BY THE STATES

The Second Circuit decision conflicts with the Supreme Court's recent decision in *Alden v. Maine*, 527 U.S. at 715, which held that in exercising its enumerated powers, *the Federal Government may not infringe upon the "residuary and inviolable sovereignty" retained by the States* under the Constitution (*quoting The Federalist No. 39* at 245).

As the Court recognized in *Alden*: "the founding document 'specifically recognizes states as sovereign entities.'" (*Id.* quoting *Seminole Tribe of Fla. v. Florida*, 517 U.S. 44, 71 n.15 (1991). Therefore, under the Constitution, "Congress is bound to treat the states in a manner consistent with their status as residuary sovereigns and joint participants in the governance of the Nation.") *Alden*, 527 U.S. at 749.

An attribute of such inviolable sovereignty is the duty to ensure that citizens are not left unprotected in the face of potentially lethal threats to their lives, health and safety. This is not merely the State's right, it is arguably the most fundamental obligation of government and the cornerstone of the social compact as understood by the Framers themselves.

Relevant historical sources (*cf. Alden*, 527 U.S. at 713, 715-16) confirm that the preservation of life was considered *a paramount duty of government* and one of the key reasons

22

it exists. No less a personage than John Locke, the esteemed political writer whose thought so influenced the Framers, declared that the "great and chief end ... of men's uniting into commonwealths, and putting themselves under government" is for "the mutual preservation of their *lives*, liberties and estates." Locke, *Second Treatise of Government*, Sections 123, 124. (Emphasis added.) Speaking through Jefferson, the founding generation incorporated Locke's principle into the Declaration of Independence itself, which declares that securing life was one of the three primary purposes for which "Governments are instituted among men."

So basic is this obligation, plaintiffs submit that it is of equal stature with sovereign immunity from lawsuits, and with those "political functions" which "lie[ ] at the heart of representative government" and are thus "reserved to the states under the Tenth Amendment." *Gregory*, *supra*, 501 U.S. at 463.[12]

The Federal Government may, of course, exercise the power to set public health standards in areas relating to interstate commerce. However, where it has defaulted on its obligation to protect public health, the Federal Government may not simultaneously *prevent the States from taking action to do so.* Such preemption would be irreconcilable with the "dignity and essential attributes inherent in" the State's status as sovereigns. (*Alden*, 527 U.S. at 714) Yet that is precisely what the Telecommunications Act and the FCC regulations

---

[12] In the present day, recent decisions of this Court also confirm that the power to protect the people from threats to health and safety is part of the traditional powers retained by the States. *U.S. v. Morrison*, 529 U.S. ___, 120 S.Ct. 1740 (2000) (confirming that the Founders reposed the plenary police power in the States.) Indeed, this Court has very recently reconfirmed that the field of health care "is a subject of traditional state regulation ..." *Pegram v. Herdich*, 530 U.S. ___, 120 S. Ct. 2143, 2158 (2000), *quoting New York State Conference of Blue Cross and Blue Shield v. Travelers Ins. Co.*, 514 U.S. 645, 654-655 (1995).

23

do, by leaving citizens exposed to the potential health effects of the radio frequency radiation from cellular towers and by simultaneously tying the hands of state and local officials who wish to intercede to protect the well-being of their citizens.

Based on the administrative record before the Second Circuit, it is apparent that the FCC has been hobbled by Congress in its ability to update emissions standards and to take meaningful regulatory steps to safeguard the public. As the scientific literature amply demonstrates, the level of Federal research on this issue by EPA is wholly inadequate to this day, at a time when findings by researchers around the world demonstrate the pressing need for a heavily-funded federal human health-oriented research program.[13]

The power and responsibility to protect public health and safety cannot lapse. When the Federal Government fails to exercise it, the power necessarily reverts to the people of the States as part of their inviolable sovereignty. This principle is also enshrined in the Declaration, wherein one of the chief complaints against the British Crown is that the king impeded

---

[13] For example, an 18-year study by Dr. Bruce Hocking in Sydney, Australia found that children living close to broadcast towers for four TV stations and an FM radio station suffered twice as many deaths from leukemia as children residing farther away. The radiation levels were no more than 8 microwatts per square centimeter, 125 times lower than the 1996 FCC standards. (Hocking B, Gordon IR, Grain HL, Hatfield GE, *Cancer Incidence and Mortality and Proximity to TV Towers. Med J Aust* 165(11-12):601-605, 1996.)

Adult leukemias were nine times higher than expected within the first half kilometer of a BBC TV and FM transmitter in Sutton Coldfield near Birmingham, England. Dr. Helen Dolk and associates observed that the leukemia incidence was almost double expected levels within two kilometers. The maximum radiation level measured was only 5.7 microwatts per square centimeter. (Helen Dolk, *et al. Cancer Incidence Near Radio and Television Transmitters in Great Britain. American Journal of Epidemiology*, Vol. 145, No. 1 (January 1997) pp. 1-9.)

24

the passage of "laws most wholesome and necessary to the public good" by "refusing his assent" and by "dissolving colonial legislatures":

> whereby the Legislative Powers, incapable of annihilation . . . returned to the People at large for their exercise. . . .

The provision of the Telecommunications Act forbidding States from filling the regulatory vacuum left by Congress and the FCC is therefore repugnant to the Tenth Amendment and basic principles of American democracy.

Congress Has Failed to Fund EPA Research Into Biological Effects of RF Emissions on Human Health

The real problem here is that the most recent FCC standards set in 1996, are still based on thermal effects, despite newer information coming from scientific sectors largely outside of the U.S. The current FCC standards were adopted from decades-old research reviewed by the National Council on Radiation Protection (*NCRP Report No. 86*, issued April 2, 1986), and from the American National Standards Institute (*EEE Standard for Safety Levels with Respect to Human Exposure to Radio Frequency Electromagnetic Fields, 3kHz to 300 GHz*, approved Sept. 26, 1991, with a cut-off date for scientific papers of December, 1985). Both Professional agencies have a 5-to-7 year built-in time lag in their review process, and their respective RF committees are comprised almost entirely of physicists, engineers and bioelectromagnetics researchers — not professionals from the public health sector. In other words, dated, inappropriate research, reviewed by authorities from inappropriate professions, is being used to reach conclusions about public safety concerning radio frequency radiation. Why has there been no better updating of the FCC standards? The answer is obvious: because

25

Congress has not appropriated adequate funds to conduct non-thermal research by the key federal agency — EPA.

The Court of Appeals premised its refusal to disturb the FCC regulations in large part on the Court's confidence in the Environmental Protection Agency (EPA) keeping the FCC informed on new developments which would require changes in the FCC's existing maximum emissions standards. As the Court of Appeals said:

> Moreover, it was not arbitrary and capricious for the FCC to conclude that it need not supply the new evidence to the other federal agencies with expertise in the area. It could reasonably expect those agencies to keep abreast of scientific developments in carrying out their missions. For instance, the EPA had participated not only in the hearings and comments leading to the promulgation of the Guidelines, but also had been on the verge of releasing its own draft guidelines pertaining to the health effects of RF radiation in 1996. *It was fully reasonable for the FCC to expect the agency with primacy in evaluating environmental impacts to monitor all relevant scientific input into the FCC's reconsideration, particularly because the EPA had been assigned the lead role in RF radiation health effects since 1970. See* 42 U.S.C. § 2021(h).

(205 F.3d at 91) (A-10) (Emphasis added.)

The Court's reliance on the EPA was technically correct but substantively naive. What the Court did not realize was that *Congress terminated funding for radiation research by EPA in 1996*, and no staff has been available at EPA to conduct such research for the past five years.

This Court can properly take judicial notice of the federal budget levels for this agency. Reproduced on the following page is a "Summary of EPA Budget and Staffing for RF Radiation Activities from FY 1990-2000" recently supplied

CELL TOWERS

26

Summary of EPA Budget and Staffing for RF Radiation Activities from FY1990–2000

(Extramural Dollars Only)

FY	90	91	92	93	94	95	96	97	98	99	00
FTE	2.3	2.2	2.1	2.1	2	2	0.5	0.5	0.5	0.5	0.5
$(K)	$0	$40	$25	$543[a]	$73[b]	$140[c]	$0	$0	$25[d]	$0	$0

[a] Includes grant funds ($510,000) under EPA/NIEHS Interagency Agreement DW75935939.

[b] Includes funds ($50,000) for Cooperative Agreement (CX823714) with the National Council on Radiation Protection and Measurements (NCRP).

[c] Includes funds ($50,000) for Cooperative Agreement (CX823714) with NCRP.

[d] $25K completes total funding ($125,000) for Cooperative Agreement (CX823714) with NCRP.

27

by the agency in response to a request from Senator Joseph I. Lieberman of Connecticut. It will be seen that only one-half of a staff member is presently assigned to perform EPA's "lead role" in RF radiation health effects, and such has been the case since 1995. It will also be seen that *total* research expenditures in the five years since 1995 amount to a final payment of *$25,000* on a cooperative agreement entered into with NCRP in 1994. Nothing more. In contrast, the EPA research expenditures from 1990 through 1995 totaled *$821,000*. While the Court of Appeals was theoretically correct in its reliance on EPA's lead research responsibility, in practical terms the Court was dead wrong. There is *no* Congressionally funded research into the biological effects of cellular tower RF emissions in the agency to which Congress assigned the "lead role" in 1970.

This is a perfect example of lack of accountability. Citizens should be allowed to decide whether inaction by their own elected Congressional delegations is the result of large campaign contributions and intense lobbying from the telecommunications industry.[14]

---

[14] The Court can take judicial notice of the official reports filed with the Federal Elections Commission (FEC), summarized on the Internet website of the Center for Responsive Politics (CRP) (website: www.crp.org). At the time the Telecommunications Act of 1996 was under discussion in 1994-95, political action committees for local and long distance phone companies contributed over $4 million to key members of Congress (data from CRP reported in *USA Today* issue of October 16, 1995).

During the period of actual passage of the Act, FEC filings, together with lobbying reports filed with the House and Senate, showed substantially greater expenditures for 1996-97, amounting to a grand total of $29,425,097.

For the current Congress, campaign contributions from telephone utilities reported to the FEC (as of August 30, 2000, even before the start of final election campaigning): $5,503,169.

29

CONCLUSION

The Petition for Certiorari should be granted.

Dated: New York, New York
September 7, 2000

WHITNEY NORTH SEYMOUR, JR.*
PETER JAMES CLINES
LANDY & SEYMOUR
Attorneys for Petitioners
363 Seventh Avenue, Room 1300
New York, New York 10001
(212) 629-0590

* *Counsel of Record*

Appendix B

Abstracts compiled by Dr. Henry Lai

Papers reporting biological effects of radiofrequency radiation at low intensities

Akoev IG, Mel'nikov VM, Usachev AV, Kozhokaru AF, [Modification of lethal radiation injury in mice by postradiation exposure to low-intensity centimeter-band radio frequency waves]. *Radiats Biol Radioecol* 34(4-5):671-674, 1994.
[Article in Russian]

A clearly pronounced modification of acute radiation injury of mice has been obtained by prolonged action (for up to 23 hours) of low-intensity (5 +/- 1.5 mu Wt/cm2) radiofrequency radiation in the ranges of 2-8, 8-18 and 19-27 GHz with a swing frequency of 12-14 Hz, applied immediately after exposure to lethal dose of gamma-radiation. Survival of mice and average life duration of killed mice were increased.

Balode, Z, Assessment of radio-frequency electromagnetic radiation by the micronucleus test in bovine peripheral erythrocytes. *Sci Total Environ* 180(1):81-85, 1996.

Previous bioindicative studies in the Skrunda Radio Location Station area have focused on the somatic influence of electromagnetic radiation on plants, but it is also important to study genetic effects. We have chosen cows as test animals for cytogenetical evaluation because they live in the same general exposure area as humans, are confined to specific locations and are chronically exposed to radiation. Blood samples were obtained from female Latvian Brown cows from a farm close to and in front of the Skrunda Radar and from cows in a control area. A simplified alternative to the Schiff method of DNA staining for identification of micronuclei in peripheral erythrocytes was applied. Microscopically, micronuclei in peripheral blood erythrocytes were round in shape and exhibited a strong red colour. They are easily detectable as the only coloured bodies in the uncoloured erythrocytes. From each individual animal 2000 erythrocytes were examined at a magnification of x 1000 for the presence of micronuclei. The counting of micronuclei in peripheral erythrocytes gave low average incidences, 0.6 per 1000 in the exposed group and 0.1 per 1000 in the control, but statistically significant (P < 0.01) differences were found in the frequency distribution between the control and exposed groups.

Belyaev IYa, Alipov YD, Shcheglov VS, Lystsov VN, Resonance effect of microwaves on the genome conformational state of E. coli cells. *Z Naturforsch [C]* 47(7-8):621-827, 1992.

The effect of low intensity microwaves on the conformational state of the genome of X-irradiated E. coli cells was studied by the method of viscosity anomalous time dependencies. It has been established that within the ranges of 51.62-51.84 GHz and 41.25-41.50 GHz the frequency dependence of the observed effect has a resonance nature with a resonance half-width of the order of 100 MHz. The power dependence of the microwave effect within the range of 0.1-200 microW/cm2 has shown that a power density of 1 microW/cm2 is sufficient to suppress radiation-induced repair of the genome conformational state. The effect of microwave suppression of repair is well reproduced and does not depend on the sequence of cell exposure to X-rays and microwave radiation in the millimeter band. The results obtained indicate the role of the cell genome in the resonant interaction of cells with low intensity millimeter waves.

Belyaev IY, Shcheglov VS, Alipov YD, Polunin VA, Resonance effect of millimeter waves in the power range from 10(-19) to 3 x 10(-3) W/cm2 on Escherichia coli cells at different concentrations. *Bioelectromagnetics* **17(4):312-321, 1996.**

The effect of millimeter waves (MMWs) on the genome conformational state (GCS) of E. coli AB1157 cells was studied by the method of anomalous viscosity time dependencies (AVTD) in the frequency range of 51.64-51.85 GHz. The 51.755 GHz resonance frequency of the cell reaction to MMWs did not depend on power density (PD) in the range from 10(-19) to 3 x 10(-3) W/cm2. The half-width of the resonant reaction of cells showed a sigmoid dependence on PD, changing from 3 MHz to 100 MHz. The PD dependence of the half-width had the same shape for different concentrations of exposed cells (4 x 10(7) and 4 x 10(8) cells/ml), whereas the magnitude of the 51.755 GHz resonance effect differed significantly and depended on the PD of MMW exposure. Sharp narrowing of the 51.755 GHz resonance in the PD range from 10(-4) to 10(-7) W/cm2 was followed by an emergence of new resonance frequencies. The PD dependence of the MMW effect at one of these resonance frequencies (51.674 GHz) differed markedly from the corresponding dependence at the 51.755 GHz resonance, the power window occurring in the range from 10(-16) to 10(-8) W/cm2. The results obtained were explained in the framework of a model of electron-conformational interactions. The frequency-time parameters of this model appeared to be in good agreement with experimental data.

Budinscak V, Goldoni J, Saric M, [Hematologic changes in workers exposed to radio wave radiation]. *Arh Hig Rada Toksikol* **42(4):367-373, 1991.**
[Article in Serbo-Croatian (Roman)]

Haematological parameters were measured in 43 radar operators employed in air traffic control occupationally exposed to microwave radiation of low intensity over a period of four years. Exposure to heat, soft X-ray radiation and noise were within maximally allowed limits. The haematological changes included a decreased number of erythrocytes, reticulocytes, platelets, segmented granulocytes and monocytes, and an increased number of leucocytes and lymphocytes. The changes were not pathologically significant and most of them were reversible.

Chiang H, Yao GD, Fang QS, Wang KQ, Lu DZ, Zhou YK, Health effects of environmental electromagnetic fields. *J. Bioelectricity* 8:127-131, 1989.

We investigated the effects of exposure to environmental electromagnetic fields (EMFs) in 1170 subjects. Neutrophil phagocytosis was enhanced in the low-intensity exposure groups, but reduced significantly at relatively higher intensities. Visual reaction time was prolonged and the scores of short-term memory tests were lower in some high-intensity exposure groups. EMFs may affect the central nervous and immune systems in man.

de Pomerai D, Daniells C, David H, Allan J, Duce I, Mutwakil M, Thomas D, Sewell P, Tattersall J, Jones D, Candido P, Non-thermal heat-shock response to microwaves, *Nature* 405:417-418, 2000.

Nematode worms (C. elegans) exposed overnight to 750-MHz microwaves at a SAR of 0.001 W/kg showed an increased in heat shock proteins (HSPs). (Heat shock proteins are induced in most organisms by adverse conditions (such as heat or toxins) that cause damage to cellular proteins, acting as molecular chaperones to rescue damaged proteins). The authors give several arguments that the microwave-induced effect on HSPs is non-thermal and suggest that 'current exposure limits for microwave equipment may need to be reconsidered.'

D'Inzeo G, Bernardi P, Eusebi F, Grassi F, Tamburello C, Zani BM, Microwave effects on acetylcholine-induced channels in cultured chick myotubes. *Bioelectromagnetics* 9(4):363-372, 1988.

The behavior of cultured myotubes from chick embryos exposed to microwaves has been experimentally analyzed. Recordings of acetylcholine-induced currents have been obtained via patch-clamp techniques using both cell-attached (single-channel current recording) and whole-cell (total current recording) configurations. During the exposure to low-power microwaves the frequency of the ACh-activated single channel openings decreased, while the ACh-induced total current showed a faster falling phase. Channel open time and conductance were not affected by microwave irradiation. It is concluded that the exposure to microwaves increases the rate of desensitization and decreases the channel opening probability. The nonthermal origin and the molecular interaction mechanisms governing these electromagnetic-induced effects are discussed.

Dolk H, Shaddick G, Walls P, Grundy C, Thakrar B, Kleinschmidt I, Elliott P, Cancer incidence near radio and television transmitters in Great Britain. I. Sutton Coldfield transmitter. *Am J Epidemiol* 145(1):1-9, 1997.

A small area study of cancer incidence in 1974-1986 was carried out to investigate an unconfirmed report of a "cluster" of leukemias and lymphomas near the Sutton Coldfield television (TV) and frequency modulation (FM) radio transmitter in the West Midlands, England. The study used a national database of postcoded cancer registrations, and population and socioeconomic data from the 1981 census.

Selected cancers were hematopoietic and lymphatic, brain, skin, eye, male breast, female breast, lung, colorectal, stomach, prostate, and bladder. Expected numbers of cancers in small areas were calculated by indirect standardization, with stratification for a small area socioeconomic index. The study area was defined as a 10 km radius circle around the transmitter, within which 10 bands of increasing distance from the transmitter were defined as a basis for testing for a decline in risk with distance, and an inner area was arbitrarily defined for descriptive purposes as a 2 km radius circle. The risk of adult leukemia within 2 km was 1.83 (95% confidence interval 1.22-2.74), and there was a significant decline in risk with distance from the transmitter (p = 0.001). These findings appeared to be consistent over the periods 1974-1980, 1981-1986, and were probably largely independent of the initially reported cluster, which appeared to concern mainly a later period. In the context of variability of leukemia risk across census wards in the West Midlands as a whole, the Sutton Coldfield findings were unusual. A significant decline in risk with distance was also found for skin cancer, possibly related to residual socioeconomic confounding, and for bladder cancer. Study of other radio and TV transmitters in Great Britain is required to put the present results in wider context. No causal implications can be made from a single cluster investigation of this kind.

Dutta SK, Verma M, Blackman CF, Frequency-dependent alterations in enolase activity in Escherichia coli caused by exposure to electric and magnetic fields. *Bioelectromagnetics* 15(5):377-383, 1994.

Some neurochemical effects of low-intensity electric and magnetic fields have been shown to be nonlinear functions of exposure parameters. These effects occurred within narrow ranges of frequency and intensity. Previous studies on membrane-associated endpoints in cell culture preparations demonstrated changes in calcium efflux and in acetylcholinesterase activity following exposure to radiofrequency radiation, amplitude modulated (AM) at 16 and at 60 Hz, at a specific absorption rate of 0.05 W/kg. In this study, these modulation frequencies were tested for their influence on the activity of a cytoplasmic enzyme, enolase, which is being tested clinically for detection of neoplasia. Escherichia coli cultures containing a plasmid with a mammalian gene for enolase were exposed for 30 min, and cell extracts were assayed for enolase activity by measuring absorbance at 240 nm. The enolase activity in exposed cultures was compared to the activity in paired control cultures. Exposure to 147 MHz carrier waves at 0.05 W/kg, AM at 16 Hz showed enolase activity enhanced by 62%, and AM at 60 Hz showed enolase activity reduced by 28%. Similarly, exposure to 16 Hz fields alone, at 21.2 V/mrms (electric) and 97 nTrms (magnetic), showed enhancement in enolase activity by 59%, whereas exposure to 60 Hz fields alone, at 14.1 V/mrms (electric) and 65 nTrms (magnetic), showed reduction in activity by 24%. Sham exposures as well as exposure to continuous-wave 147 MHz radiation at 0.05 W/kg showed no change in enolase activity.

Fesenko EE, Novoselova EG, Semiletova NV, Agafonova TA, Sadovnikov VB, [Stimulation of murine natural killer cells by weak electromagnetic waves in the centimeter range]. *Biofizika* **44(4):737-741, 1999.**
[Article in Russian]

Irradiation with electromagnetic waves (8.15-18 GHz, 1 Hz within, 1 microW/cm2) in vivo increases the cytotoxic activity of natural killer cells of rat spleen. In mice exposed for 24-72 h, the activity of natural killer cells increased by 130-150%, the increased level of activity persisting within 24 h after the cessation of treatment. Microwave irradiation of animals in vivo for 3.5 and 5 h, and a short exposure of splenic cells in vitro did not affect the activity of natural killer cells.

Fesenko, EE, Makar, VR, Novoselova, EG, Sadovnikov, VB, Microwaves and cellular immunity. I. Effect of whole body microwave irradiation on tumor necrosis factor production in mouse cells. *Bioelectrochem Bioenerg* **49(1):29-35, 1999.**

Whole body microwave sinusoidal irradiation of male NMRI mice with 8.15-18 GHz (1 Hz within) at a power density of 1 microW/cm2 caused a significant enhancement of TNF production in peritoneal macrophages and splenic T lymphocytes. Microwave radiation affected T cells, facilitating their capacity to proliferate in response to mitogenic stimulation. The exposure duration necessary for the stimulation of cellular immunity ranged from 5 h to 3 days. Chronic irradiation of mice for 7 days produced the decreasing of TNF production in peritoneal macrophages. The exposure of mice for 24 h increased the TNF production and immune proliferative response, and these stimulatory effects persisted over 3 days after the termination of exposure. Microwave treatment increased the endogenously produced TNF more effectively than did lipopolysaccharide, one of the most potential stimuli of synthesis of this cytokine. The role of microwaves as a factor interfering with the process of cell immunity is discussed.

Galat VV, Mezhevikina LM, Zubin MN, Lepikhov KA, Khramov RN, Chailakhian LM, [Effect of millimeter waves on the early development of the mouse and sea urchin embryo]. *Biofizika* **44(1):137-140, 1999.**
[Article in Russian]

The action of nonthermal electromagnetic radiation (EMR) of the millimeter range on the early development of murine and sea urchin embryos was investigated. An MRTA-01E-03 generator with a frequency of 54-78 GHz and radiation intensity of 0.06 mWt/cm2 was used. The embryos were irradiated during 30 min at the stage of two blastomeres. The number of murine embryos that reached the blastocyst stage increased (up to 97.3% in comparison with 87.5% in control). The total time of cultivation up to the blastocyst stage was also shorter (72 h) than in control (96 h). The irradiation had effect on the development of sea urchin embryos only if embryos with a weakened viability were tested. The results indicate that millimeter electromagnetic radiation has a stimulating effect on the early development of embryos, increasing the resistance of embryos to unfavorable environmental conditions.

Gapeev AB, Lakushina VS, Chemeris NK, Fesenko EE [Modulated extremely high frequency electromagnetic radiation of low intensity activates or inhibits respiratory burst in neutrophils depending on modulation frequency]. *Biofizika* **42(5):1125-1134, 1997.**
[Article in Russian]

The influence of low-intensity modulated electromagnetic radiation of extremely high frequencies (EHF EMR) on synergistic reaction of calcium ionophore A23187 and phorbol ester PMA in activation of the respiratory burst of the peritoneal neutrophils of mice line NMRI was investigated. The production of reactive oxygen species by the neutrophils was estimated by luminol-dependent chemiluminescence technique. The cells were irradiated in the far field zone of the channel radiator for 20 min in the presence of A23187 and then were activated by PMA after switching off the irradiation. It was shown, that continuous EHF EMR (50 microW/cm2) inhibited quasi-resonantly the synergistic reaction. The maximum effect was about 25% at carrier frequency of 41.95 GHz. Modulated radiation with carrier frequency of 41.95 GHz and modulation frequency of 1 Hz activated the synergistic reaction, but at modulation frequencies of 0.1, 16 and 50 Hz inhibited one. At fixed modulation frequency of 1 Hz the nonlinear dependence of the effect on the carrier frequency was found. The synergistic reaction was activated in the frequency range of 41.95-42.05 GHz and was inhibited at the frequencies of 41.8-41.9 GHz. The effect was observed only at raised intracellular free calcium concentration and at calcium fluxes through plasma membrane. The obtained results prove the possibility of control over cell functioning by low-intensity modulated EHF EMR, presumably, manipulating by connected systems of enzyme reactions.

Hjollund NH, Bonde JP, Skotte J, Semen analysis of personnel operating military radar equipment. *Reprod Toxicol* **11(6):897, 1997.**

This is a preliminary survey of semen quality among Danish military personnel operating mobile ground-to-air missile units that use several microwave emitting radar systems. The maximal mean exposure was estimated to be 0.01 mW/cm2. The median sperm density of the military personnel was significantly low compared to the references. The difference is either due to chance, uncontrolled bias, or nonthermal effects of transitory microwaves.

Hocking B, Gordon IR, Grain HL, Hatfield GE, Cancer incidence and mortality and proximity to TV towers. *Med J Aust* **165(11-12):601-605, 1996.**

(Published erratum appears in *Med J Aust* 166(2):80, 1997.)
OBJECTIVE: To determine whether there is an increased cancer incidence and mortality in populations exposed to radiofrequency radiations from TV towers.
DESIGN: An ecological study comparing cancer incidence and mortality, 1972-1990,

in nine municipalities, three of which surround the TV towers and six of which are further away from the towers. (TV radiofrequency radiation decreases with the square of the distance from the source.) Cancer incidence and mortality data were obtained from the then Commonwealth Department of Human Services and Health. Data on frequency, power, and period of broadcasting for the three TV towers were obtained from the Commonwealth Department of Communications and the Arts. The calculated power density of the radiofrequency radiation in the exposed area ranged from 8.0 microW/cm2 near the towers to 0.2 microW/cm2 at a radius of 4km and 0.02 microW/cm2 at 12 km. SETTING: Northern Sydney, where three TV towers have been broadcasting since 1956. OUTCOME MEASURES: Rate ratios for leukaemia and brain tumour incidence and mortality, comparing the inner with the outer areas. RESULTS: For all ages, the rate ratio for total leukaemia incidence was 1.24 (95% confidence interval [CI], 1.09-1.40). Among children, the rate ratio for leukaemia incidence was 1.58 (95% CI, 1.07-2.34) and for mortality it was 2.32 (95% CI, 1.35-4.01). The rate ratio for childhood lymphatic leukaemia (the most common type) was 1.55 (95% CI, 1.00-2.41) for incidence and 2.74 (95% CI, 1.42-5.27) for mortality. Brain cancer incidence and mortality were not increased. CONCLUSION: We found an association between increased childhood leukaemia incidence and mortality and proximity to TV towers.

Ivaschuk OI, Jones RA, Ishida-Jones T, Haggren W, Adey WR, Phillips JL, Exposure of nerve growth factor-treated PC12 rat pheochromocytoma cells to a modulated radiofrequency field at 836.55 MHz: effects on c-jun and c-fos expression. *Bioelectromagnetics* 18(3):223-229, 1997.

Rat PC12 pheochromocytoma cells have been treated with nerve growth factor And then exposed to athermal levels of a packet-modulated radiofrequency field At 836.55 MHz. This signal was produced by a prototype time-domain multiple-access (TDMA) transmitter that conforms to the North American digital cellular telephone standard. Three slot average power densities were used: 0.09, 0.9, and 9 mW/cm2. Exposures were for 20, 40, and 60 min and included an intermittent exposure regimen (20 min on/20 min off), resulting in total incubation times of 20, 60, and 100 min, respectively. Concurrent controls were sham exposed. After extracting total cellular RNA, Northern blot analysis was used to assess the expression of the immediate early genes, c-fos and c-jun, in all cell populations. No change in c-fos transcript levels were detected after 20 min exposure at each field intensity (20 min was the only time period at which c-fos message could be detected consistently). Transcript levels for c-jun were altered only after 20 min exposure to 9 mW/cm2 (average 38% decrease).

Kolodynski AA, Kolodynska VV, Motor and psychological functions of school children living in the area of the Skrunda Radio Location Station in Latvia. *Sci Total Environ* 180(1):87-93, 1996.

This paper presents the results of experiments on school children living in the area of the Skrunda Radio Location Station (RLS) in Latvia. Motor function, memory and attention significantly differed between the exposed and control groups. Children living in front of the RLS had less developed memory and attention, their reaction time was slower and their neuromuscular apparatus endurance was decreased.

Lebedeva NN, Sulimov AV, Sulimova OP, Kotrovskaya TI, Gailus T, Cellular phone electromagnetic field effects on bioelectric activity of human brain. *Crit Rev Biomed Eng* 28(1-2):323-337, 2000.

24 volunteers participated in the experiments. The investigation of EEG reactions to cellular phone (EMF frequency 902.4 MHz and intensity 0.06 mW/cm2) was conducted. Two experiments were performed with each subject--cellular phone exposure and Placebo Duration of the experiment was 60 min: 15 min--background; 15 min--EMF exposure or Placebo; 30 min--afterexposure. EEG was recorded in 16 standard leads with "eyes open" and "eyes closed". Special software with non-linear dynamics was developed for EEG analyses. One parameter, multichannel (global) correlation dimension, was calculated. The changes of these parameters can be evidence of brain functional state changes. As a result of EEG record processing, a significant increase of global correlation dimension during the exposure and afterexposure period was discovered, more pronounced in the case of "eyes closed". That can be viewed as the manifestation of cortex activation under phone EMF exposure.

Loscher W, Kas G, Extraordinary behavior disorders in cows in proximity to transmission stations. *Der Praktische Tierarz* 79:437-444, 1998. [Article in German]

In addition to reduction of milk yield and increased health problems, behavioral abnormalities were observed over a period of two years in a herd of diary cows maintained in close proximity to a TV and cell phone transmitting antenna. Evaluation of possible factors which could explain the abnormalities in the live stock did not disclose any factors other than the high-frequency electromagnetic fields. An experiment in which a cow with abnormal behavior was brought to a stable 20 km away from the antenna resulted in a complete normalization of the cow within five days, whereas symptoms returned when the cow was brought back to the stable nearby the antenna. In view of the previous described effects of electromagnetic fields, it might be possible that the observed abnormalities in cows are related to electromagnetic field exposure. (power densities measured 0.02-7 mW/m2).

Magras, IN, Xenos, TD, RF radiation-induced changes in the prenatal development of mice. *Bioelectromagnetics* 18(6):455-461, 1997.

The possible effects of radiofrequency (RF) radiation on prenatal development has been investigated in mice. This study consisted of RF level measurements and in vivo experiments at several places around an "antenna park." At these locations RF power densities between 168 nW/cm2 and 1053 nW/cm2 were measured. Twelve pairs of mice, divided in two groups, were placed in locations of different power densities and were repeatedly mated five times. One hundred eighteen newborns were collected. They were measured, weighed, and examined macro- and microscopically. A progressive decrease in the number of newborns per dam was observed, which ended in irreversible infertility. The prenatal development of the newborns, however, evaluated by the crown-rump length, the body weight, and the number of the lumbar, sacral, and coccygeal vertebrae, was improved.

Mann, K, Wagner, P, Brunn, G, Hassan, F, Hiemke, C, Roschke, J, Effects of pulsed high-frequency electromagnetic fields on the neuroendocrine system. *Neuroendocrinology* **67(2):139-144, 1998.**

The influence of pulsed high-frequency electromagnetic fields emitted from a circularly polarized antenna on the neuroendocrine system in healthy humans was investigated (900 MHz electromagnetic field, pulsed with 217 Hz, average power density 0.02 mW/cm2). Nocturnal hormone profiles of growth hormone (GH), cortisol, luteinizing hormone (LH) and melatonin were determined under polysomnographic control. An alteration in the hypothalamo-pituitary-adrenal axis activity was found with a slight, transient elevation in the cortisol serum level immediately after onset of field exposure which persisted for 1 h. For GH, LH and melatonin, no significant effects were found under exposure to the field compared to the placebo condition, regarding both total hormone production during the entire night and dynamic characteristics of the secretion pattern. Also the evaluation of the sleep EEG data revealed no significant alterations under field exposure, although there was a trend to an REM suppressive effect. The results indicate that weak high-frequency electromagnetic fields have no effects on nocturnal hormone secretion except for a slight elevation in cortisol production which is transient, pointing to an adaptation of the organism to the stimulus.

Michelozzi P, Ancona C, Fusco D, Forastiere F, Perucci CA, Risk of leukemia and residence near a radio transmitter in Italy. *Epidemiology* **9 (Suppl) 354p, 1998.**

We conducted a small area study to investigate a cluster of leukemia near a high power radio-transmitter in a peripheral area of Rome. The leukemia mortality within 3.5 km (5,863 inhabitants) was higher than expected (SMR=2.5, 95% confident interval 1.07-4.83); the excess was due to a significant higher mortality among men (7 cases observed, SMR=3.5). The results of the Stone's test, after adjusting for socio-economic confounding, showed a significant decline in risk with distance from the transmitter only among men (p=0.005), whereas the p-value for both sexes was p=0.07.

Navakatikian MA, Tomashevskaya LA, Phasic behavioral and endocrine effects of microwaves of nonthermal intensity. In "Biological Effects of Electric and Magnetic Fields, Volume 1," D.O. Carpenter (ed) Academic Press, San Diego, CA, 1994, pp.333-342.

Microwaves at nonthermal levels are able to induce behavioral and endocrine changes at low power densities (0.01-0.1 mW/cm2). Our studies have demonstrated several phases of inhibition and activation. We suggest that inhibition of behavior by microwaves has many mechanisms depending on the strength and duration of exposure, and most inhibitory effects from direct actions on the nervous system. Activation, on the other hand, is correlated well with decreases in serum concentrations of testosterone and insulin. CW microwaves, however, have no influence on the secretion of insulin.

Novoselova ET, Fesenko EE, [[Stimulation of production of tumor necrosis factor by murine macrophages when exposed in vio and in vitro to weak electromagnetic waves in the centimeter range]]. *Biofizika* 43(6):1132-1333, 1998.
[Article in Russian]

Whole-body microwave sinusoidal irradiation of male NMRI mice, exposure of macrophages in vitro, and preliminary irradiation of culture medium with 8.15-18 GHz (1 Hz within) at a power density of 1 microW/cm2 caused a significant enhancement of tumor necrosis factor production in peritoneal macrophages. The role of microwaves as a factor interfering with the process of cell immunity is discussed.

Novoselova, EG, Fesenko, EE, Makar, VR, Sadovnikov, VB, Microwaves and cellular immunity. II. Immunostimulating effects of microwaves and naturally occurring antioxidant nutrients. *Bioelectrochem Bioenerg* 49(1):37-41, 1999.

The effect of 8.15-18 GHz (1 Hz within) microwave radiation at a power density of 1 microW/cm2 on the tumor necrosis factor (TNF) production and immune response was tested. A single 5 h whole-body exposure induced a significant increase in TNF production in peritoneal macrophages and splenic T cells. The mitogenic response in T lymphocytes increased after microwave exposure. The activation of cellular immunity was observed within 3 days after exposure. The diet containing lipid-soluble nutrients (beta-carotene, alpha-tocopherol and ubiquinone Q9) increased the activity of macrophages and T cells from irradiated mice. These results demonstrate that irradiation with low-power density microwaves stimulates the immune potential of macrophages and T cells, and the antioxidant treatment enhances the effect of microwaves, in particular at later terms, when the effect of irradiation is reduced.

Pashovkina MS, Akoev IG, [Changes in serum alkaline phosphatase activity during in vitro exposure to amplitude-modulated electromagnetic field of ultrahigh frequency (2375 MHz) in guinea pigs]. *Biofizika* 45(1):130-136, 2000.
[Article in Russian]

The activity of alkaline phosphatase by the action of pulse-modulated microwave radiation was studied. The carrier frequency of radiation was 2375 MHz, the range of modulation pulse rate was 10-390 Hz with the on-off time ratio 2, and the specific absorption rate was 8 and 0.8 microW/cm2. Time of exposure was 1 and 3 min under conditions of continuous temperature control. It was shown that the activity of alkaline phosphatase depends on both modulation frequency and intensity of superhigh-frequency electromagnetic radiation. At a frequency of 70 Hz, the activity of alkaline phosphatases increased 1.8-2.0 times.

Persson BRR, Salford LG, Brun A, Blood-brain barrier permeability in rats exposed to electromagnetic fields used in wireless communication. *Wireless Network* 3:455-461, 1997.

Biological effects of radio frequency electromagnetic fields (EMF) on the blood-brain barrier (BBB) have been studied in Fischer 344 rats of both sexes. The rats were not anesthetised during the exposure. The brains were perfused with saline for 3-4 minutes, and thereafter perfusion fixed with 4% formaldehyde for 5-6 minutes. Whole coronal sections of the brains were dehydrated and embedded in paraffin and sectioned at 5 micrometers. Albumin and fibinogen were demonstrated immunochemically and classified as normal versus pathological leakage. In the present investigation we exposed male and female Fischer 344 rats in a Transverse Electromagnetic Transmission line camber to microwaves of 915 MHz as continuous wave (CW) and pulse-modulated with different pulse power and at various time intervals. The CW-pulse power varied from 0.001 W to 10 W and the exposure time from 2 min to 960 min. In each experiment we exposed 4-6 rats with 2-4 controls randomly placed in excited and non-excited TEM cells, respectively. We have in total investigated 630 exposed rats at various modulation frequencies and 372 controls. The frequency of pathological rats is significantly increased (P< 0.0001) from 62/372 (ratio 0.17 $\pm$ 0.02) for control rats to 244/630 (ratio: 0.39 $\pm$ 0.043) in all exposed rats. Grouping the exposed animals according to the level or specific absorption energy (J/kg) give significant difference in all levels above 1.5 J/kg. The exposure was 915 MHz microwaves either pulse modulated (PW) at 217 Hz with 0.57 ms pulse width, at 50 Hz with 6.6 ms pulse width or continuous wave (CW). The frequency of pathological rats (0.17) among controls in the various groups is not significantly different. The frequency of pathological rats was 170/480 (0.35 $\pm$ 0.03) among rats exposed to pulse modulated (PW) and 74/149 (0.50 $\pm$ 0.07) among rats exposed to continuous wave exposure (CW). These results are both highly significantly different to their corresponding controls (p< 0.0001) and the frequency of pathological rats after exposure to pulsed radiation (PW) is significantly less (p< 0.002) than after exposure to continuous wave radiation (CW).

Phillips, J.L., Ivaschuk, O., Ishida-Jones, T., Jones, R.A., Campbell-Beachler, M. and Haggren, W. DNA damage in Molt-4 T- lymphoblastoid cells exposed to cellular telephone radiofrequency fields in vitro. *Bioelectrochem. Bioenerg.* **45:103-110, 1998.**

Molt-4 T-lymphoblastoid cells have been exposed to pulsed signals at cellular telephone frequencies of 813.5625 MHz (iDEN signal) and 836.55 MHz (TDMA signal). These studies were performed at low SAR (average = 2.4 and 24 microwatt/g for iDEN and 2.6 and 26 microwatt/g for TDMA) in studies designed to look for athermal RF effects. The alkaline comet, or single cell gel electrophoresis, assay was employed to measure DNA single-strand breaks in cell cultures exposed to the radiofrequency (RF) signal as compared to concurrent sham-exposed cultures. Tail moment and comet extent were calculated as indicators of DNA damage. Statistical differences in the distribution of values for tail moment and comet extent between exposed and control cell cultures were evaluated with the Kolmogorov-Smirnoff distribution test. Data points for all experiments of each exposure condition were pooled and analyzed as single groups. It was found that: 1) exposure of cells to the iDEN signal at an SAR of 2.4 microwatt/g for 2 h or 21 h significantly decreased DNA damage; 2) exposure of cells to the TDMA signal at an SAR of 2.6 microwatt/g for 2 h and 21 h significantly decreased DNA damage; 3) exposure of cells to the iDEN signal at an SAR of 24 microwatt/g for 2 h and 21 h significantly increased DNA damage; 4) exposure of cells to the TDMA signal at an SAR of 26 microwatt/g for 2 h significantly decreased DNA damage. The data indicate a need to study the effects of exposure to RF signals on direct DNA damage and on the rate at which DNA damage is repaired.

Ray S, Behari J, Physiological changes in rats after exposure to low levels of microwaves. *Radiat Res* **123(2):199-202, 1990.**

The effects of exposure to sublethal levels of microwaves were studied. Young albino rats of both sexes were exposed for 60 days to 7.5-GHz microwaves (1.0-KHz square wave modulation, average power 0.6 mW/cm2) for 3 h daily. During and after microwave exposure several physiological parameters were measured in both control and exposed animals. It was found that the animals exposed to microwaves tended to eat and drink less and thus showed a smaller gain in body weight. Some of the hematological parameters and organ weights were also significantly different. It is proposed that a nonspecific stress response due to microwave exposure and mediated through the central nervous system is responsible for the observed physiological changes.

Schwartz JL, House DE, Mealing GA, Exposure of frog hearts to CW or amplitude-modulated VHF fields: selective efflux of calcium ions at 16 Hz. *Bioelectromagnetics* 11(4):349-358, 1990.

Isolated frog hearts were exposed for 30-min periods in a Crawford cell to a 240-MHz electromagnetic field, either continuous-wave or sinusoidally modulated at 0.5 or 16 Hz. Radiolabeled with calcium (45Ca), the hearts were observed for movement of Ca2+ at calculated SARs of 0.15, 0.24, 0.30, 0.36, 1.50, or 3.00 mW/kg. Neither CW radiation nor radiation at 0.5 Hz, which is close to the beating frequency of the frog's heart, affected movement of calcium ions. When the VHF field was modulated at 16 Hz, a field-intensity-dependent change in the efflux of calcium ions was observed. Relative to control values, ionic effluxes increased by about 18% at 0.3 mW/kg (P less than .01) and by 21% at 0.15 mW/kg (P less than .05), but movement of ions did not change significantly at other rates of energy deposition. These data indicate that the intact myocardium of the frog, akin to brain tissue of neonatal chicken, exhibits movement of calcium ions in response to a weak VHF field that is modulated at 16 Hz.

Somosy Z, Thuroczy G, Kubasova T, Kovacs J, Szabo LD, Effects of modulated and continuous microwave irradiation on the morphology and cell surface negative charge of 3T3 fibroblasts. *Scanning Microsc* 5(4):1145-1155, 1991.

Mouse embryo 3T3 cells were irradiated with 2450 MHz continuous and low frequency (16 Hz) square modulated waves of absorbed energy ranging from 0.0024 to 2.4 mW/g. The low frequency modulated microwave irradiation yielded more morphological cell changes than did the continuous microwave fields of the same intensity. The amount of free negative charges (cationized ferritin binding) on cell surfaces decreased following irradiation by modulated waves but remained unchanged under the effect of a continuous field of the same dose. Modulated waves of 0.024 mW/g dose increased the ruffling activity of the cells, and caused ultrastructural alteration in the cytoplasm. Similar effects were experienced by continuous waves at higher (0.24 and 2.4 mW/g) doses.

Stagg RB, Thomas WJ, Jones RA, Adey WR, DNA synthesis and cell proliferation in C6 glioma and primary glial cells exposed to a 836.55 MHz modulated radiofrequency field. *Bioelectromagnetics* 18(3):230-236, 1997.

We have tested the hypothesis that modulated radiofrequency (RF) fields may act as a tumor-promoting agent by altering DNA synthesis, leading to increased cell proliferation. In vitro tissue cultures of transformed and normal rat glial cells were exposed to an 836.55 MHz, packet-modulated RF field at three power densities: 0.09, 0.9, and 9 mW/cm2, resulting in specific absorption rates (SARs) ranging from 0.15 to 59 muW/g. TEM-mode transmission-line cells were powered by a prototype time-domain multiple-access (TDMA) transmitter that conforms to the North American digital cellular telephone standard. One sham and one

energized TEM cell were placed in standard incubators maintained at 37 degrees
C and 5% CO2. DNA synthesis experiments at **0.59-59 muW/g SAR** were
performed on log-phase and serum-starved semiquiescent cultures after 24 h
exposure. Cell growth at 0.15-15 muW/g SAR was determined by cell counts of
log-phase cultures on days 0, 1, 5, 7, 9, 12, and 14 of a 2 week protocol. Results
from the DNA synthesis assays differed for the two cell types. Sham-exposed
and RF-exposed cultures of primary rat glial cells showed no significant
differences for either log-phase or serum-starved condition. *C6 glioma cells*
exposed to RF at 5.9 muW/g SAR (0.9 mW/cm2) exhibited small (20-40%)
significant increases in 38% of [3H]thymidine incorporation experiments.
Growth curves of sham and RF-exposed cultures showed no differences in either
normal or transformed glial cells at any of the power densities tested. Cell
doubling times of C6 glioma cells [sham (21.9 +/- 1.4 h) vs. field (22.7 +/- 3.2 h)]
also demonstrated no significant differences that could be attributed to altered
DNA synthesis rates. Under these conditions, this modulated RF field did not
increase cell proliferation of normal or transformed cultures of glial origin.

Stark KD, Krebs T, Altpeter E, Manz B, Griot C, Abelin T, Absence of
chronic effect of exposure to short-wave radio broadcast signal on
salivary melatonin concentrations in dairy cattle. *J Pineal Res* 22(4):171-
176, 1997.

A pilot study was conducted to investigate the influence of electromagnetic
fields in the short-wave range (3-30 MHz) radio transmitter signals on salivary
melatonin concentration in dairy cattle. The hypothesis to be tested was
whether EMF exposure would lower salivary melatonin concentrations, and
whether removal of the EMF source would be followed by higher concentration
levels. For this pilot study, a controlled intervention trial was designed. Two
commercial dairy herds at two farms were compared, one located at a distance
of 500 m (exposed), the other at a distance of 4,000 m (unexposed) from the
transmitter. At each farm, five cows were monitored with respect to their salivary
melatonin concentrations over a period of ten consecutive days. Saliva samples
were collected at two-hour intervals during the dark phase of the night. As an
additional intervention, the short-wave transmitter was switched off during
three of the ten days (off phase). The samples were analyzed using a
radioimmunoassay. The average nightly field strength readings were 21-fold
greater on the exposed farm (1.59 mA/m) than on the control farm (0.076 mA/m).
The mean values of the two initial nights did not show a statistically significant
difference between exposed and unexposed cows. Therefore, a chronic
melatonin reduction effect seemed unlikely. *However, on the first night of*
re-exposure after the transmitter had been off for three days, the difference
in salivary melatonin concentration between the two farms (3.89 pg/ml, CI:
2.04, 7.41) was statistically significant, indicating a two- to seven-fold
increase of melatonin concentration. Thus, a delayed acute effect of EMF
on melatonin concentration cannot completely be excluded. However,

results should be interpreted with caution and further trials are required in order to confirm the results.

Velizarov, S, Raskmark, P, Kwee, S, The effects of radiofrequency fields on cell proliferation are non-thermal. *Bioelectrochem Bioenerg* 48(1):177-180, 1999.

The number of reports on the effects induced by radiofrequency (RF) electromagnetic fields and microwave (MW) radiation in various cellular systems is still increasing. Until now no satisfactory mechanism has been proposed to explain the biological effects of these fields. One of the current theories is that heat generation by RF/MW is the cause, in spite of the fact that a great number of studies under isothermal conditions have reported significant cellular changes after exposure to RF/MW. Therefore, this study was undertaken to investigate which effect MW radiation from these fields in combination with a significant change of temperature could have on cell proliferation. The experiments were performed on the same cell line, and with the same exposure system as in a previous work [S. Kwee, P. Raskmark, Changes in cell proliferation due to environmental non-ionizing radiation: 2. Microwave radiation, Bioelectrochem. Bioenerg., 44 (1998), pp. 251-255]. The field was generated by signal simulation of the Global System for Mobile communications (GSM) of 960 MHz. Cell cultures, growing in microtiter plates, were exposed in a specially constructed chamber, a Transverse Electromagnetic (TEM) cell. The Specific Absorption Rate (SAR) value for each cell well was calculated for this exposure system. However, in this study the cells were exposed to the field at a higher or lower temperature than the temperature in the field-free incubator i.e., the temperature in the TEM cell was either 39 or 35 +/- 0.1 degrees C. The corresponding sham experiments were performed under exactly the same experimental conditions. The results showed that there was a significant change in cell proliferation in the exposed cells in comparison to the non-exposed (control) cells at both temperatures. On the other hand, no significant change in proliferation rate was found in the sham-exposed cells at both temperatures. This shows that biological effects due to RF/MW cannot be attributed only to a change of temperature. Since the RF/MW induced changes were of the same order of magnitude at both temperatures and also comparable to our previous results under isothermal conditions at 37 degrees C, cellular stress caused by electromagnetic fields could initiate the changes in cell cycle reaction rates. It is widely accepted that certain classes of heat-shock proteins are involved in these stress reactions.

Veyret B, Bouthet C, Deschaux P, de Seze R, Geffard M, Joussot-Dubien J, le Diraison M, Moreau JM, Caristan A, Antibody responses of mice exposed to low-power microwaves under combined, pulse-and-amplitude modulation. *Bioelectromagnetics* 12(1):47-56, 1991.

Irradiation by pulsed microwaves (9.4 GHz, 1 microsecond pulses at 1,000/s), both with and without concurrent amplitude modulation (AM) by a sinusoid at discrete frequencies between 14 and 41 MHz, was assessed for effects on the immune system of Balb/C mice. The mice were immunized either by sheep red blood cells (SRBC) or by glutaric-anhydride conjugated bovine serum albumin (GA-BSA), then exposed to the microwaves at a low rms power density (30 microW/cm2; whole-body-averaged SAR approximately 0.015 W/kg). Sham exposure or microwave irradiation took place during each of five contiguous days, 10 h/day. The antibody response was evaluated by the plaque-forming cell assay (SRBC experiment) or by the titration of IgM and IgG antibodies (GA-BSA experiment). In the absence of AM, the pulsed field did not greatly alter immune responsiveness. In contrast, exposure to the field under the combined-modulation condition resulted in significant, AM-frequency-dependent augmentation or weakening of immune responses.

Wolke S, Neibig U, Elsner R, Gollnick F, Meyer R, Calcium homeostasis of isolated heart muscle cells exposed to pulsed high-frequency electromagnetic fields. *Bioelectromagnetics* 17(2):144-153, 1996.

The intracellular calcium concentration ($[Ca(2+)]i$) of isolated ventricular cardiac myocytes of the guinea pig was measured during the application of pulsed high-frequency electromagnetic fields. The high-frequency fields were applied in a transverse electromagnetic cell designed to allow microscopic observation of the myocytes during the presence of the high-frequency fields. The $[Ca(2+)]i$ was measured as fura-2 fluorescence by means of digital image analysis. Both the carrier frequency and the square-wave pulse-modulation pattern were varied during the experiments (carrier frequencies: 900, 1,300, and 1,800 MHz pulse modulated at 217Hz with 14 percent duty cycle; pulsation pattern at 900 MHz: continuous wave, 16 Hz, and 50 Hz modulation with 50 percent duty cycle and 30 kHz modulation with 80 percent duty cycle). The mean specific absorption rate (SAR) values in the solution were within one order of magnitude of **1 mW/kg**. They varied depending on the applied carrier frequency and pulse pattern. The experiments were designed in three phases: 500 s of sham exposure, followed by 500 s of field exposure, then chemical stimulation without field. The chemical stimulation (K+ -depolarization) indicated the viability of the cells. The K+ depolarization yielded a significant increase in $[Ca(2+)]i$. Significant differences between sham exposure and high-frequency field exposure were not found except when a very small but statistically significant difference was detected in the case of 900 MHz/50 Hz. However, this small difference was not regarded as a relevant effect of the exposure.

Appendix C

II

106TH CONGRESS
1ST SESSION **S. 1538**

To amend the Communications Act of 1934 to clarify State and local authority to regulate the placement, construction, and modification of broadcast
transmission and telecommunications facilities, and for other purposes.

IN THE SENATE OF THE UNITED STATES

AUGUST 5, 1999

Mr. LEAHY (for himself, Mr. JEFFORDS, Mrs. HUTCHISON, Mr. FEINGOLD,
and Mr. MOYNIHAN) introduced the following bill; which was read twice
and referred to the Committee on Commerce, Science, and Transportation

A BILL

To amend the Communications Act of 1934 to clarify State
and local authority to regulate the placement, construction, and modification of broadcast transmission and telecommunications facilities, and for other purposes.

1   *Be it enacted by the Senate and House of Representa-*

2 *tives of the United States of America in Congress assembled,*

3 **SECTION 1. FINDINGS AND PURPOSES.**

4   (a) FINDINGS.—Congress makes the following find-

5 ings:

6   (1) The placement of telecommunications facili-

7   ties near residential properties can greatly reduce

3

1   (5) On August 19, 1997, the Federal Commu-
2   nications Commission issued a proposed rule, MM
3   Docket No. 97–182, which would preempt the appli-
4   cation of State and local zoning and land use ordi-
5   nances regarding the placement, construction, and
6   modification of broadcast transmission facilities. It
7   is in the interest of the Nation that the Commission
8   not adopt this rule.

9   (6) It is in the interest of the Nation that the
10   memoranda opinions and orders and proposed rules
11   of the Commission with respect to application of cer-
12   tain ordinances to the placement of such towers
13   (WT Docket No. 97–192, ET Docket No. 93–62,
14   RM–8577, and FCC 97–303, 62 F.R. 47960) be
15   modified in order to permit State and local govern-
16   ments to exercise their zoning and land use authori-
17   ties, and their power to protect public health and
18   safety, to regulate the placement of telecommuni-
19   cations or broadcast facilities and to place the bur-
20   den of proof in civil actions, and in actions before
21   the Commission and State and local authorities re-
22   lating to the placement, construction, and modifica-
23   tion of such facilities, on the person or entity that
24   seeks to place, construct, or modify such facilities.

5

1   of their representations, assertions, and promises to

2   governmental authorities.

3   (11) There has been a substantial effort by the

4   Federal Government to determine the effects of elec-

5   tric and magnetic fields on biological systems, as is

6   evidenced by the Electric and Magnetic Fields Re-

7   search   and   Public   Information   Dissemination

8   (RAPID) Program, which was established by section

9   2118 of the Energy Policy Act of 1992 (Public Law

10   102–486; 42 U.S.C. 13478). This five-year program,

11   which was coordinated by the National Institute of

12   Environmental Health Sciences and the Department

13   of Energy, examined the possible effects of electric

14   and magnetic fields on human health. Despite the

15   success of this program, there has been no similar

16   effort by the Federal Government to determine the

17   possible effects on human health of radio frequency

18   emissions associated with telecommunications facili-

19   ties. The RAPID program could serve as the excel-

20   lent   model   for   a   Federally-sponsored   research

21   project.

22   (b) PURPOSES.—The purposes of this Act are as fol-

23   lows:

24   (1) To repeal certain limitations on State and

25   local authority regarding the placement, construc-

7

1 record of hearings for such permits, licenses, or

2 approvals.

3 **SEC. 2. STATE AND LOCAL AUTHORITY OVER PLACEMENT,**

4 **CONSTRUCTION, AND MODIFICATION OF**

5 **TELECOMMUNICATIONS FACILITIES.**

6 (a) REPEAL OF LIMITATIONS ON REGULATION OF

7 PERSONAL WIRELESS FACILITIES.—Section 332(c)(7)(B)

8 of the Communications Act of 1934 (47 U.S.C.

9 332(c)(7)(B)) is amended—

10 (1) in clause (i), by striking "thereof—" and all

11 that follows through the end and inserting "thereof

12 shall not unreasonably discriminate among providers

13 of functionally equivalent services.";

14 (2) by striking clause (iv);

15 (3) by redesignating clause (v) as clause (iv);

16 and

17 (4) in clause (iv), as so redesignated—

18 (A) in the first sentence, by striking "30

19 days after such action or failure to act" and in-

20 serting "30 days after exhaustion of any admin-

21 istrative remedies with respect to such action or

22 failure to act"; and

23 (B) by striking the third sentence and in-

24 serting the following: "In any such action in

25 which a person seeking to place, construct, or

9

1 ner that is inconsistent with State or local law, or contrary

2 to an official decision of the appropriate State or local gov-

3 ernment entity having authority to approve, permit, li-

4 cense, modify, or deny an application to place, construct,

5 or modify a tower, if alternate technology is capable of

6 delivering the broadcast or telecommunications signals

7 without the use of a tower.

8 "(b) AUTHORITY REGARDING PRODUCTION OF SAFE-

9 TY AND INTERFERENCE STUDIES.—No provision of this

10 Act may be interpreted to prohibit a State or local govern-

11 ment from—

12 "(1) requiring a person or entity seeking au-

13 thority to place, construct, or modify telecommuni-

14 cations facilities or broadcast transmission facilities

15 within the jurisdiction of such government to

16 produce—

17 "(A) environmental studies, engineering re-

18 ports, or other documentation of the compliance

19 of such facilities with radio frequency exposure

20 limits established by the Commission and com-

21 pliance with applicable laws and regulations

22 governing the effects of the proposed facility on

23 the health, safety, and welfare of local residents

24 in the community; and

11

1 sessment through grants to appropriate public and private

2 entities selected by the Secretary for purposes of the inde-

3 pendent assessment.

4   (b). AUTHORIZATION OF APPROPRIATIONS.—There

5 are hereby authorized to be appropriated for the Secretary

6 of Health and Human Services for fiscal year 2000,

7 $10,000,000 for purposes of grants for the independent

8 assessment required by subsection (a). Amounts appro-

9 priated pursuant to the authorization of appropriation in

10 the preceding sentence shall remain available until ex-

11 pended.

12   (c) The Secretary of Health and Human Services

13 shall produce a report on existing research evaluating the

14 biological effects to human health of short term, high-level,

15 as well as long-term, low-level exposures to radio frequency

16 emissions to Congress no later than January 1, 2001.

○

TOWN OF CABOT

PROPOSED AMENDMENT TO ZONING REGULATIONS
FOR
NEW TELECOMMUNICATIONS
FACILITIES AND TOWERS BYLAW

PRESENTED BY THISTLE HILL NEIGHBORHOOD ALLIANCE

August 22, 1997

As Amended by the Cabot Planning Commission December 9, 1997
After Consultation With Mark Hutchins, Telecommunications Engineer

ARTICLE V

Telecommunication Facilities and Towers Article

SECTION 5.1   PURPOSE

The purpose of this Article is to:
A. Preserve the character and appearance of the Town of Cabot while allowing adequate telecommunications services to be developed.
B. Protect the scenic, historic, environmental, and natural or human resources of Cabot.
C. Provide standards and requirements for the regulation, placement, design, appearance, construction, monitoring, modification and removal of telecommunication facilities and towers.
D. Preserve property values, and protect scenic areas within the town.
E. Locate towers and/or antennas in a manner which promotes the general safety, health, welfare and quality of life of the citizens of Cabot and all those who visit this community.
F. Require the sharing of existing communications facilities, towers, and sites where possible.

SECTION 5.2   CONSISTENCY WITH FEDERAL LAW

These regulations are intended to be consistent with state and federal law, particularly the Telecommunications Act of 1996 in that: a) they do not prohibit or have the effect of prohibiting the provision of personal wireless services; b) they are not intended to be used to unreasonably discriminate among providers of functionally equivalent services, and; c) they do not regulate personal wireless services on the basis of the environmental effects of radio frequency emissions to the extent that the regulated services and facilities comply with the regulations of the Federal Communications Commission concerning such emissions. A finding that a particular portion of this article is not in accordance with any state or federal law shall only affect the validity of that portion of the article.

SECTION 5.3   DEFINITIONS AND WORD USAGE

The following terms shall have the meanings indicated. The word "shall" or "will" indicate mandatory requirements: "may" is advisory and indicates recommendations which are not mandatory.

ADEQUATE COVERAGE - Coverage is considered to be "adequate" within that area surrounding a base station where the predicted or measured median field strength of the transmitted signal is such that the majority of the time, transceivers properly installed and operated will be able to communicate with the base station without objectionable noise (or excessive bit-error-rate for digital) and without calls being dropped. In the case of cellular communications in a rural environment like Cabot, this would be a signal strength of at least -90dbm. It is acceptable for there to be holes within the area of

1

adequate coverage as long as the signal regains its strength further away from the base station. For the limited purpose of determining whether the use of a repeater is necessary or desirable, there shall be deemed not to be adequate coverage within said holes. The outer boundary of the area of adequate coverage, however, is that location past which the signal does not regain.

ADEQUATE CAPACITY - Capacity is considered to be "adequate" if the grade of service is p.05 or better for at least 50% of the days in a preceding month, prior to the date of application, as measured using direct traffic measurement of the telecommunications facility in question, where the call blocking is due to frequency contention at the antenna(s).

ANTENNA - A device which is attached to a tower, or other structure for transmitting and receiving electromagnetic waves.

AVAILABLE SPACE - The space on a tower or structure to which antennas of a telecommunications provider are both structurally able and electromagnetically able to be attached.

BASE STATION - The primary sending and receiving site in a wireless telecommunications network. More than one base station and/or more than one variety of telecommunications provider can be located on a single tower or structure.

BULLETIN 65 - Published by the FCC Office of Engineering and Technology specifying radiofrequency radiation levels and methods to determine compliance.

CHANNEL - The segment of the radiation spectrum from an antenna which carries one signal. An antenna may radiate on many channels simultaneously.

COMMUNICATION EQUIPMENT SHELTER - A structure located at a base station designed principally to enclose equipment used in connection with telecommunications transmissions.

dBm - Unit of measure of the power level of an electromagnetic signal expressed in decibels referenced to 1 milliwatt.

ELECTROMAGNETICALLY ABLE - The determination that the new signal from and to the proposed new antennas will not significantly interfere with the existing signals from and to other facilities located on the same tower or structure as determined by a qualified professional telecommunications engineer. The use of available technologies to alleviate such interference shall be considered when making this determination.

FACILITY SITE - A property, or any part thereof, which is owned or leased by one or more telecommunications providers and upon which one or more telecommunications facility(s) and required landscaping are located.

FCC - Federal Communications Commission. The government agency responsible for regulating telecommunications in the United States.

FCC 97-303 - A report and order which sets new national standards for exposure to radio-frequency emissions from FCC-regulated transmitters.

GHz - GigaHertz: One billion Hertz.

GRADE OF SERVICE - A measure of the percentage of calls which are able to connect to the base station, during the busiest hour of the day. Grade of service is expressed as a number, such as p.05 - which means that 95% of callers will connect on their first try. A lower number (p.04) indicates a better grade of service.

2

HERTZ - One Hertz is the frequency of an electric or magnetic field which reverses polarity once each second, or one cycle per second.

LOCATION - References to site location as the exact longitude and latitude, to the nearest tenth of a second with bearing or orientation referenced to true North.

MAJOR MODIFICATION OF AN EXISTING FACILITY - Any change, or proposed change in power input or output, number of antennas, change in antenna type or model, repositioning of antenna(s),or change in number of channels per antenna above the maximum number approved under an existing conditional use permit.

MAJOR MODIFICATION OF AN EXISTING TOWER - Any change, or proposed change in dimensions of an existing and permitted tower or other structure designed to support telecommunications transmission, receiving and/or relaying antennas and/or equipment.

MHz - MegaHertz: One million Hertz.

MONITORING - The measurement, by the use of instruments in the field, of non-ionizing radiation exposure at a site as a whole, or from individual telecommunications facilities, towers, antennas or repeaters.

MONITORING PROTOCOL - The testing protocol, such as the Cobbs Protocol, (or one substantially similar, including compliance determined in accordance with the National Council on Radiation Protection and Measurements, Reports 86 and 119) which is to be used to monitor the emissions and determine exposure risk from existing and new telecommunications facilities upon adoption of this article.

MONOPOLE - A single self-supporting vertical pole with no guy wire anchors, usually consisting of a galvanized or other unpainted metal, or a wooden pole with below grade foundations.

PERSONAL WIRELESS SERVICES - Commercial mobile services, unlicensed wireless services, and common carrier wireless exchange access services. These services include: cellular services, personal communications services, specialized mobile radio services, and paging services.

RADIAL PLOTS - Radial plots are the result of drawing equally-spaced lines (radials) from the point of the antenna, calculating the expected signal and indicating this graphically on a map. The relative signal strength may be indicated by varying the size or color at each point being studied along the radial; a threshold plot uses a mark to indicate whether that point is strong enough to provide adequate coverage - i.e., the points meeting the threshold of adequate coverage. The drawback is the concentration of points close to the antenna and the divergence of points far from the site near the ends of the radials.

RADIATED-SIGNAL PROPAGATION STUDIES OR COVERAGE PLOTS - Computer generated estimates of the signal emanating, and prediction of coverage, from antennas or repeaters sited on a specific tower or structure. The height above ground, power input and output, frequency output, type of antenna, antenna gain, topography of the site and its surroundings are all taken into account to create these simulations. They are the primary tool for determining whether a site will provide adequate coverage for the telecommunications facility proposed for that site.

REPEATER - A small receiver/relay transmitter of relatively low power output designed to provide service to areas which are not able to receive adequate coverage directly from a base or primary station.

3

STRUCTURALLY ABLE - The determination that a tower or structure is capable of carrying the load imposed by the proposed new antennas under all reasonably predictable conditions as determined by professional structure engineering analysis.

TELECOMMUNICATIONS FACILITY - All equipment (including repeaters) with which a telecommunications provider broadcasts and receives the radiofrequency waves which carry their services and all locations of said equipment or any part thereof. This facility may be sited on one or more towers or structure(s) owned and permitted by another owner or entity.

TELECOMMUNICATIONS PROVIDER - An entity, licensed by the FCC to provide telecommunications services to individuals or institutions.

TILED COVERAGE PLOTS – Tiled plots result from calculating the signal at uniformly spaced locations on a rectangular grid, or tile, of the area of concern. Unlike radial plots, tiled plots provide a uniform distribution of points over the area of interest; usually the same grid will be used as different sites are examined, and it is not necessary that the transmitter site be within the grid or area of interest. As with radial plots, the graphic display or plot can be either signal strength or adequate threshold. This method requires substantially more topographic data and longer (computer) execution time than radial plots, but is preferable for comparative analysis.

TOWER - A lattice structure or framework, either self-supporting or guyed, or monopole, that is designed to support telecommunications transmission, receiving and/or relaying antennas and/or equipment.

SECTION 5.4 EXEMPTIONS

The following wireless telecommunications facilities are exempt: police, fire, ambulance and other emergency dispatch; amateur (ham) radio; citizens band radio; any existing commercial radio tower; and radio dispatch services for local businesses. No personal wireless service facility shall be considered exempt from this article for any reason whether or not said facility is proposed to share a tower or other structure with such exempt uses.

SECTION 5.5 PROVISION FOR HIRING INDEPENDENT CONSULTANTS

A. Upon submission of an application for a conditional use permit under this article, the Cabot zoning board of adjustment and/or the Cabot planning commission may hire independent consultants whose services shall be paid for by the town. These consultants shall be qualified professionals with an appropriate combination of training, record of service, and/or certification in one of the following fields: a) telecommunications/radiofrequency engineering; b) structural engineering; c) assessment of electromagnetic fields; and, if determined necessary by the Cabot zoning board of adjustment and/or planning commission, d) other fields.

B. Upon submission of a complete application for a conditional use permit under this article, the Cabot zoning board of adjustment and/or planning commission may provide its independent consultant(s) with the full application for their analysis and review.

4

SECTION 5.6   FINDINGS OF THE ZONING BOARD OF ADJUSTMENT

A. **Conditional Uses:** No tower or telecommunications facility shall be erected, constructed, or installed without first obtaining a conditional use permit from Cabot zoning board of adjustment. A conditional use permit is required for: a) new tower construction (or major modification of an existing towers); b) telecommunications facilities (or major modification of existing facilities) to be mounted on a tower or structure.

B. **Applicable Bylaws:** In acting on the conditional use permit application, the Cabot zoning board of adjustment shall proceed in accordance with Section 2.7 of the Cabot zoning regulations (conditional uses).

C. **Findings:** All applicable conditions in the following sections 5.7 and 5.8 of this article shall be substantially complied with. In addition, Cabot zoning board of adjustment shall in consultation with independent consultant(s), make all of the following applicable findings before granting the conditional use permit:

1. Applicant is not already providing adequate coverage and/or adequate capacity to the town of Cabot;

2. Applicant is not able to use existing tower/facility sites either with or without the use of repeaters to provide adequate coverage and/or adequate capacity to the town of Cabot;

3 Applicant has endeavored to provide adequate coverage and adequate capacity to the town of Cabot with the least number of towers and antennas which is technically and economically feasible;

4. Efforts have been made to locate new towers adjacent to existing towers;

5. Applicant has agreed to rent or lease available space on the tower, under the terms of a fair-market lease, with reasonable conditions and without discrimination to other telecommunications providers;

6. Proposed telecommunications facility or tower should make use of available municipal lands and suitable existing municipal and privately owned structures;

7. The proposal shall comply with rules as adopted in FCC 97-303 and procedures outlined in FCC Bulletin 65 regarding emissions and exposure from electromagnetic radiation and that the required monitoring program has been developed and shall be paid for by the applicant;

8. Towers and telecommunications facilities shall be located so as to minimize the following potential impacts:

   a. Visual/Aesthetic: Towers shall, when possible, be sited off ridge lines, and where their visual impact is least detrimental to highly rated scenic areas. In determining whether or not a tower will have an undue adverse visual impact on the scenic or natural beauty of a ridge or hillside, the board shall consider:

      i. The period of time during which the proposed tower would be viewed by the traveling public on a public highway;

      ii. The frequency of the view of the proposed tower as experienced by the traveling public;

5

        iii. The degree to which the view of the tower is screened by topographic features;

        iv. Background features in the line of sight to the proposed tower that obscure the facility or make it more conspicuous;

        v. The distance of the proposed tower from the viewing vantage point and the proportion of the facility that is visible above the skyline;

        vi. The number of vehicles traveling on a public highway or waterway at or near the critical vantage point;

        vii. The sensitivity or unique value of the particular view affected by the proposed development.

    b. Devaluation of property values. Siting shall be in as low population density areas as possible.

    c. Safety hazards: In cases of structural failure, ice accumulation and discharge, and attractive nuisance.

    d. Electromagnetic radiation: In case the tower, guys wires or telecommunications facility is found to exceed the FCC guidelines.

D. **Documentation of Denial**: Any decision by the Cabot zoning board of adjustment to deny an application for a conditional use permit under this article shall be in conformance with 47 U.S.C. §332 (7)(B)(iii) of the Act, in that it shall be in writing and supported by substantial evidence contained in a written record.

SECTION 5.7   GENERAL PROJECT REQUIREMENTS

A. **Access Roads and Above Ground Utilities:** Where new telecommunications towers and facilities require construction of or improvement to access roads, to the extent practicable, roads shall follow the contour of the land, and be constructed or improved within existing forest or forest fringe areas, and not in open fields. Utility or service lines shall be designed and located so as to minimize or prevent disruption to the scenic character or beauty of the area.

B. **Landscaping/Screening:** Screening shall be required at the perimeter of the site. A natural or planted vegetative screen of a minimum of 20 feet in depth and 6 feet in height shall be maintained at all times. Vegetation shall be of a type that has the potential to reach a height of at least 15 feet at maturity. Existing vegetation surrounding the site shall be preserved and maintained to the greatest extent possible. Applicant shall obtain a financial surety to cover the cost of the remediation of any damage to the landscape which occurs during the clearing of the site.

C. **Fencing and Signs:** The area around the tower and communication equipment shelter(s) shall be completely fenced for security to a height of six feet and gated. Use of razor wire is not permitted. A sign no greater than two (2) square feet indicating the name of the facility owner(s) and a 24 hour emergency telephone number, either local or toll-free, shall be posted adjacent to the entry gate. In addition, No Trespassing or other warning signs, and the federal tower registration plate, where applicable, may be posted on the fence or as required to meet federal requirements.

D. **Building Design:** Communication equipment shelters and accessory buildings shall be designed to be architecturally similar and compatible with each other, and shall be no more than 12 feet high. The buildings shall be used only for the housing of equipment related to this particular site. Whenever possible, the buildings shall be joined or clustered so as to appear as one building.

E. **Height of Towers:** New towers shall not exceed the minimum height necessary to provide adequate coverage for the telecommunications facilities proposed for use on the tower. Applicant may submit a request for additional height to accommodate future sharing, or to provide indirect service as described in Section 5.8, A, 3, and shall provide design information to justify such additional height. Repeaters shall not be closer than 25 feet to the ground.

F. **Tower Finish:** New towers shall have a galvanized finish unless otherwise required. The Cabot zoning board of adjustment may require the tower(s) to be painted or otherwise camouflaged to minimize the adverse visual impact.

G. **Tower Sharing:** Tower(s) must be of a type which will maximize potential sharing. Lattice type structures are preferred, but where a monopole is required, applicant must demonstrate the future utility of such structure for expansion of service for applicant and other future applicants.

H. **Use of Repeaters:** The use of repeaters to assure adequate coverage, or to fill holes within areas of otherwise adequate coverage, while minimizing the number of required towers is permitted and encouraged. Applicants shall detail the number, location, power output, and coverage of any proposed repeaters in their systems and provide engineering data to justify their use.

I. **Coverage Area:** If primary coverage (greater than 50%) from proposed telecommunications facility is outside Cabot, then the permit may be denied unless the applicant can demonstrate an inability to locate within the town which is primarily receiving service from the proposed facility.

J. **Commercial Advertising** shall not be allowed on any antenna, tower, or accessory building or communication equipment shelter.

K. **Lighting:** No external lighting is permitted, except for manually operated emergency lights for use only when operating personnel are on site.

L. **Air Navigation:** No tower or telecommunications facility that would be classified as a hazard to air navigation, as defined by the Federal Aviation regulations (Title 14 CFR) is permitted.

M. **Setback Requirements:** No repeater shall be located closer than 100' to a dwelling unit, nor closer than 25' to the ground. No other telecommunications facility or tower, including guy-wire anchors and protective fencing, if any, shall be located:

    1. Closer than 300' horizontally to any boundary of the site on which the tower is located.

    2. Closer than 1,500' horizontally to any structure existing at the time of application which is used as a primary or secondary residence, to the property of any school (both public and private), or to any other public building. Primary or secondary residences are those dwelling units that include toilet facilities, and facilities for food preparation and sleeping.

3. Within the habitat of any state-listed rare or endangered wildlife or plant species;
4. Within 200' horizontally of any Vermont or federally regulated wetland;
5. Within the 200' horizontally of the outer riparian zone measured horizontally from any river or perennial stream;
6. Within 1,500' horizontally of any historic district or property listed on the state or Federal Register of Historic Places;
7. Within 500' horizontally of any known archaeological site.

SECTION 5.8   REQUIRED DOCUMENTATION

A. **Evidence of Need:**
1. **Existing Coverage:** Applicant shall provide written documentation demonstrating that existing telecommunications facility Sites and other existing structures of suitable height in Cabot, in abutting towns, and within a 30 mile radius of the proposed site cannot reasonably be made to provide adequate coverage and/or adequate capacity to the town of Cabot. The documentation shall include, for each facility site listed which is owned or operated by the applicant, the exact location (in longitude and latitude, to degrees, minutes and seconds to the nearest tenth), ground elevation, height of tower or structure, type of antennas, antenna gain, height of antennas on tower or structure, output frequency, number of channels, power input and maximum power output per channel. Potential adjustments to these existing facility sites, including changes in antenna type, orientation, gain, height or power output shall be specified. Radial or tiled coverage plots showing each of these facility sites, as they exist, and with adjustments as above, shall be provided as part of the application.
2. **Repeaters:** Applicant shall demonstrate with written documentation that they have analyzed the feasibility of repeaters in conjunction with all facility sites listed in compliance with 5.8. A. 1 (above) to provide adequate coverage and/or adequate capacity to the town of Cabot. Radial or tiled coverage plots of all repeaters considered for use in conjunction with these facility sites shall be provided as part of the application.
3. **Indirect Service:** Applicant shall demonstrate which portion of a tower or structure and which antennas, if any, are to reduce or eliminate reliance on land-lines, or otherwise provide communications capability to the applicant, as opposed to providing direct service to customers. Such provision of indirect service may be considered if reasonable alternatives are not available and the incremental effect is consistent with the purposes set forth in Section 5.1 of this article.
4. **Five Year Plan:** All applications shall be accompanied by a written five-year plan for the utilization of the proposed facilities. This plan should include justification for capacity in excess of immediate needs, as well as plans for any further development within the town.

B. **Legal and Technical Documentation for Telecommunications Towers and Facilities:**
1. **Federal Permits:** Applicant shall submit copies of all pertinent submittals and showings pertaining to: FCC permitting/licensing; Environmental Assessments

8

and Environmental Impact Statements; FAA Notice of Construction or Alteration; aeronautical studies; all pertinent data, assumptions and calculations relating to service coverage; and all pertinent calculations and/or measurement data related to non-ionizing radiation emissions and exposure, regardless of whether categorical exemption from routine environmental evaluation under the FCC rules is claimed.

2. **Contacts:** Applicant shall submit the exact legal name, address or principal place of business and phone number of the following:
   a. Applicant. If any applicant is not a natural person, it shall also give the type of business entity and the state in which it is registered.
   b. Person to whom correspondence or communications in regard to the application are to be sent. Notice, orders and other papers may be served upon the person so named, and such service shall be deemed to be service upon the applicant.
   c. Person to be contacted in the event of an emergency involving the facility. This should be someone available on a 24-hour basis who is authorized by the applicant to act on behalf of the applicant regarding an emergency situation.
   d. Owner of the property on which the proposed tower shall be located, and of the owner(s) of the tower or structure on which the proposed facility shall be located. Written permission of the owner(s) to apply for a conditional use permit shall also be submitted along with written permission from the owner(s) of the proposed property(s) or facilities site(s) for the town's independent consultant(s), to conduct any necessary site visit(s).
   e. Names and addresses of the record owners of all abutting properties.

3. **Surety:** Details of proposed method of financial surety as required in Sections 5.7.b (Landscaping/Screening) and 5.10 (Removal Requirements) of this article.

4. **Commitment to Available Space:** Applicants for new tower construction or modification permits shall provide a written, irrevocable commitment valid for the duration of the existence of the tower, to rent or lease available space for collocation on the tower at fair market prices and terms, without discrimination to other telecommunications providers.

5. **Lease of Tower:** Applicants for a conditional use permit for a facility to be installed on an existing structure shall provide a copy of its lease/contract with the owner of the existing structure.

6. **Contract with Provider:** Applicants for a telecommunications tower or facility conditional use permit must be a telecommunications provider or must provide a copy of its lease/contract with an existing telecommunications provider. A conditional use permit shall not be granted for a tower to be built on speculation.

7. **Plans and Maps:** Required physical plant plans, prepared, stamped and signed by a professional engineer licensed to practice in Vermont. Survey plans shall be stamped and signed by a land surveyor registered in Vermont. Signal propagation and radio-frequency studies, plots and related material shall be prepared, clearly identified and signed by a qualified radiofrequency engineer. Plans shall be on

9

24" x 36" sheets, on as many sheets as necessary, and at scales which are no smaller (i.e. no less precise) than listed below. Each plan sheet shall have a title block indicating the project title, sheet title, sheet number, date, revision dates, scale(s), and original seal(s) and signature(s) of the professional(s) who prepared the plan.

a. **Location Map:** Copy of a portion of the most recent U.S.G.S. Quadrangle map, at a scale of 1:25,000, and showing the area within at least two miles from the proposed tower site. Indicate the tower location and the exact latitude and longitude (degrees, minutes and seconds to the nearest tenth).

b. **Vicinity Map** at a scale of 1" = 416' (1:5000) with contour intervals no greater than 10 feet (3 meter) showing the entire vicinity within a 2500' radius of the tower site, and including the topography, public and private roads and driveways, buildings and structures, bodies of water, wetlands, landscape features, historic sites, habitats for endangered species. Indicate the property lines of the proposed tower site parcel and of all abutters to the tower site parcel, (from assessors maps or available surveys). Indicate any access easement or right of way needed for access from a public way to the tower, and the names of all abutters or property owners along the access easement or who have deeded rights to the easement.

c. **Existing Conditions Plan:** A recent survey of the area within 500 feet of the tower site at a scale no smaller than 1" = 40' (1:480 or metric equivalent 1:500) with topography drawn with a minimum of 10' (3 meter) contour intervals, showing existing utilities, property lines, existing buildings or structures, stone walls or fence lines, wooded areas, existing water wells and springs. Show the boundary of any wetlands or floodplains or watercourses, and of any bodies of water included in the Watershed Protection District within 500' from the tower or any related facilities or access ways or appurtenances. The survey plan must have been completed, on the ground, by a land surveyor (registered in Vermont) within two years prior to the application date.

d. **Proposed Site Plans:** Proposed facility site layout, grading and utilities at the same scale or larger than the existing conditions plan.
    i. Proposed tower location and any appurtenances, including supports and guy wires, if any, and any accessory building (communication equipment shelter or other). Indicate property boundaries and setback distances to the base(s) of the tower and to the nearest corners of each of the appurtenant structures to those boundaries, and dimensions of all proposed improvements. Where protective fencing is proposed, indicate setback distances from the edge of the fencing.
    ii. Indicate proposed spot elevations at the base of the proposed tower and at the base of any guy wires, and the corners of all appurtenant structures.

    iii. Proposed utilities, including distance from source of power, sizes of
        service available and required, locations of any proposed utility of
        communication lines, and whether underground or above ground.
        Detailed plans for emergency power generation, including:
        1. Demonstration of percent of electrical demand being proposed
           in event of loss of commercial power.
        2. Type of fuel, storage method, and expected means and
           frequency of fuel delivery to the site for power generation.
        3. Amount of generator time based on historical power reliability
           for the area of the facility, proposed frequency and duration
           of tests, and description of muffler system and methods for
           noise abatement.
        4. Feasibility of wind and/or solar power in conjunction with
           storage batteries.
    iv. Any direct or indirect wetlands alteration proposed.
    v. Detailed plans for drainage of surface and/or sub-surface water; plans
       to control erosion and sedimentation both during construction and
       as a permanent measure.
    vi. Plans indicating locations and specifics of proposed screening,
       landscaping, ground cover, fencing, etc.; any exterior light or
       signs.
    vii. Plans of proposed access driveway or roadway and parking area at the
       tower site. Include grading, drainage, traveled width. Include a
       cross section of the access drive indicating the width, depth of
       gravel, paving or surface materials.
    viii Plans showing any changes to be made to an existing facility's
       landscaping, screening, fencing, lighting, drainage, wetlands,
       grading, driveways or roadways, parking, or other infrastructure as
       a result of a proposed modification of the facility.

e. **Proposed Tower and Appurtenances:**
    i. Plans, elevations, sections and details at appropriate scales but no
      smaller than 1" = 10'.
    ii. Two cross sections through proposed tower drawn at right angles to
      each other, and showing the ground profile to at least 100 feet
      beyond the limit of clearing, and showing any guy wires or
      supports. Dimension the proposed height of tower above average
      grade at tower base. Show all proposed antennas, including their
      location on the tower.
    iii. Details of proposed tower foundation, including cross sections and
      details. Show all ground attachments, specifications for anchor
      bolts and other anchoring hardware.
    iv. Detail proposed exterior finish of the tower.

v. Indicate relative height of the tower to the tops of surrounding trees as they presently exist, and the height to which they are expected to grow in ten years.

vi. Illustration of the modular structure of the proposed tower indicating the heights of sections which could be removed or added in the future to adapt to changing communications conditions or demands.

vii. A professional structural engineer's written description of the proposed tower structure and its capacity to support additional antennas or other communications facilities at different heights and the ability of the tower to be shortened if future communications facilities no longer require the original height.

viii. A description of available space on the tower, providing illustrations and examples of the type and number of telecommunications facilities which could be mounted on the structure.

f. **Plans of Proposed Communications Equipment Shelter** including 1) Floor plans, elevations and cross sections at a scale of no smaller than 1/4" = 1' (1:48) of any proposed appurtenant structure, and 2) Representative elevation views, indicating the roof, facades, doors and other exterior appearance and materials.

g. **Proposed Equipment Plan:**

i. Plans, elevations, sections and details at appropriate scales but no smaller than 1" = 10'.

ii. Number of antennas and repeaters, as well as the exact locations, of antenna(s) and of all repeaters (if any) located on a map as well as by degrees, minutes and seconds to the nearest tenth of latitude and longitude.

iii. Mounting locations on tower or structure, including height above ground.

Iv A recent survey of the facility site at a scale no smaller than 1" = 40' (1:480 or metric equivalent 1:500) showing horizontal and radial distances of antenna(s) to nearest point on property line, and to the nearest dwelling unit

v. Antenna type(s), manufacturer(s), model number(s).

vi. For each antenna, the antenna gain and antenna radiation pattern.

vii. Number of channels per antenna, projected and maximum.

viii. Power input to the antenna(s).

ix. Power output, in normal use and at maximum output for each antenna and all antennas as an aggregate.

x. Output frequency of the transmitter(s).

xi. For modification of an existing facility with multiple emitters, the results of an intermodulation study to predict the interaction of the additional equipment with existing equipment.

h. **Visibility Maps:**

12

i. A minimum of eight (8) view lines in a zero (0) to two (2) mile radius from the site, shown beginning at True North and continuing clock-wise at forty-five degree intervals.

ii. A map of the town of Cabot on which any visibility of the proposed tower from a public way (including all existing public rights of way) shall be indicated.

j. **Balloon Test.** Within 35 days of submitting an application, applicant shall arrange to fly, or raise upon a temporary mast, a three foot diameter brightly colored balloon at the maximum height of the tower and within fifty horizontal feet of the center of the proposed tower. The date time and location of this balloon test shall be advertised by the applicant, at 7 and 14 days in advance of the test date in *The Hardwick Gazette, The Times Argus* and *The Caledonia Record.* The applicant shall inform the Cabot zoning board of adjustment, the planning commission, and abutting property owners in writing, of the dates and times of the test, at least 14 days in advance. The balloon shall be flown for at least four consecutive hours sometime between 9:00 a.m. and 5:00 p.m. of the dates chosen.

k. **Visual Analysis.** The applicant shall develop and submit a written analysis of the visual impact of the proposed tower. This analysis shall include photographs of the balloon test taken from at least 10 different perspectives within the Town of Cabot.

SECTION 5.9   MONITORING AND EVALUATION OF COMPLIANCE

A. **Monitoring Protocol**: The planning commission may, as the technology changes, require and accept the use of testing protocols other than the Cobbs Protocol. A copy of the monitoring protocol shall be on file with the board of selectmen and the town clerk.

B. **Pre-testing:** After the granting of a conditional use permit and before applicant's telecommunications facilities begin transmission, the applicant shall submit a report, prepared by an independent qualified telecommunications or radiofrequency engineer, on the background levels of non-ionizing radiofrequency radiation around the proposed facility site and/or any repeater locations to be utilized for applicant's telecommunications facilities. The independent engineer shall use the monitoring protocol, or one substantially similar. This report shall be submitted to the board of selectmen, zoning administrative officer, the planning commission, and the town clerk.

C. **Post-testing:** After transmission begins, the owner(s) of any telecommunications facility(s) located on any facility site shall submit reports prepared by an independent qualified telecommunications or radiofrequency engineer regarding any non-ionizing radiofrequency radiation emission or exposure from said site, and to report results as follows:

1. There shall be routine annual monitoring of emissions/exposure by the independent engineer using actual field measurement of radiation, utilizing the monitoring protocol. This monitoring shall measure levels of non-ionizing radiofrequency radiation exposure at the facility site as well as from repeaters (if any). A report

of the monitoring results shall be prepared by the independent engineer and submitted to the board of selectmen, the Cabot zoning board of adjustment, the planning commission, the town clerk, and abutting property owners.

2. Any major modification of existing facility, or the activation of any additional permitted channels, shall require new monitoring.

D. **Excessive Exposure:** Should the monitoring of a facility site reveal that the site exceeds the current FCC standard and guidelines, the owner(s) of all facilities utilizing that site shall be so notified. In accordance with FCC requirements, the owner(s) must immediately reduce power or cease operation as necessary to protect persons having access to the site, tower or antennas. Additionally, the owner(s) shall submit to the Cabot zoning board of adjustment and the zoning administrator a plan for the correction of the situation that resulted in excessive exposure. Failure to act as described above shall be a violation of the conditional use permit and violations are subject to penalties as provided by Section 2.5 of these regulations.

E. **Structural Inspection:** Tower owner(s) shall arrange for an independent consultant (a licensed professional structural engineer), to conduct inspections of the tower's structural integrity and safety. Guyed towers shall be inspected every three years. Monopoles and non-guyed lattice towers shall be inspected every five years. A report of the inspection results shall be prepared by the independent consultant and submitted to the board of selectmen, Cabot zoning board of adjustment, the planning commission and the town clerk. Any major modification of existing facility which includes changes to tower dimensions or antenna numbers or type shall require new structural inspection.

F. **Unsafe Structure:** Should the inspection of any tower reveal any structural defect(s) which, in the opinion of the independent consultant render(s) that tower unsafe, the following actions must be taken. Within 10 business days of notification of unsafe structure, the owner(s) of the tower shall submit a plan to remediate the structural defect(s). This plan shall be initiated within 10 days of the submission of the remediation plan, and completed as soon as reasonably possible. Failure to accomplish this remediation of structural defect(s) within 10 business days of initial notification shall be a violation of the conditional use permit and subject to penalties as specified in Section 2.5 of these regulations.

SECTION 5.10   REMOVAL REQUIREMENTS

Any telecommunications facility which ceases to operate for a period of one year shall be removed. Cease to operate is defined as not performing the permitted functions associated with the telecommunications facility and its equipment on a continuous and ongoing basis for a period of one year. At the time of removal, the facility site shall be remediated such that all telecommunications facility improvements which have ceased to be utilized are removed. If all facilities on a tower have ceased to operate, the tower shall also be removed, and the site shall be revegetated. Existing trees shall only be removed if necessary to complete the required removal. Applicant shall, as a condition of the conditional use permit provide a financial surety bond payable to the town of Cabot and acceptable to the Cabot zoning board of adjustment to cover the cost of removal of the telecommunications facility and the remediation of the landscape, should the facility cease to operate.

SECTION 5.11   FEES

A schedule of fees for towers and telecommunications facilities permitting and renewal, any monitoring of exposure and inspection of structures, and any other fees shall be established by the Cabot board of selectmen as provided for in 24 V.S.A. §1446. This schedule may be amended from time to time.

SECTION 5.12   SEVERABILITY CLAUSE

The invalidity of any section or provision of this article shall not invalidate any other section or provision hereof.

Suggested Field Test Protocol For Comprehensive EMF Assessment of Telecommunications Transmitter Sites - By C.A. Cobbs

EMF Parameter to be Assessed	Suggested Test Equipment	Suggested Method or Technique	Comments
Broadband Radio Frequency Field Density	Broadband RF Survey Meter with Isotropic, omnidirectional probe (Holaday Instruments, HP/Agilent, etc.)	Record pre-existing conditions and repeat post-installation. Probe sensor should be tripod-mounted (non-metallic) using fiber optic cables to eliminate possible coupling effects between probe and operator.	A hand-held Global Positioning Satellite Receiver (GPS) should be used to position all readings. Make measurements at 1m above ground. Flag all 'Hot Spots' or 'nulls' in signal density/intensity.
Broadband Spectrum Analysis Covering the Frequency Range of 60Hz to 3GHz.	HP/Agilent E4402B ESA-E Series SpectrumAnalyzer or Equivalent with 1/4 Wave Dipole, Biconical, Log-Periodic and Horn Antennas. Analyzer MUST be capable of measuring the 2.4MHz Bluetooth Telecommunications Standard Parameters	Record the spectrum of pre-existing frequencies at selected GPS coordinates. Repeat upon site completion. Note any displayed interference or constructive/destructive harmonics.	Spectrum Analysis readings at antenna and at 4-positions encompassing the near field. Spectrum readings must also be taken at all GPS locations where RF or MW 'Hot Spots' or 'Nulls' were previously detected. Measurements must include horizontal and vertical polarizations at each portion of the spectrum.
Low-Frequency (60Hz) Electric and Magnetic Fields from Overhead or Underground Powerlines	Holaday Instruments, Magnetic Sciences or Equivalent Low-Frequency Measurement System (Electric and Magnetic Fields) with Fiber Optic Isolation Cables and 3-Axis Magnetic Field Sensors	Record electric(E) and magnetic(H) field readings at multiple locations including GPS data, within 50m from center of site. Also measure at 10m, fields from existing powerlines and sub-stations within site area.	Powerline towers and cables, transformers, substations, etc. as well as cyclone fences and other metallic structures can cause constructive/destructive harmonics, signal interference, re-radiation and attenuation or amplification of transmitter signals.
Transmitter Test and Signal Characterization	HP 8901 Modulation Analyzer or Updated Equivalent	Make readings at four GPS-designated points on using the appropriate antenna, within the manufacturer-specified near-field range of the specified transmitters to a maximum of 100m.	Make baseline readings before transmitters are activated. Then record operational characteristics of transmitters at approved maximum configuration during test installation and note interference or intermodulation with existing signals.

Suggested Field Test Protocol For Comprehensive EMF Assessment of Telecommunications Transmitter Sites - By C.A. Cobbs

Identification of Potential Sources of Strong Interference	Use Broad-Band Spectrum Analyzer and appropriate antennas as decribed above for Broadband Spectrum Analysis	Record **pre-existing** signals around proposed site at distances to 100M. Make measurements at 1m above ground in open areas **and in occupancy areas in buildings** within 100m of proposed site. **Repeat measurements** after transmitter test installation.	This method is useful when proposed site is in near-field proximity to powerful existing RF/MW sources (Radio/TV/Police/Commercial/Ham). Use frequency-specific antenna to document emissions from existing facilities or source.
Data Acquisition	Digital Data Loggers, Hard Disks, Floppy Drives and Other Digital Media are available for Use with All Equipment Specified in This Test Protocol	To simplify data analysis and insure accuracy, some form of **digital data acquisition** should be used to record all measurements.	All the suggested test equipment has digital interface capability. Where anomalies are detected, notes describing the GPS location and anomaly should be flagged and detailed comments entered.
Data Presentation	It is suggested that 2-copies of the Comprehensive Site Report be filed with the local permit-granting authority. To support federal paperwork reduction, a brief summary referencing the ID-numbered and filed report can be submitted to the FCC.	The data described above will constitute a comprehensive picture of the existing and post-installation ELF/RF/MW environment. The final report should be signed by the senior engineer for the project	Final report of the data should include a print out of all measurements by type, GPS coordinate and readings in the appropriate units. Anomalies and findings should be discussed in detail, along with any suggested or implemented site remediations.
Reporting of Human Health Risks Per ANSI/IEEE C.95 Guidelines	Findings of exposure risks in excess of ANSI/IEEE guidelines should be reported immediately to the FCC and to the local permit-granting Authority.	The suggested protocol is broad enough in scope to disclose unexpected or unpredicted potentially harmful EMR levels to impacted populations. Knowledge of potential hazards is also important to facility maintenance personnel.	Given the competition, co-location and siting issues associated with the emerging telecommunications technologies, obtaining comprehensive site data is a prudent way to minimize disputes, litigation and controversy.

Suggested Test Data and Documentation To Comprise A Comprehensive Site Report - Submitted By: C.A.Cobbs

Operational Characteristic to Be Documented	Suggested Test Documentation	Comments
Detailed Description of FCC-Approved Use(s) For Transmitting Facilities at This Site	Summary of Approved Site License, Application or Permit, Listing Approved Use(s) [Cellular, PCS, Bluetooth, etc.] Equipment and Accessory Equipment	Copies of this information may be available from municipal or Federal sources. Details of approved, on-site equipment buildings, electrical requirements, etc.should also be included.
FCC-Allocated Operational Frequency Band For This Facility	Copy of Operator's approved FCC Frequency Allocation showing frequency band(s), side bands and ermissible Signal Deviation	State or Municipal Licensing or Permit-Granting Entities, or Regional FCC Offices Can Provide This Information
Documented Municipal Authority Location Approval for Wireless Telecom Facilities and List of Responsible Parties for All Aspects of Facility (Construction Defects, Accidents, Natural Disasters, Ecological/Health Impacts)	Local Site Approval Agreement Detailing Exact Geographical Location of Facility, Including Municipal Plat Map, Easements, Use Conditions and Survey Coordinates.	Documentation of approval should list site owner/operator, tower construction company, wireless affiliate companies (including co-located facilities) insurance coverages **and responsible parties for all complaints/lawsuits including full names, contact numbers and addresses**
Manufacturer Specifications for Transmitting Equipment To Be Installed at Site Including Subsequent Co-Located Transmitter/Antenna Specifications	Copies of Manufacturer Specification Sheets or Detailed Engineering Specifications for the model(s) of transmitters, antenna(s) and accessory equip[ment to be installed at site.	This documentation should include models to be installed and any possible substitutions. If replacements are made during the Permit Term, specifications and performance characteristics of alternatives must be submitted to the Local Authority.
FCC-Allocated Maximum Number of Transmitters and/or Total Maximum Allowed Operational Output Power of The Proposed Facility	Listing from Site Operator, of minimum and maximum number of transmitters and configuration to be installed at Site	Operator's reported installation and operation plans can be compared with FCC Site License specifications.

Suggested Test Data and Documentation To Comprise A Comprehensive Site Report - Submitted By: C.A.Cobbs

Comprehensive Pre and Post-Installation Test Report	The previously-described "Suggested Test Protocol" should be performed by Site Operator and submitted to the Local Authority. By thoroughly defining the pre and post EMF environment, many issues related to co-location can be avoided.	Upon completion of Operator's own Final Tests, it is recommended that Operator be required to conduct, at minimum, RF/MW Power Density, Spectrum Analysis and Intermodulation assessment at maximum output.
Reporting and Remediation of EMF Problems and Transmission Anomalies	Accurate data will be pertinent in transmission disputes and litigation. When any signals are found to exceed authorized specifications, offending party should be required to pay for re-test by a competent 3rd.Party after remediation has been effected.	Also, signal anomalies found during pre-installation should be re-assessed when new facility is tested at maximum. Intensification of former problems should be recorded with Authority and Operator, with remediation contingent to severity.
Implementing The Federal Paperwork Reduction Act: Establishment of Local Permit-Granting Authorities as Repositories For Site Test Data and As First-Line Arbitrators of Local Disputes	Local authorities presently grant site construction permits. These local authorities are the logical repositories for Comprehensive Site Test Reports, and with FCC guidance, can serve as the primary arbitratators of transmission or co-location disputes.	Where local EM fields of any frequency range are found to exceed any of the adopted standards, appropriate warning signs should be placed. 'Hot Spots' in presently open areas should be marked by Authority to prevent human access or future construction.

A NON-PROFIT CORPORATION   www.EMRNetwork.org
CITIZENS AND PROFESSIONALS FOR THE RESPONSIBLE USE OF ELECTROMAGNETIC RADIATION (EMR)
P. O. Box 221, MARSHFIELD, VT 05658   TEL: (802) 426-3035 FAX: (802)426-3030

SITE PLANNING – HAZARDS AND LIABILITIES OF WIRELESS TELECOMMUNICATIONS BASE STATION INSTALLATIONS

This list contains URL's for articles **from various industry and government web sites** that discuss safety hazards and liability issues from wireless telecommunications installations. These include back-up battery problems including fire, explosion, and leaking of sulfuric acid as well as liability for RF interference with a variety of industrial, medical and home electronic equipment in the neighborhood and real estate property devaluation.

These articles address the "public safety" and "preserving property values" arguments and provide "substantial evidence in a written record" to deny permits for wireless telecommunications facilities in close proximity to schools, homes, and day care and nursing home facilities such as on the community water tower, as well as those proposed for existing structures such as roof tops, historic structures and churches. The equipment shelter/hut that is required for the operation of the antennas presents a clear hazard to the safety of the neighborhood. The cost of liability insurance to cover all of these hazards along with decreases in property values must be considered by churches and historic sites before hosting wireless facilities despite the promise of revenue from the wireless provider.

REAL ESTATE DEVALUATION

http://www.cba.uiuc.edu/orer/V13-1-1.pdf
From *The Illinois Real Estate Letter,* published by the Office of Real Estate Research, University of Illinois at Urbana-Champaign, Winter 1999, "The Price of Zoning Revisited: Zoning Issues Raised by the Telecommunications Act of 1996", by Carol C. McDonough, Ph.D., Professor of Economics at the University of Massachusetts – Lowell. She also serves as Clerk of the Andover, MA Zoning Board of Appeals. Dr. McDonough cites two cases where courts "did not requires **proof** that the power line posed a health risk, but only that the **perception** of danger led to a drop in property value. The court held that whether the danger is scientifically genuine is irrelevant to the central issue of market value impact." She also states, " it is certainly possible to infer that transmission towers impose negative externalities to property values, if not to human health," and "... with cell towers still in their infancy, it is far too soon to develop reliable scientific information on health effects."

http://www.appraisalinstitute.org/pubs/aipub125.htm
The Home Environmental Sourcebook: 50 Environmental Hazards to Avoid When Buying, Selling, or Maintaining a Home.
Although published in 1996, it is currently out of print. Try to borrow a copy from your state's Appraisal Board's library. Wireless base stations are included in the list of 50.

http://www.abanet.org/publicserv/envguide.html
1998 American Bar Association Annual Meeting - Environmental Law Activities
Session on Monday, August 3, 1998, 9:30-11:30 AM – PRESIDENTIAL SHOWCASE PROGRAM; Environmental Impacts of the Telecommunications Revolution and at 3:15-5:00 PM -Stigmas, Contamination and the Environment: Their Influence on Property Valuation for Tax Purposes. Microwave and cellular towers are included in the list of stigmas.

http://library.northernlight.com/UU20010820020000576.html?cb=0&sc=0#doc
Real Estate appraisal expert testifies at zoning board hearing that a mobile phone tower would cut property value $50,000. Sprint Spectrum disputes analysis in Springfield Township (PA) case. Residents say they'll keep fighting the construction. *Allentown (PA) Morning Call,* August 17, 2001.
http://www.vernontwp.com/public/planningzoning/minutes-082900zs.
MAI appraiser cites *Appraiser Journal & Institute* as source for information that cell towers act as an "external obsolescence" which will devalue residential property. This site provides minutes from the Vernon Township (NJ) Board of Adjustment hearing of August 29, 2000. It cites facts and figures showing just how much

devaluation can occur.

http://www.weconnect.com/citizens/articles/Lawyersweeklyfiles/article1.
Lawyers Weekly USA, **The National Newsletter for Small Firm Lawyers**
"Towns can Reject Cellular Towers" April 16, 2001 - Details aesthetic basis for
rejecting towers, property values mentioned. Cite number - 2001 LWUSA 289

BATTERY HAZARDS

Several of the authors of these articles were asked to describe a typical battery array for a cellular or PCS base station supporting an antenna site. Typically there are 24 one hundred pound, Lead-Acid 48 volt batteries that are most often filled with sulfuric acid. Their chemistry is similar to automobile batteries. There is some controversy as to whether the EPA regulations that require notification of the presence of hazardous materials to local fire and safety authorities should apply. Sulfuric Acid is on the EPA list of "Extremely Hazardous Substances" and is present in an array of 24 batteries in sufficient amount to require this notification. As more and more antennas are sited on rooftops, in steeples, and in residential neighborhoods, notification becomes more critical.

http://www.calicorp.com/articles/batteries-hazards.html
Lead-Acid Battery Hazards

http://www.ncs.gov/n5_hp/information_Assurance/HazSec2.htm
Web site of the National Communications System (NCS). In 1962 after the Cuban missile crisis, President Kennedy directed the National Security Council (NSC) to form this interdepartmental committee to examine the communications networks and institute changes. NCS keeps ongoing records of all hazards that have affected telecommunications systems in the United States.
From this on-line NCS Report - **2.0 NATURAL AND TECHNOLOGICAL HAZARDS:**
This section provides information concerning major natural and technological hazard threats to NS/EP telecommunications and supporting systems.

2.2.1.3 Experiential Data
Properties wholly dedicated to computer or telecommunications activities are actually a comparatively small part of the U.S. fire problem. From 1990 to 1994, computer and data processing centers annually averaged 29 structure fires, no reported deaths, 1 injury, and $1.31 million in direct property damage. All communications, defense, and document facilities combine - including defense radio and radar sites, police and fire communications centers, telephone exchanges, and document centers and record repositories- annually averaged 249 structure fires, no deaths, 6 injuries, and $7.21 million in direct property damage. **The large problem actually occurs in electronic equipment rooms or areas where more than 1,000 structure fires are reported each year to U.S. fire departments.**

See section entitled **"1994 Los Angeles Telephone Exchange Fire"** and paragraph under **Table 2-8 Causes of Fires at Telecommunications Facilities.**

http://www.telecomclick.com
Type in "A battery for all seasons?" in the SEARCH box. Click on GO.

http://www.calicorp.com/advisory.htm
Advisory: Lead-acid Batteries

http://www.telecomclick.com
Type in "Power Struggle: Battling over battery technologies" in the SEARCH box. Click on GO.

http://www.zomeworks.com/tech/H2/H2FAQ.html

Hydrogen FAQ [This article discusses how complex proper venting of a battery shelter/room is. This company sells shelters as well as designs to properly vent existing shelters.]

"What is the danger of explosion during battery charging?
    Battery rooms and cabinets are notorious for explosions when hydrogen created by electrolysis and mixed with oxygen is ignited by a spark.
    The proliferation of back up batteries at communications sites has spread the hazard from the private concern of the battery's users to the public at large. Battery cabinets, vaults, and rooms are now scattered like time bombs all around the world, many where explosion could injure or kill unaware bystanders. The danger is not imagined. Many vaults have exploded and recently a communications shelter in Yuma, Arizona, exploded shattering the windows of a neighboring house..."

http://www.powerquality.com/art0060/art1.htm

From the industry journal, *Power Quality Journal.*
The cogent point in this article is in the first paragraph:
". . . Most battery owners, including some of the biggest companies is the country, do not follow IEEE recommendations. They claim that the full program is too expensive. That is short-term thinking and sooner or later they will pay for it."

http://www.calicorp.com/articles/open-house.html
Fire Department Safety Officers Association - "Open House" Battery Incident

http://www.firehouse.com/news/2000/6/14_APstate.html
Fire Knocks Out State Department Phones

http://www.wa.gov/lni/news/pr051800.htm
All telecommunications contractors must register with Labor & Industry by June 8

http://www.telecomclick.com
Type "Powering wireless telecom basestations" in the SEARCH box. Click on "GO."

http://www.ospmag.com/features/1999/h2_ohno.htm
H2-OhNo! Hydrogen Build-Up Can Cause Battery Cabinets to EXPLODE

http://www.telecomclick.com
Type in "Flirting with disaster" in SEARCH box. Click on GO.

http://www.calicorp.com/articles/osha_special_equip.htm
Electrical Safety Requirements for Special Equipment -
OSHA Regulatory Profile - Special Equipment

http://www.calicorp.com/articles/batteries-buildings.html
Lead-Acid Batteries in Buildings

ENVIRONMENTAL HAZARDS OF BATTERY CHEMICALS

http://www.calicorp.com/articles/osha-articles.html
Industrial Lead-Acid Batteries Are Not Considered "Articles"

http://www.calicorp.com/epa_news_release.htm
EPA News Release - Ten Telecommunications Companies Voluntarily Disclose and Correct Environmental Violations

http://es.epa.gov/oeca/ore/enfalert/vol3num6.html
EPA's "Audit Policy" Offers Opportunity for Telecommunications Industry to Remedy Violations

http://www.americasnetwork.com/issues/2000supplements/20000915cc/cc20000915_finesprint.htm
Smart builders: The Fine(s) Print - EPA takes kindly to telecom companies that catch and report their own mistakes

RADIO FREQUENCY RADIATION LIABILITY ISSUES - RF IN THE NEIGHBORHOOD

http://www.telecomclick.com
Type in "The case for testing electromagnetic radiation at the mobile radio sites" in the SEARCH box. Click GO.

From the United Kingdom-based web site of The Institution of Electrical Engineers. IEE represents the public, professional and educational interest of over 140,000 electrical, electronic and manufacturing engineers world-wide. Key activities include publishing, the organisation of conferences, the maintenance of technical standards, interaction with government departments and the provision of scientific and technical information services.

http://www.iee.org.uk/PAB/EMC/core.htm
IEE Guidance Document on EMC (Electromagnetic Compatibility) and Functional Safety
[From "Introduction and Purpose"]
    "One of the problems peculiar to all electronic technologies is electromagnetic (EM) interference. All electrical and electronic technologies emit EM disturbances that can interfere with the correct operation of radio-communications or other electronics. Modern electronic technologies are in general more likely to cause such disturbances than those they replace.
    All electronic technologies can also suffer from degraded functionality (including complete failure) when exposed to EM disturbances. Modern electronic technologies are in general more likely to be susceptible in this way than those they replace. . .
    Electronic technology is increasingly used in safety-related applications. Consequently, errors and misoperation of electronic devices due to inadequate EMC can result in hazardous situations with an increased risk of harm to people's health and safety."

http://www.gcfa.org/ChurchSteeplesMainMemo.html
    Another URL for a Memorandum from the General Counsel on Finance and Administration for the United Methodist Church on legal considerations for wireless sites on churches, etc. Key paragraph below:

"The legal and tax considerations covered by these two memos do not cover the full range of issues that a local church or other church organization needs to consider when invited to rent steeple space to a cellular phone company. For example, the very first question that needs to be addressed is whether this activity is in keeping with the mission and ministry of the local church. In addition, we are aware of two local churches that have been severely criticized by their neighbors for agreeing to rent steeple space for cellular phone antennas, because of possible health concerns. We are not experts on these issues but can tell you that some people are very fearful of possible adverse health effects from living in the vicinity of these antennas."

It also takes special note of lightning hazards:
"From a risk management perspective, churches should consider the potential risk of attracting lightning and ask the cell phone company(s) to install lightning protection, at their own expense."

LIGHTNING HAZARDS AND LIABLITY RELATED TO WIRELESS FACILITIES

http://lightningsafety.com/nlsi_info/little_known_facts.html
Little-Known Lightning Information from the National Lightning Safety Institute Technical Information. Information on how to obtain the article described in this abstract:

    The number of tower structures to support cellular-telephone and wireless communications in North America has grown dramatically in the last ten years. In addition to cell-phone antenna towers, there are hundreds of thousands of towers with heights between thirty and two hundred meters. These towers include ham radio towers, water towers, microwave repeater and VHF communication towers. Tall towers are in some cases erected in residential and industrial areas. Some municipalities now lease public spaces for tower sites. Measurements of lightning strikes to towers between 30 and 200 m in height have shown that such towers increase the incidence of lightning at the tower location and that the probability of lightning to a tower increases roughly as the square of the tower height. Recent work has characterized the multiple ground attachments of natural, negative discharges and the electromagnetic environment near the ground strike point. We review the tower/lightning problem in light of these findings and relate a recent case of multiple lightning incidents at a water tower in which it appears that the tall structure is a land-use-nuisance to people nearby. We use lightning ground flash density data to show the skew of lightning incidence near towers of 300m or more in height. We review mitigation measures for some lightning effects at towers.

http://www.hive4telecom.com/telecom/newstrends/articledetail.jhtml?ontologyID=11282&contentType=ArticleS
tandard&headerGif=pix.gif&siteNavigationLocation=/&
Lightning and Liability
It's common knowledge that if you seek shelter from a thunderstorm
by hiding near a tree, you increase your risk of death or injury from a lightning strike. By the same token,
lightning strikes isolated communications towers more frequently than undisturbed ground in the same area.

Towers are productive sites for lightning laboratories. In 1998, a radio tower was struck by five flashes
in a single storm – an occurrence that would be highly unlikely in the same area if the tower were not present.
Studies of lightning to instrumented towers of various heights show that the probability of lightning striking
towers of moderate height increases roughly as the square of the tower height.

http://science.msfc.nasa.gov/newhome/headlines/essd18jun99_1.htm
From a NASA site – **Human Voltage: What happens when people and lightning converge.**
Note especially pp. 3 and 4 – increased amount of lightning strikes in areas near towers, and an estimate of $4
to $5 billion dollars a year in lightning costs and losses each year in the U.S. Includes links to severe weather
sites.

http://www.unco.edu/safety/lightning.htm
Lightning Safety Group Recommendations
In 1998, twelve business and government organizations discussed, drafted and jointly published a
cohesive and unified lightning safety document in the public interest.

> **AVOID being in or near:**
> *High places and open fields, isolated trees, unprotected gazebos, rain or
> picnic shelters, baseball dugouts, communications towers, flagpoles,
> light poles, bleachers (metal or wood), metal fences, convertibles,
> golf carts, water (ocean, lakes, swimming pools, rivers, etc.).*

http://www.newton.dep.anl.gov/askasci/wea00/wea00006.htm
Ask a Scientist – Lightning Damage
*Trees, chimneys, towers, etc. are prime targets as they are tall and can provide some distance of path
that takes the place of the leader. They can also build up charge more easily, especially if not grounded. In our
lightning research, we use a rocket to send a wire up into the air; this serves the same purpose as a wet tree or
tall tower, by providing a path for the lightning energy; in this way, lightning is "triggered" and can be studied
in a more controlled way.*

http://www.glatmos.com/lightinfo/techPapers.html
Lightning Information
This site provides links to several technical and scientific papers on lightning safety, the physics of
lightning, lightning detection, and meteorological applications.

http://www.allcompc.com/page-surge/ABC.htm
Lightning Surge Suppression
*Stepped leaders (lightning bolts) take the path of least impedance (resistance + inductance) to ground.
Metal towers, antennas, wet trees, wires, and people usually provide a lower impedance path to ground than
the surrounding air.*

*No single protection device can fully protect a communications site. Maximum protection is provided by
a comprehensive, fully integrated, low impedance grounding system.*

Appendix F

Websites:

Government/Professional:

www.fcc.gov/oet/rfsafety	(FCC)
www.fda.gov/cdrh/newpg.html	(FDA)
www.who.int	(World Health Organization)
www.fws.gov/r9mbmo/issues/tower.html	(Fish & Wildlife Services)
www.ortho.lsumc.edu/Faculty/Marino/Marino.html	(Andrew Marino)
www.microwavenews.com	(Microwave News)
www.rcrnews.com	(Wireless News Source)
www.emfinterface.com	(James Beal)
www.towerkill.com	(bird kills)

Legal/Activist/Informational:

www.EMRNetwork.org

www.wave-guide.org

www.c-a-r-e.org

www.ccwti.org

www.emfguru.com

www.millervaneaton.com

www.als.edu   (Albany Law School, source for
                                telecommunications case law.)

www.sageassociates.net

Radiofrequency Interagency Work Group Members

Alphabetical Listing

Cleveland, Robert
Senior Scientist
Federal Communications Commission
Office of Eng & Technology, Room 230
2000 M St., MW
Washington, DC 20554
(202) 418-2422
(202) 418-1918 (fax)
rclevela@fcc.gov

Cress, Larry
US FDA, CDRH
Radiation Biology Branch, DLS, OST
9200 Corporate Blvd. (HFZ-114)
Rockville, MD 20850
(301) 443-7173
(301) 594-6775 (fax)
lwc@cdrh.fda.gov

Curtis, Robert A.
OSHA
Dir-U.S. Dept. of Labor/OSHA
OSHA Health Response Team
1781 S. 300 W.
Salt Lake City, UT 84115-1802
(801) 487-0521, ext. 243
(801) 487-1190 (fax)
rac@osha-slc.gov

Elder, Joseph A.
US Environmental Protection Agency
U.S. EPA, NHEERL (MD-87)
2525 Highway 54
Research Triangle Park, NC 27711
(919) 541-2542
(919) 541-4201 (fax)
elder.joe@epamail.epa.gov

Hankin, Norbert N.
U.S. Environmental Protection Agency
Mailcode 6604J
U.S. EPA
Washington, DC 20460
(202) 564-9235
(202) 565 2038 (fax)
hankin.norbert@epamail.epa.gov

Healer, H. Janet
NTIA
Department of Commerce (H-4099)
14th & Constitution Ave., NW
Washington, DC 20230
(202) 482-1850
(202) 482-4396 (fax)
jhealer@ntia.doc.gov

Lotz, W. Gregory
Chief, Physical Agents Effects Branch
National Institute for Occupational Safety
and Health
4676 Columbia Parkway C-27
Cincinnati, OH 45226-1998
(513) 533-8153
(513) 533-8139 (fax)
wgl0@cdc.gov

Owen, Russell D.
U.S. FDA/CDRH (HFZ-114)
Chief, Radiation Biology Branch (HFZ-114)
9200 Corporate Blvd.
Rockville, MD 20850
(301) 443-7153
(301) 761-1842 (fax)
rdo@cdrh.fda.gov

RF Guideline Issues
Identified by members of the federal RF Interagency Work Group, June 1999

Issue: Biological basis for local SAR limit

The C95.1 partial body (local) exposure limits are based on an assumed ratio of peak to whole body SAR; that is, they are dosimetrically, rather than biologically based. Instead of applying a dosimetric factor to the whole body SAR to obtain the local limits, an effort should be made to base local SAR limits on the differential sensitivity of tissues to electric fields and temperature increases. For example, it seems intuitive that the local limits for the brain and bone marrow should be lower than those for muscle, fat and fascia; this is not the case with the current limits which implicitly assume that all tissues are equally sensitive (except for eye and testicle). If no other data are available, differential tissue sensitivity to ionizing radiation should be considered.

If it is deemed necessary to incorporate dosimetric factors into the resulting tissue-specific SAR limits these should be based on up-to-date dosimetric methods such as finite-difference time-domain calculations utilizing MRI data and tissue-specific dielectric constants: For certain exposure conditions FDTD techniques and MRI data may allow better simulation of peak SAR values. Consideration should be given to the practical tissue volume for averaging SAR and whether this volume is relevant to potential effects on sensitive tissues and organs.

Issue: Selection of an adverse effect level

Should the thermal basis for exposure limits be reconsidered, or can the basis for an unacceptable/adverse effect still be defined in the same manner used for the 1991 IEEE guidelines? Since the adverse effect level for the 1991 guidelines was based on acute exposures, does the same approach apply for effects caused by chronic exposure to RF radiation, including exposures having a range of carrier frequencies, modulation characteristics, peak intensities, exposure duration, etc., that does not elevate tissue temperature on a macroscopic scale?

Selection criteria that could be considered in determining unacceptable/adverse effects include:

        a) adverse effects on bodily functions/systems
        b) minimal physiological consequences
        c) measurable physiological effects, but no known consequences

If the adverse effect level is based on thermal effects in laboratory animals, the literature on human studies (relating dose rate to temperature elevation and temperature elevation to a physiological effect) should be used to determine if the human data could reduce uncertainties in determination of a safety factor.

RFIAWG Issues, June 1999, page 3

Issue: <u>Acute and chronic exposures</u>

There is a need to discuss and differentiate the criteria for guidelines for acute and chronic
exposure conditions. The past approach of basing the exposure limits on acute effects data with
an extrapolation to unlimited chronic exposure durations is problematic. There is an extensive
data base on acute effects with animal data, human data (e.g. MRI information), and modeling to
address thermal insult and associated adverse effects for acute exposure (e.g., less than one day)
For lower level ("non-thermal"), chronic exposures, the effects of concern may be very different
from those for acute exposure (e.g., epigenetic effects, tumor development, neurologic
symptoms). It is possible that the IEEE RF radiation guidelines development process may
conclude that the data for these chronic effects exist but are inconsistent, and therefore not
useable for guideline development. If the chronic exposure data are not helpful in determining a
recommended exposure level, then a separate rationale for extrapolating the results of acute
exposure data may be needed. In either case (chronic effects data that are useful or not useful), a
clear rationale needs to be developed to support the exposure guideline for chronic as well as
acute exposure.

Issue: <u>One tier vs two tier guidelines:</u>

A one tier guideline must incorporate all exposure conditions and subject possibilities (e g., acute
or chronic exposure, healthy workers, chronically ill members of the general public, etc.). A two
tier guideline, as now exists, has the potential to provide higher limits for a specific, defined
population (e.g., healthy workers), and exposure conditions subject to controls, while providing a
second limit that addresses greater uncertainties in the data available (about chronic exposure
effects, about variations in the health of the subject population, etc.). A greater safety factor
would have to be incorporated to deal with greater uncertainty in the scientific data available.
Thus, a two-tier guideline offers more flexibility in dealing with scientific uncertainty, while a
one-tier guideline would force a more conservative limit to cover all circumstances including the
scientific uncertainties that exist.

Issue: <u>Controlled vs uncontrolled</u> (applicability of two IEEE exposure tiers)

The current "controlled" and "uncontrolled" definitions are problematic, at least in the civilian
sector, particularly since there are no procedures defined in the document to implement the
"controlled" condition. The new guidelines should offer direction for the range of controls to be
implemented and the training required for those who knowingly will be exposed (e.g. workers),
along the lines of the existing ANSI laser safety standards. This essential element needs to be
included for whatever limits are defined, be they one-tier or two-tier.

For example, the OSHA position is that the "uncontrolled" level is strictly an "action" level which

RF·IAWG Issues, June 1999, page 4

indicates that there is a sufficiently high exposure (compared to the vast majority of locations) to merit an assessment to determine what controls and training are necessary to ensure persons are not exposed above the "controlled" limit. Many similar "action" levels are part of OSHA and public health standards. Should this interpretation be incorporated into the IEEE standard as a means to determine the need to implement a safety plan? [The laser standard has a multi-tiered (Class I, II, III, IV) standard which similarly requires additional controls for more powerful lasers to limit the likelihood of an excess exposure, even though the health effect threshold is the same.]

On the other hand, if it is determined that certain populations (due to their health status or age) are more susceptible to RF exposures, then a multi-tiered standard, applicable only to those specific populations, may be considered

The ANSI/IEEE standard establishes two exposure tiers for controlled and uncontrolled environments. The following statement is made in the rationale (Section 6, page 23): "The important distinction is not the population type, but the nature of the exposure environment." If that is the case, consideration should be given to providing a better explanation as to why persons in uncontrolled environments need to be protected to a greater extent than persons in controlled environments. An uncontrolled environment can become a controlled environment by simply restricting access (e.g., erecting fences) and by making individuals aware of their potential for exposure. After such actions are taken, this means that the persons who previously could only be exposed at the more restrictive uncontrolled levels could now be exposed inside the restricted area (e.g., inside the fence) at controlled levels.

What biologically-based factor changed for these people? Since the ostensible public health reason for providing greater protection for one group of persons has historically been based on biological considerations or comparable factors, it is not clear why the sentence quoted above is valid.

Issue: Uncertainty factors

The uncertainties in the data used to develop the guideline should be addressed. An accepted practice in establishing human exposure levels for agents that produce undesirable effects is the application of factors representing each area of uncertainty inherent in the available data that was used to identify the unacceptable effect level. Standard areas of uncertainty used in deriving acceptable human dose for agents that may produce adverse (but non-cancer) effects include

(1) extrapolation of acute effects data to chronic exposure conditions,
(2) uncertainty in extrapolating animal data to humans in prolonged exposure situations,
(3) variation in the susceptibility (response/sensitivity) among individuals,
(4) incomplete data bases,
(5) uncertainty in the selection of the effects basis, inability of any single study to adequately address all possible adverse outcomes.

RFIAWG Issues, June 1999, page 5

If guidelines are intended to address nonthermal chronic exposures to intensity modulated RF radiation, then how could uncertainty factors be used; how would this use differ from the historical use of uncertainty factors in establishing RF radiation guidelines to limit exposure to acute or sub-chronic RF radiation to prevent heat-related effects?

There is a need to provide a clear rationale for the use of uncertainty factors.

Issue: Intensity or frequency modulated (pulsed or frequency modulated) RF radiation

Studies continue to be published describing biological responses to nonthermal ELF-modulated and pulse-modulated RF radiation exposures that are not produced by CW (unmodulated) RF radiation. These studies have resulted in concern that exposure guidelines based on thermal effects, and using information and concepts (time-averaged dosimetry, uncertainty factors) that mask any differences between intensity-modulated RF radiation exposure and CW exposure, do not directly address public exposures, and therefore may not adequately protect the public. The parameter used to describe dose/dose rate and used as the basis for exposure limits is time-averaged SAR; time-averaging erases the unique characteristics of an intensity-modulated RF radiation that may be responsible for producing an effect.

Are the results of research reporting biological effects caused by intensity-modulated, but not CW exposure to RF radiation sufficient to influence the development of RF exposure guidelines? If so, then how could this information be used in developing those guidelines? How could intensity modulation be incorporated into the concept of dose to retain unique characteristics that may be responsible for a relationship between exposure and the resulting effects?

Issue: Time averaging

Time averaging of exposures is essential in dealing with variable or intermittent exposure, e.g., that arising from being in a fixed location of a rotating antenna, or from moving through a fixed RF field. The 0.1 h approach historically used should be reassessed, but may serve this purpose adequately. Time averaging for other features of RF exposure is not necessarily desirable, however, and should be reevaluated specifically as it deals with modulation of the signal, contact and induced current limits, and prolonged, or chronic exposure. These specific conditions are discussed in a little more detail elsewhere.

If prolonged and chronic exposures are considered to be important, then there should be a reconsideration of the time-averaging practices that are incorporated into existing exposure guidelines and used primarily to control exposure and energy deposition rates in acute/subchronic exposure situations.

Issue: Lack of peak (or ceiling) limits for induced and contact current

A recent change in the IEEE guidelines allows for 6 minute, rather than 1 second, time-weighted-averaging for induced current limits. This change increases the concern about the lack of a peak limit for induced and contact currents. Will the limits for localized exposure address this issue, i.e., for tissue along the current path?

Issue: Criteria for preventing hazards caused by transient discharges

The existing IEEE recommendation states that there were insufficient data to establish measurable criteria to prevent RF hazards caused by transient discharges. If specific quantitative criteria are still not available, can qualitative requirements be included in the standard to control this hazard (e.g., metal objects will be sufficiently insulated and/or grounded, and/or persons will utilize sufficient insulating protection, such as gloves, to prevent undesirable transient discharge.)?

ISSUE: Limits for exposure at microwave frequencies

Concerns have been expressed over the relaxation of limits for continuous exposures at microwave frequencies above 1500 MHz. The rationale provided in the current guideline (Section 6 8) references the fact that penetration depths at frequencies above 30 GHz are similar to those at visible and near infrared wavelengths and that the literature for skin burn thresholds for optical radiation "is expected to be applicable." The rationale then implies that the MPE limits at these high frequencies are consistent with the MPE limits specified in ANSI Z136.1-1986 for 300 GHz exposures. This is apparently the rationale for "ramping up" to the MPE limits for *continuous* exposure of 10 mW/cm^2 at frequencies above 3 GHz (controlled) or 15 GHz (uncontrolled). The rationale should be given as to why this ramp function has been established at relatively low microwave frequencies (i e , 1500 MHz and above), rather than being implemented at higher frequencies that are truly quasi-optical. For example, one option could be two ramp functions, one beginning at 300 MHz, based on whole- or partial-body dosimetry considerations, and another at higher frequencies (say 30-100 GHz) to enable consistency with the laser standard. Such a revision should help reduce concern that the standard is not restrictive enough for continuous exposures at lower microwave frequencies where new wireless applications for consumers could make this an issue in the future.

Issue: Replication/Validation

Published peer-reviewed studies that have been independently replicated/validated should be used to establish the adverse effects level from which exposure guidelines are derived. The definition of "replicated/validated" should not be so restrictive to disallow the use of a set of reports that

RFIAWG Issues, June 1999, page 7

are scientifically valid but are not an <u>exact</u> replication/validation of specific experimental procedures and results.

Peer-reviewed, published studies that may not be considered to be replicated/validated, but are well done and show potentially important health impacts provide important information regarding uncertainties in the data base used to set the adverse effect level (e.g., incomplete data base).

Issue: <u>Important Health Effects Literature Areas:</u>

Documentation should be provided that the literature review process included a comprehensive review of the following three areas:

       1) long-term, low-level exposure studies (because of their importance to environmental and chronic occupational RFR exposure);
       2) neurological/behavioral effects (because of their importance in defining the adverse effect level in existing RFR guidelines); and
       3) micronucleus assay studies (because of their relevance to carcinogenesis)

Issue: <u>Compatibility of RFR guidelines</u>

Compatibility of national and international RFR guidelines remains a concern. It is important for the IEEE Committee to address this issue by identifying and discussing similarities and differences in a revised IEEE guideline and other RFR guidelines. Compatibility/noncompatibility issues could be discussed in the revised IEEE guideline or as a companion document distributed at the time the revised IEEE guideline is released to the public.

Appendix H

VIDEO ORDER FORM:

<u>CELL TOWERS FORUM, STATE OF THE SCIENCE/STATE OF THE LAW</u>
DECEMBER 2, 2000.

Sponsored by the Berkshire-Litchfield Environmental Council
and others...

. 3-Tape video package, VHS, 2-hours each.

. PRICE: $90.00. Includes shipping & handling.

Name: _____

Business: _____

Mailing Address:
Town/City:_____

State: _____   Zip: _____

Day Phone:_____   Evening Phone: _____

MAKE CHECKS PAYABLE TO: The Berkshire-Litchfield Environmental
Council (or BLEC)

PAYMENT METHOD:

Check:( ) #_____   Purchase Order# _____

MC ( ) or Visa ( )

Card #: _____

Card Holder: _____

Home address:_____

_____

Signature: _____

Expiration Date: _____

FOR INFORMATION, OR TO FAX OR SEND YOUR ORDER BY PHONE, CONTACT
THE BERKSHIRE-LITCHFIELD ENVIRONMENTAL COUNCIL, 860-435-2004. C
SEND YOUR ORDER WITH PAYMENT TO BLEC, P.O. BOX 552, LAKEVILLE,
CT. 06039

Index

C-D

U-W

weather problems, 22
West Point, 165
WGY, 108, 112, 113, 114
white blood cell activity, 107
White House Office of Science and
    Technology Policy, 86
whole-body resonance, 31
whole-body SAR, 119
wireless1,2. 10, 169
wireless-free areas, 20
Wisconsin Department of Natural
    Resources, 77
World Health Organization (WHO),
    122
www.fcc.gov/oet/rfsafety, 117, 235
www.findlaw.com, 143

X-Z

Xenos, Thomas, 40, 67, 68, 74
zoners, 45, 190, 193
zoning, 3, 8, 13, 14, 17, 18, 23, 25, 42,
    46, 48, 83, 100, 142, 143, 144, 145,
    146, 147, 148, 149, 150, 152, 154,
    161, 186, 187, 188, 189, 192, 194,
    206, 222, 223
Zoning Board of Adjustment, 146
zoning decisions, 8, 149